Robert Herrick, B. Grosart Alexander

The Complete Poems Of Robert Herrick

Vol. III

Robert Herrick, B. Grosart Alexander

The Complete Poems Of Robert Herrick
Vol. III

ISBN/EAN: 9783348011990

Printed in Europe, USA, Canada, Australia, Japan

Cover: Foto ©ninafisch / pixelio.de

More available books at **www.hansebooks.com**

Early English Poets.

THE

COMPLETE POEMS

OF

ROBERT HERRICK

EDITED,

WITH

Memorial-Introduction and Notes,

BY THE

REV. ALEXANDER B. GROSART.

IN THREE VOLUMES.—VOL. III.

London:

CHATTO AND WINDUS, PICCADILLY.

1876.

Contents.

HESPERIDES.

The showre of Blossomes.

OVE in a showre of Blossomes came
Down, and halfe drown'd me with the same
The Blooms that fell were white and red ;
But with such sweets comminglèd,
As whether (this) I cannot tell
My sight was pleas'd more, or my smell :
But true it was, as I rowl'd there,
Without a thought of hurt, or feare ;
Love turn'd himselfe into a Bee,
And with his Javelin wounded me :
From which mishap this use I make,
Where most sweets are, there lyes a Snake:
Kisses and Favours are sweet things ;
But Those have thorns, and These have stings.

Upon Spenke.

SPENKE has a strong breath, yet short Prayers
   saith :
Not out of want of breath, but want of faith.

A Defence for Women.

NAUGHT are all Women : I say no,
    Since for one Bad, one Good I know :
For *Clytemnestra* most unkind,
Loving *Alcestis* there we find :
For one *Medea* that was bad,
A good *Penelope* was had :
For wanton *Lais*, then we have
Chaste *Lucrece*, or a wife as grave :
And thus through Woman-kind we see
A Good and Bad.   *Sirs credit me.*

Upon Lulls.

LULLS swears he is all heart ; but you'l suppose
    By his *Probossis* that he is all nose.

Slavery.

'TIS liberty to serve one Lord ; but he
    Who many serves, serves base servility.[1]

Charmes.

BRING the holy crust of Bread,
    Lay it underneath the head ;

---

[1] Cf. the Page's argument that servants are less servants than their masters, in Massinger's Unnatural Combat : Act iii. sc. 2.

'Tis a certain Charm to keep
Hags away, while Children sleep.

Another.

LET the superstitious wife
   Neer the child's heart lay a knife :
Point be up, and Haft be downe ;
(While she gossips in the towne)
This 'mongst other mystick charms
Keeps the sleeping child from harms.[2]

Another to bring in the Witch.

TO house[3] the Hag, you must doe this ;
   Commix with Meale a little Pisse
Of him bewitcht : then forthwith make
A little Wafer or a Cake :
And this rawly bak't will bring
The old Hag in.   No surer thing.

Another Charme for Stables.[4]

HANG up Hooks, and Sheers to scare
   Hence the Hag, that rides the Mare,

---

[2] Folk-lore.   [3] Curious use of ' house '—to bring into your
house. See last line.   [4] Folk-lore.

Till they be all over wet,
With the mire, and the sweat :
This observ'd, the Manes shall be
Of your horses, all knot-free.

Ceremonies for Candlemasse Eve.[5]

DOWN with the Rosemary and Bayes,
　　Down with the Misleto ;
Instead of Holly, now up-raise
　　The greener Box[6] (for show.)

The Holly hitherto did sway ;
　　Let Box now domineere ;
Untill the dancing Easter-day,
　　Or Easters Eve appeare.

---

[5] In former times, foliage and flowers were much more frequently employed in the internal decoration of houses than at present; and different kinds were allotted to different seasons. The bay, holly, and misletoe, at Christmas, are not yet exploded. Strutt, in his *Manners and Customs of the English*, informs us, from Hollingshed, that our ancestors used to strew their houses with rushes, which were carefully spread over the floors, till carpets came in fashion; and it is still a practice to cover the ground with rushes in many churches, at Whitsuntide. N. The last custom has been finely celebrated by Wordsworth. See Notes and Queries, December 25th, 1875. The date is 1st February, or Eve of Purification of V. Mary.

[6] Boxwood plant.

Then youthfull Box which now hath grace,
  Your houses to renew ;
Grown old, surrender must his place,
  Unto the crispèd Yew.

When Yew is out, then Birch comes in,
  And many Flowers beside ;
Both of a fresh, and fragrant kinne
  To honour Whitsontide.

Green Rushes then, and sweetest Bents,[7]
  With cooler Oken boughs ;
Come in for comely ornaments,
  To re-adorn the house.
Thus times do shift ; each thing his turne do's hold ;
New things succeed, as former things grow old.

The Ceremonies for Candlemasse day.[8]

KINDLE the Christmas Brand [9] and then
  Till Sunne-set, let it burne ;
Which quencht, then lay it up agen,
  Till Christmas next returne.

---

[7] = long coarse moor growing grass.

[8] These two stanzas are curious, inasmuch as they record an old superstitious ceremony, which I do not recollect to have before met with. N.   [9] = Log.

Part must be kept wherewith to teend [1]
   The Christmas Log next yeare;
And where 'tis safely kept, the Fiend,
   Can do no mischiefe (there.)

Upon Candlemasse day.

END now the White-loafe, & the Pye,
   And let all sports with Christmas dye.

Surfeits.

BAD are all surfeits : but Physitians call
   That surfeit tooke by bread, the worst of all.

Upon Nis.

N *IS*, he makes Verses; but the Lines he writes,
   Serve but for matter to make Paper-kites.

To Biancha, *to blesse him.*

WO'D I wooe, and wo'd I winne,
   Wo'd I well my worke begin?
Wo'd I evermore be crown'd
With the end that I propound?
Wo'd I frustrate, or prevent
All Aspects malevolent?

   [1] See Glossarial Index s. v.

Thwart all Wizzards, and with these
Dead all black contingencies :
Place my words, and all works else
In most happy Parallels?
All will prosper, if so be
I be kist, or blest by thee.

Julia's *Churching*, or *Purification*.

PUT on thy *Holy Fillitings*, and so
    To th' Temple with the sober *Midwife* go.
Attended thus (in a most solemn wise)
By those who serve the Child-bed misteries.
Burn first thine incense ; next, whenas thou see'st
The candid [2] Stole thrown ore the *Pious Priest;*
With reverend Curtsies come, and to him bring
Thy free (and not decurted [3]) offering.
All Rites well ended, with faire Auspice [4] come
(As to the breaking of a Bride-Cake) home :
Where ceremonious *Hymen* shall for thee
Provide a second *Epithalamie.*
She who keeps chastly to her husbands side
Is not for one, but every night his Bride :
And stealing still with love, and feare to Bed,
Brings him not one, but many a Maiden-head.

---

[2] =white. [3] =shortened: used now only in 'curt' and 'curtly.'
. [4] See Glossarial Index s. v.

To his Book.

BEFORE the Press scarce one co'd see
 A little-peeping-part of thee :
But since th' art Printed, thou dost call
To shew thy nakedness to all.
My care for thee is now the less,
(Having resign'd thy shamefac'tness :)
Go with thy Faults and Fates ; yet stay
And take this sentence, then away ;
Whom one belov'd will not suffice,
She'l runne to all adulteries.

Teares.

TEARES most prevaile ; with teares too thou
  mayst move
Rocks to relent, and coyest maids to love.

To his friend to avoid contention of words.

WORDS beget Anger ; Anger brings forth blowes :
 Blowes make of dearest friends immortall Foes.
For which prevention (Sociate [5]) let there be
Betwixt us two no more *Logomachie.*[6]
Farre better 'twere for either to be mute,
Then for to murder friendship, by dispute.   [*than*

---

[5] =companion, friend.   [6] =war of words.

Truth.

TRUTH is best found out by the time, and eyes ;
    Falsehood winnes credit by uncertainties.

Upon Prickles.   *Epig.*

PRICKLES is waspish, and puts forth his sting,
    For Bread, Drinke, Butter, Cheese ; for every
        thing
That *Prickles* buyes, puts *Prickles* out of frame ;
How well his nature's fitted to his name !

The Eyes before the Eares.

WE credit most our sight ; one eye doth please
    Our trust farre more then ten eare-witnesses.

                        [*than*

Want.

WANT is a softer Wax, that takes thereon,
    This, that, and every base impression.

To a Friend.

LOOKE in my Book, and herein see,
    Life endlesse sign'd to thee and me.
  We o're the tombes, and Fates shall flye ;
  While other generations dye.

Upon M. William Lawes, *the rare Musitian.*[7]

SHO'D I not put on Blacks, when each one here
  Comes with his Cypresse, and devotes a teare?
Sho'd I not grieve (my *Lawes*) when every Lute,
Violl, and Voice, is (by thy losse) struck mute ?
Thy loss, brave man ! whose Numbers have been
      hurl'd,
And no less prais'd, then spread throughout the
      world.   [*than*
Some have Thee call'd *Amphion ;* some of us,
Nam'd thee *Terpander*, or sweet *Orpheus :*
Some this, some that, but all in this agree,
Musique had both her birth and death with Thee.

A Song upon Silvia.

FROM me my *Silvia* ranne away,
      And running therewithall,
A *Primrose* Banke did cross her way,
      And gave my Love a fall.

But trust me now, I dare not say,
      What I by chance did see ;
But such the Drap'ry did betray
      That fully ravisht me.

---

[7] See Memorial-Introduction.

The Hony-combe.

I F thou hast found an honie-combe,
  Eate thou not all, but taste on some :
For if thou eat'st it to excess ;
That sweetness turnes to Loathsomness.
Taste it to Temper[8]; then 'twill be
Marrow, and Manna unto thee.

Vpon Ben. Johnson.[9]

H ERE lyes *Johnson* with the rest
  Of the Poets ; but the Best.
Reader, wo'dst thou more have known ?
Aske his Story, not this Stone.
That will speake what this can't tell
Of his glory. *So farewell.*

An Ode for him.

A H *Ben !*
    Say how, or when
  Shall we thy Guests
  Meet at those *Lyrick* Feasts,
    Made at the *Sun,*
  The *Dog,* the triple *Tunne ?*

---

[8] =temperance, moderation.   [9] On this and next see Memorial-Introduction.

Where we such clusters had,
As made us nobly wild, not mad;
And yet each Verse of thine
Out-did the meate, out-did the frolick wine.

My *Ben !*
Or come agen :
Or send to us,
Thy wits great over-plus ;
But teach us yet
Wisely to husband it ;
Lest we that Tallent spend :
And having once brought to an end
That precious stock; the store
Of such a wit the world sho'd have no more.

Upon a Virgin.

SPEND Harmless shade, thy nightly Houres,
    Selecting here, both Herbs, and Flowers ;
Of which make Garlands here, and there,
To dress thy silent sepulchre.
Nor do thou feare the want of these,
In everlasting Properties.
Since we fresh strewings will bring hither,
Farre faster then the first can wither.   [*than*

Blame.

IN Battailes what disasters fall,
  The King he beares the blame of all.

A request to the Graces.

PONDER my words, if so that any be
  Known guilty here of incivility :
Let what is graceless, discompos'd, and rude,
With sweetness, smoothness, softness, be endu'd.
Teach it to blush, to curtsie, lisp, and shew
Demure, but yet, full of temptation too.
Numbers ne'r tickle, or but lightly please,
Unlesse they have some wanton carriages.[1]
This if ye do, each Piece will here be good,
And gracefull made, by your neate[2] Sisterhood.

Upon himselfe.

I LATELY fri'd,[3] but now behold
  I freeze as fast, and shake for cold.

---

[1] Thus the poet of Verona, in a similar strain :—

    Nam castum esse decet pium poetam
    Ipsum : versiculos nihil necesse est :
    Qui tum denique habent salem ac leporem,
    Si sunt molliculi, ac parum pudici,
    Et quod prunat, incitare possunt.
                          Catul. Carmen 16. N.

[2] =elegant.   [3] See Glossarial Index under 'frie.'

And in good faith I'd thought it strange
T'ave found in me this sudden change ;
But that I understood by dreames,
These only were but Loves extreames ;
Who fires with hope the Lovers heart,
And starves with cold the self-same part.

Multitude.

WE Trust not to the multitude in Warre,
    But to the stout ; and those that skilfull are.

Feare.

MAN must do well out of a good intent ;
    Not for the servile feare[4] of punishment.

To M. Kellam.[5]

WHAT! can my *Kellam* drink his Sack
    In Goblets to the brim,
And see his *Robin Herrick* lack,
    Yet send no Boules to him ?

---

[4] " Oderunt peccare boni virtutis amore :
    Tu nihil admittes in te fomidine pœnae."
            Horace : Epist. i. xvi. 10, ll 52-3.

[5] A parishioner, probably.

For love or pitie to his Muse,
    (That she may flow in Verse)
Contemne to recommend a Cruse,
    But send to˙ her a Tearce.[6]

Happinesse to hospitalitie, or a hearty
to good house-keeping.

FIRST, may the hand of bounty bring
    Into the daily offering
Of full provision ; such a store,
Till that the Cooke cries, Bring no more.
Upon your hogsheads never fall
A drought of wine, ale, beere (at all ;)
But, like full clouds, may they from thence
Diffuse their mighty influence.
Next, let the Lord, and Ladie here
Enjoy a Christning yeare by yeare ;
And this *good blessing* back them still,
T'ave Boyes, and Gyrles too, as they will.
Then from the porch may many a Bride
Unto the Holy Temple ride :
And thence return, (short prayers seyd)
A wife most richly marrièd.

[6] = cask, one-third of a pipe, 42 gallons.

Last, may the Bride and Bridegroome be
Untoucht by cold *sterility ;*
But in their springing blood so play,
As that in *Lusters* few they may,
By laughing too, and lying downe,
People a *City* or a *Towne.*

Cunctation [7] in Correction.

THE *Lictors*[8] bundl'd up their rods : beside,
   Knit them with knots (with much adoe unty'd)
That if (unknitting) men wo'd yet repent,
They might escape the lash of punishment.

Present Government grievous.

MEN are suspicious ; prone to discontent :
   Subjects still loath the present Government.[9]

Rest Refreshes.

LAY by the good a while ; a resting field
   Will, after ease, a richer harvest yeild :
Trees this year beare ; next, they their wealth with-
       hold :
Continuall reaping makes a land wax old.

---

[7] = delay.   [8] = ligatores ?
[9] So Hooker begins his " Ecclesiastical Polity.'

Revenge.

MANS *disposition is for to requite*
An injurie, before a benefite :
Thanksgiving is a burden,[1] *and a paine ;*
Revenge is pleasing to us, as our gaine.

The first marrs or makes.

IN all our high designments, 'twill appeare,
The first event breeds confidence or feare.

Beginning, difficult.

HARD *are the two first staires unto a Crowne ;*
Which got, the third, bids him a King come downe.

Faith four-square.[2]

FAITH is a thing that's four-square ; let it fall
This way or that, it not declines at all.

---

[1] Cf. the remarks by which Reynolds attracted the notice of Dr. Johnson : "You have the comfort of being released from a burden of gratitude." (Boswell sub. anno, 1752.)

[2] See Glossarial Index s. v.

The present time best pleaseth.

PRAISE they that will Times past, I joy to see
My selfe now live : *this age best pleaseth mee.*

Cloathes, are conspirators.

THOUGH from without no foes at all we feare ;
We shall be wounded by the cloathes we weare.

Cruelty.

TIS *but a dog-like madnesse in bad Kings,*
For to delight in wounds and murderings.
As some plants prosper best by cuts and blowes ;
So Kings by killing doe encrease their foes.

Faire after foule.

TEARES *quickly drie : griefes will in time decay :*
A cleare, will come after a cloudy, day.

Hunger.

ASKE me what hunger is, and Ile reply,
'Tis but a fierce desire of hot and drie.

Bad wages for good service.

IN this misfortune Kings doe most excell,
To heare the worst from men, when they doe well.

The End.

CONQUER we shall, but we must first contend;
  'Tis not the Fight that crowns us, but the end.[3]

The Bondman.

BIND me but to thee with thine haire,
  And quickly I shall be
Made by that fetter or that snare
  A bondman unto thee.

Or if thou tak'st that bond away,
  Then bore me through the care;
And by the Law [4] I ought to stay
  For ever with thee here.

Choose for the best.

GIVE house-roome to the best; *'Tis never known*
  Vertue and pleasure, both to dwell in one.

To Silvia.

PARDON my trespasse (Silvia,) I confesse,
  My kisse out-went the bounds of shamfastnesse:
None is discreet at all times; no, *not Jove*
Himselfe, at one time, can be wise and Love.

---

[3] "*Finis coronat opus*" (a Proverb).   [4] See Exodus xxi. 6.

Faire shewes deceive.

SMOOTH was the Sea, and seem'd to call
   To prettie girles to play withall :
Who padling there, the Sea soone frown'd,
And on a sudden both were drown'd.
What credit can we give to seas,
Who, kissing, kill such Saints as these ?

His wish.

FAT be my Hinde ; unlearnèd be my wife ;
   Peacefull my night ; my day devoid of strife :
To these a comely off-spring I desire,
Singing about my everlasting fire.

Upon Julia's *washing her self in the river.*

HOW fierce was I, when I did see
   My *Julia* wash her self in thee !
So *Lillies* thorough Christall look :
So purest pebbles in the brook :
As in the River *Julia* did,
Halfe with a Lawne of water hid,
Into thy streames my self I threw,
And strugling there, I kist thee too ;
And more had done (it is confest)
Had not thy waves forbad the rest.

A Meane in our Meanes.

THOUGH Frankinsense the *Deities* require,
    We must not give all to the hallowed fire.
Such be our gifts, and such be our expence,
As for our selves to leave some frankinsence.[5]

Upon Clunn.

A ROWLE of Parchment *Clunn* about him beares,
    Charg'd with the Armes of all his Ancestors :
And seems halfe ravisht, when he looks upon
That Bar, this *Bend* ; that *Fess*, this *Cheveron ;*
This *Manch*, that *Moone ;* this *Martlet*, and that
    Mound ;
This counterchange of *Perle* and *Diamond*.[6]
What joy can *Clun* have in that Coat, or this,
Whenas his owne still out at elboes is ?

Upon Cupid.[7]

LOVE, like a Beggar, came to me
    With Hose and Doublet torne :

---

[5] " Sure none need be more bountifull in giving then the Sunne is in shining, which though freely bestowing his beames on the world keeps notwithstanding the body of light to himself. Yea it is necessary that Liberality should as well have banks as a stream."
               Fuller's Holy and Profane State (1648), p. 29.

[6] = mode of blazon sometimes used in case of Peers. The others are also heraldic terms.

[7] Our poet has before pourtrayed a fairy beggar. He now gives us

His Shirt bedangling from his knee,
  With Hat and Shooes out-worne.

He askt an almes ; I gave him bread,
  And meat too, for his need :
Of which, when he had fully fed,
  He wished me all *Good speed.*

Away he went, but as he turn'd
  (In faith I know not how)
He toucht me so, as that I burn,
  And am tormented now.

Love's silent flames, and fires obscure
  Then crept into my heart ;
And though I saw no Bow, I'm sure,
  His finger was the dart.

Vpon Blisse.

B*LISSE* (last night drunk) did kisse his mothers
    knee :
Where he will kisse (next drunk) conjecture yc.

Vpon Burr.

B*URR* is a smell-feast, and a man alone,
  That (where meat is) will be a hanger on.

Love in a mendicant form. The style of this little Anacreontic sketch
will somewhat remind us of the third Ode of the sportive Teian. N.

Vpon Megg.

M*EGG* yesterday was troubled with a Pose,
 Which, this night hardned, sodders up her
  nose.[8]

An Hymne to Love.

1.　　　I WILL confesse
　　　With Cheerfulnesse,
 Love is a thing so likes me,
　　　That let her lay
　　　On me all day,
 Ile kiss the hand that strikes me.

2.　　　I will not, I
　　　Now blubb'ring, cry,
 It (Ah!) too late repents me,
　　　That I did fall
　　　To love at all,
 Since love so much contents me.

3.　　　No, no, Ile be
　　　In fetters free :
 While others they sit wringing
　　　Their hands for paine ;
　　　Ile entertaine
 The wounds of love with singing.

[8] = rheum—a cold in the head.

4.   With Flowers and Wine,
               And Cakes Divine,
         To strike me I will tempt thee :
               Which done ; no more
               Ile come before
         Thee and thine Altars emptie.

To his honoured and most ingenious friend
Mr. Charles Cotton.[9]

FOR brave comportment, wit without offence,
    Words fully flowing, yet of influence :
Thou art that man of men, the man alone,
Worthy the Publique Admiration :
Who with thine owne eyes read'st what we doe
    write,
And giv'st our Numbers *Euphonie*, and weight.
Tel'st when a Verse springs high, how understood
To be, or not borne of the Royall-blood.
What State above, what *Symmetrie* below,
Lines have, or sho'd have, thou the best canst show.
For which (my *Charles*) it is my pride to be,
Not so much knowne, as to be lov'd of thee.
Long may I live so, and my wreath of *Bayes*,
Be lesse anothers *Laurell*, then thy praise.   [*than*

---

[9] The translator of Montaigne and associate of Isaak Walton.

Women uselesse.

WHAT need we marry Women, when
    Without their use we may have men?
And such as will in short time be,
For murder fit, or mutinie ;
As *Cadmus* once a new way found,
By throwing teeth into the ground ;[10]
(From which poore seed, and rudely sown)
Sprung up a War-like Nation.
So let us Yron, Silver, Gold,
Brasse, Leade, or Tinne, throw into th' mould ;
And we shall see in little space
Rise up of men, a fighting race.
If this can be, say then, what need
Have we of Women or their seed ?

Love is a sirrup.

L*OVE is a sirrup ;* and who er'e we see
    Sick and surcharg'd with this sacietie : [1]
Shall by this pleasing trespasse quickly prove,
Ther's loathsomnesse[2] e'en in the sweets of love.

---

[10] Ovid, Metamorph.   [1] = satiety.

[2] " Medio de fonte leporum
    surgit amari aliquid." Lucretius.

Leven.[3]

LOVE is a Leven, and a loving kisse
  The Leven of a loving sweet-heart is.

Repletion.

PHYSITIANS say Repletion springs
  More from the sweet then sower things. [*than*

On Himselfe.

WEEPE for the dead, for they have lost this
        light :
And weepe for me, lost in an endlesse night.
Or mourne, or make a Marble Verse for me,
Who writ for many.   *Benedicite.*

No Man without Money.

NO man such rare parts hath, that he can swim,
  If favour or occasion helpe not him.

On Himselfe.

LOST to the world ; lost to my selfe ; alone
  Here now I rest under this Marble stone :
In depth of silence, heard, and seene of none.

[3] = leaven.

To M. Leonard Willan [4] *his*
peculiar friend.

I WILL be short, and having quickly hurl'd
  This line about, live Thou throughout the world;
Who art a man for all Sceanes;[5] unto whom
(What's hard to others) nothing's troublesome.
Can'st write the *Comick, Tragick* straine, and fall
From these to penne the pleasing Pastorall:
Who fli'st at all heights: Prose and Verse run'st
      through;
Find'st here a fault, and mend'st the trespasse too:
For which I might extoll thee, but speake lesse,
Because thy selfe art comming to the Presse:
And then sho'd I in praising thee be slow,
Posterity will pay thee what I owe.

To his worthy Friend M. John Hall,
Student of Grayes-Inne.[6]

TELL me, young man, or did the Muses bring
  Thee lesse to taste, then to drink up their
      Spring;
That none hereafter sho'd be thought, or be
A Poet, or a Poet-like but Thee?

---

[4] Nothing seems to be known of this Willan in dramatic history.
[5] See Glossarial Index s. v.   [6] See Memorial-Introduction.

What was thy Birth, thy starre that makes thee
      knowne,
At twice ten yeares, a prime and publike one ?
Tell us thy Nation, kindred, or the whence
Thou had'st, and hast thy *mighty influence,*
That makes thee lov'd, and of the men desir'd,
And no lesse prais'd, then of the maides admir'd. [*than*
Put on thy Laurell then ; and in that trimme
Be thou *Apollo,* or the type of him :
Or let the *Unshorne God* lend thee his Lyre,
And next to him, be Master of the Quire.

To Julia.

OFFER thy gift ; but first the Law commands
    Thee, *Julia,* first, to *sanctifie* thy hands :
Doe that, my *Julia* which the rites require,
Then boldly give thine incense to the fire.

To the most comely and proper M. Elizabeth Finch.[7]

HANSOME you are, and Proper you will be
    Despight of all your infortunitie : [8]

---

[7] Sir Moyle Finch, 1st Baronet of Eastwell, co. Kent, had a d.
Elizabeth, who died young, but there were others of the name, so
that it would be unsafe to identify this M. Elizabeth Finch.

[8] = ill fortune.

Live long and lovely, but yet grow no lesse
In that your owne prefixèd comelinesse :
Spend on that stock : and when your life must fall,
Leave others Beauty, to set up withall.

Upon Ralph.

RALPH pares his nayles, his warts, his cornes,
   and *Ralph*
In sev'rall tills and boxes, keepes 'em safe ;
Instead of Harts-horne (if he speakes the troth)
To make a lustie-gellie⁹ for his broth.

To his Booke.

IF hap it must, that I must see thee lye
  Absyrtus-like,¹ all torne confusedly :
With solemne tears, and with much grief of heart,
Ile recollect thee (weeping) part by part ;
And having washt thee, close thee in a chest
With spice ; that done, Ile leave thee to thy rest.

---

⁹ =jelly, condiment.
¹ Absyrtus, son of the king of Colchis, torn to pieces by Medea
when she fled with Jason.

TO THE KING,

Upon his welcome to Hampton-Court.

Set and Sung.[2]

WELCOME, *Great Cesar*, welcome now you are,
    As dearest Peace, after destructive Warre :
Welcome as slumbers ; or as beds of ease
After our long, and peevish sicknesses.
O *Pompe of Glory* ! Welcome now, and come
To re-possess once more your long'd-for home.
A thousand Altars smoake ; a thousand thighes
Of Beeves here ready stand for Sacrifice.
Enter and prosper ; while our eyes doe waite
For an *Ascendent* throughly *Auspicate :* [3]
Under which signe we may the former stone
Lay of our safeties new foundation :
That done ; *O Cesar* ! live, and be to us,
Our *Fate*, our *Fortune*, and our *Genius ;*
To whose free knees we may our temples tye
As to a still protecting Deitie :

[2] The King was settled at Hampton Court under the protection of the army, Aug. 24, 1647 : but this poem seems to celebrate an earlier and happier occasion.

[3] Term of Astrology : a rising of such part of the ecliptic as may be auspicious.

That sho'd you stirre, we and our Altars too
May *(Great Augustus) goe along with You.*
Chor. Long live the King; and to accomplish this,
We'l from our owne, adde far more years to his.

Ultimus Heroum :
or, *To the most Learned, and to the right Honourable,*
Henry, *Marquesse of* Dorchester.[4]

A ND as time past when *Cato* the Severe
    Entred the circum-spacious Theater ;
In reverence of his person, every one
Stood as he had been turn'd from flesh to stone :
E'ne so my numbers will astonisht be
If but lookt on ; struck dead, if scan'd by Thee.

To his Muse, another to the same.
T ELL that Brave Man, fain thou wo'dst have
    access
To kiss his hands, but that for fearfullness ;
Or else because th' art like a modest Bride,
Ready to blush to death, sho'd he but chide.

---

[4] Henry Pierrepont, 2nd Earl of Kingston, was created Marquis of Dorchester, 25th March, 1644. He died in 1680. He was eldest son of the " brave Newark."

Upon Vineger.

VINEGER is no other I define,
     Then the dead Corps, or Carkase of the Wine.

                                [*than*

Upon Mudge.[5]

M UDGE every morning to the Postern comes,
     (His teeth all out) to rince and wash his
         gummes.

To his learned Friend M. Jo. Harmar,[6]
Phisitian to the Colledge of Westminster.

WHEN first I find those Numbers thou do'st
         write,
To be most soft, terce, sweet, and perpolite :[7]
Next, when I see Thee towring in the skie,
In an expansion no less large, then high ;   [*than*
Then, in that compass, sayling here and there,
And with Circumgyration[8] every where ;

---

[5] A Devonshire name.

[6] A native of Churchdoune, co. Gloucester : M. A. at Oxford in
1617, and (according to Anthony a-Wood) was always afterwards
called " Doctor," though he had taken no higher degree than M. A).
He was sometime under-master of Westminster School, and Herrick
no doubt playfully transmuted " Doctor " into " physician." He
wrote Latin verse : died 1st Nov., 1670.   [7] = thoroughly polished.

[8] See Glossarial Index under 'circum.'

Following with love and active heate thy game,
And then at last to truss [9] the Epigram ;
I must confess, distinction none I see
Between *Domitians Martiall* [1] then, and Thee.
But this I know, should *Jupiter* agen
Descend from heaven, to re-converse with men ;
The Romane Language full, and superfine,
If *Jove* wo'd speake, he wo'd accept of thine.

Upon his Spaniell Tracie. [2]

NOW thou art dead, no eye shall ever see,
    For shape and service, *Spaniell* like to thee.
This shall my love doe, give thy sad death one
Teare, that deserves of me a million.

The Deluge.

DROWNING, drowning, I espie
    Coming from my *Julia's* eye :
'Tis some solace in our smart,
To have friends to beare a part :
I have none ; but must be sure
Th' inundation to endure.

---

[9] As the whole metaphor is a hawking one, 'truss' must here mean, to seize and carry aloft.   [1] Domitiani Martiall.

[2] See Glossarial Index.

Shall not times hereafter tell
This for no meane *miracle ;*
When the waters by their fall
Threatn'd ruine unto all?
Yet the deluge here was known,
Of a world to drowne but One.

Upon Lupes.

L *UPES* for the outside of his suite has paide ;
 But for his heart, he cannot have it made :
The reason is, his credit cannot get
The inward carbage [3] for his cloathes as yet.

Raggs.

W HAT are our patches, tatters, raggs, and rents,
 But the base dregs and lees of vestiments ?

Strength to support Soveraignty.

L ET Kings and Rulers learne this line from me ;
 Where power is weake, unsafe is Majestie.

Upon Tubbs.

F OR thirty yeares, *Tubbs* has been proud and
  poor ;
'Tis now his habit, which he can't give ore.

[3] = garbage, as from ' garb,' trimming.

Crutches.

THOU seest me *Lucia* this year droope,
  Three *Zodiaks* fill'd more I shall stoope ;
Let Crutches then provided be
To shore[4] up my debilitie.
Then while thou laugh'st ; Ile, sighing, crie,
A *Ruine underpropt* am I :
Do'n[5] will I then my *Beadsmans*[6] gown,
And when so feeble I am grown,
As my weake shoulders cannot beare
The burden of a *Grashopper :*
Yet with the bench of agèd sires,
When I and they keep tearmly fires ;[7]
With my weake voice I'le sing, or say
Some Odes I made of *Lucia :*[8]

---

[4] =support.   [5] Note the transition-form 'D'on ' = do on.

[6] An almsman, or one that prays for a benefactor. Selden says,
in his *Titles of Honour*, that he had seen a petition from a bishop to
our king, Henry V., subscribed with "your worship's beadsman."
Glossographia. N. Burns signed himself in a charming poem,
" The beadsman of Nithsdale."

[7] This couplet may imply a wish to spend his old age with his
former ancestors at the college where he was educated, or afterwards
resided.

[8] From the preceding mention of the grasshopper, connected with
his weak voice, it may be presumed that our poet had in view
Homer's similitude with respect to feeble garrulous old men, in his
third Iliad: ἀλλ' ἀγορηταὶ, &c. N. The reference is rather to
Ecclesiastes xii. 5.

Then will I heave my wither'd hand
To *Jove* the Mighty, for to stand
Thy faithfull friend, and to poure downe
Upon thee many a *Benizon.*

To Julia.

HOLY waters hither bring
    For the sacred sprinkling :
Baptize me and thee, and so
Let us to the Altar go.
And (ere we our rites commence)
Wash our hands in innocence.
Then I'le be the *Rex Sacrorum,*
Thou the Queen of *Peace and Quorum.*[9]

Upon Case.

CASE is a Lawyer, that near pleads alone,   [*nere*
    But when he hears the like confusion,
As when the disagreeing Commons throw
About their House, their clamorous I,[1] or No :
Then *Case*, as loud as any *Serjant* there,
Cries out (My lord, my Lord) the Case is clear :
But when all's hush't, *Case* then a fish more mute,[2] [*than*
Bestirs his Hand, but starves in hand the Suite.

---

[9] =of Peace and *Law.*   [1] See Glossarial Index s. v.
[2] A classical epithet ἄλλος.

To Perenna.

I A *Dirge* will pen for thee ;
    Thou a *Trentall*[3] make for me :
That the Monks and Fryers together,
Here may sing the rest of either :
Next, I'm sure, the Nuns will have
Candlemas to grace the Grave.

To his Sister in Law, M. Susanna Herrick.[4]

THE Person crowns the Place ; your lot doth fall
    Last, yet to be with These a Principall.
Howere it fortuned ; know for Truth, I meant
You a fore-leader in this Testament.

Upon the Lady Crew.[5]

THIS Stone can tell the storie of my life,
    What was my Birth, to whom I was a Wife :
In teeming years, how soon my Sun was set,
Where now I rest, these may be known by *Jet.*[6]
For other things, my many Children be
The best and truest *Chronicles* of me.

---

[3] See Glossarial Index s. v.   [4] See Memorial-Introduction.

[5] She died 2nd December, 1639. See the various Crewe poems.

[6] Qu—ink? or the black-painted inscription? or the jet-black marble or other stone ?

On Tomasin Parsons.[7]

GROW up in Beauty, as thou do'st begin,
    And be of all admirèd, *Tomasin.*

Ceremony upon Candlemas Eve.

DOWN with the Rosemary, and so
    Down with the Baies, & misletoe :
Down with the Holly, Ivie, all,
Wherewith ye drest the Christmas Hall :
That so the superstitious find
No one least Branch there left behind :
For look, how many leaves there be
Neglected there (maids trust to me)
So many *Goblins* you shall see.[8]

Suspicion makes secure.

HE that will live of all cares dispossest,
    Must shun the bad, I,[9] and suspect the best.

Upon Spokes.

SPOKES, when he sees a rosted Pig, he swears
    Nothing he loves on't but the chaps and ears :
But carve to him the fat flanks ; and he shall
Rid these, and those, and part by part eat all.

---

[7] A forgotten woman ('Thomasina').   [8] Folk-lore.
[9] = ay, as before.

To his Kinsman, *M.* Tho : Herrick, *who*
desired to be in his Book.[10]

WELCOME to this my Colledge, and though late
    Th'ast got a place here (standing candidate)
It matters not, since thou art chosen one
Here of my great and good foundation.

A Bucolick betwixt Two : Lacon *and* Thyrsis.[1]

Lacon. FOR a kiss or two, confesse,
        What doth cause this pensiveness,
    Thou most lovely Neat-heardesse ?[2]
    Why so lonely on the hill ?
    Why thy pipe by thee so still,
    That erewhile was heard so shrill ?
    Tell me, do thy kine now fail
    To fulfill [3] the milkin-paile ?
    Say, what is't that thou do'st aile ?

Thyr. None of these ; but out, alas !
    A mischance is come to pass,
    And I'le tell thee what it was :
    See mine eyes are weeping ripe,

[10] See Memorial-Introduction.
  [1] Thyrsis in this poem is applied to a female character. I do not recollect to have seen it before given to a shepherdess by any pastoral writer. [2] = Cattle shepherdess. [3] See Glossarial Index s. v.

Lacon. Tell, and I'le lay down my Pipe.

Thyr. I have lost my lovely steere,
  That to me was far more deer
  Then these kine, which I milke here. [*than*
  Broad of fore-head, large of eye,
  Party-colour'd like a Pie ; [4]
  Smooth in each limb as a die ;
  Clear of hoof, and clear of horn ;
  Sharply pointed as a thorn :
  With a neck by yoke unworn.
  From the which hung down by strings,
  Balls of Cowslips, Daisie rings,
  Enterplac't with ribbanings.
  Faultless every way for shape ;
  Not a straw co'd him escape ;
  Ever gamesome as an ape :
  But yet harmless as a sheep.
  (Pardon, *Lacon* if I weep)
  Tears will spring, where woes are deep.
  Now (ai me !) (ai me !) Last night
  Came a mad dog, and did bite,
  I,[5] and kil'd my dear delight.

Lacon. Alack, for grief !

    [4] = pye.   [5] = ay.

Thyr. But I'le be brief.

> Hence I must, for time doth call
> Me, and my sad Play-mates all,
> To his Ev'ning Funerall.
> Live long, *Lacon,* so *adew !*

Lacon. Mournfull maid, farewell to you ;

> *Earth afford ye flowers to strew.*

Upon Sapho.

LOOK upon *Sapho's* lip, and you will swear,
   There is a love-like leven [6] rising there.

Upon Faunus.

WE read how *Faunus,*[7] he the shepheards *God,*
   His wife to death whipt with a *Mirtle Rod.*
The Rod (perhaps) was better'd by the name ;
But had it been of Birch, the death's the same.

The Quintell.[8]

UP with the Quintill, that the Rout,
   May fart for joy, as well as shout :
Either's welcome, Stinke or Civit,
   If we take it, as they give it.

---

[6] Leaven.   [7] Mythical.

[8] See Glossarial Index. There used to be a Quintain Club at Oxford (1830-49), chiefly supported by the wealthier under-graduate members of Christ's Church.

A Bachanalian Verse.

1.   DRINKE up
    Your Cup,
But not spill Wine ;
For if you
Do,
'Tis an ill signe ;

2.   That we
Foresee,
.You are cloy'd here,
If so, no
Hoe,[9]
But avoid here.

Care a good keeper.

CARE keepes the Conquest ; 'tis no lesse renowne,
  To keepe a Citie, then to winne a Towne.

Rules for our reach.

MEN must have Bounds[10] how farre to walke; for we
  Are made farre worse, by lawless liberty.

[9] Cf. ' Ho ' in Halliwell : =stop.
[10] " Est modus in rebus," &c., Horace, Sat. i. 1, 106-7: Ep. i, 1, 32.

To Biancha.

AH *Biancha!* now I see,
 It is Noone and past with me :
In a while it will strike one ;
Then, *Biancha*, I am gone.
Some *effusions* [1] let me have,
Offer'd on my holy Grave ;
Then, *Biancha*, let me rest
With my face towards the East. [2]

To the handsome Mistresse Grace Potter. [3]

AS is your name, so is your comely face,
 Toucht everywhere with such diffusèd grace,
As that in all that *admirable round*,
There is not one least *solecisme* found ;
And as that part, so every portion else,
Keepes line for line with *Beauties Parallels*.

Anacreontike.

I MUST
 Not trust
Here to any ;
Bereav'd,
Deceiv'd

---

[1] = outpourings.
[2] The usual position—to salute the Sun of Righteousness at the Resurrection. [3] See Memorial-Introduction.

By so many :
    As one
    Undone
By my losses ;
    Comply
    Will I
With my crosses.
    Yet still
    I will
Not be grieving ;
    Since thence
    And hence
Comes relieving.
    But this
    Sweet is
In our mourning ;
    Times bad
    And sad
Are a turning :
    And he
    Whom we
See dejected ;
    Next day
    Wee may
See erected.

More modest, more manly.

'TIS still observ'd, those men most valiant are,
  That are most modest ere they come to warre.

Not to covet much where little is the charge.

WHY sho'd we covet much, whenas we know,
  W'ave more to beare our charge, then way
    to go ?   [*than*

Anacreontick Verse.

BRISK methinks I am, and fine,
  When I drinke my capring [4] wine :
Then to love I do encline,
  When I drinke my wanton wine :
And I wish all maidens mine,
  When I drinke my sprightly wine :
Well I sup, and well I dine,
  When I drinke my frolick wine :
But I languish, lowre, and Pine,
  When I want my fragrant wine.

Upon Pennie.

BROWN bread *Tom Pennie* eates, and must of right,
  Because his stock will not hold out for white.

---

[4] = leaping, sparkling, with the under-thought, that inclines him
to dance or 'caper' and be merry. So when he drinks of the
wanton making wine he inclines to love, &c., &c.

Patience in Princes.

K INGS *must not use the Axe for each offence :*
Princes cure some faults by their patience.

Feare gets force.

D ESPAIRE *takes heart, when ther's no hope to*
speed :
The Coward then takes Armes, and do's the deed.

Parcell-gil't-Poetry.

L ET'S strive to be the best; the Gods, we know it,
Pillars and men, hate an indifferent Poet.

Upon Love, by way of question and answer.

I BRING ye Love.　　*Quest.* What will love do ?
　　Ans. Like, and dislike ye :
I bring ye love :　　*Quest.* What will Love do?
　　Ans. Stroake ye to strike ye.
I bring ye love :　　*Quest.* What will Love do ?
　　Ans. Love will be-foole ye :
I bring ye love :　　*Quest.* What will love do?
　　Ans. Heate ye to coole ye :
I bring ye love :　　*Quest.* What will love do ?
　　Ans. Love gifts will send ye :

I bring ye love :   *Quest.* What will love do ?

    Ans. Stock ye to spend ye :

I bring ye love :   *Quest.* What will love do ?

    Ans. Love will fulfill ye :

I bring ye love :   *Quest.* What will love do ?

    Ans. Kisse ye, to kill ye.

To the Lord Hopton, *on his fight in* Cornwall.[5]

GO on, brave *Hopton*, to effectuate that

    Which wee, and times to come, shall wonder at.

Lift up thy Sword ; next, suffer it to fall,

And by that *One blow* set an end to all.

His Grange.

HOW well contented in this private *Grange*

    Spend I my life (that's subject unto change :)

Under whose Roofe with *Mosse-worke* wrought,

      there I

Kisse my *Brown wife,* and *black Posterity.*

---

[5] Sir Ralph Hopton, of Stratton, co. Cornwall : created a Knight of the Bath at the coronation of Charles I. He took up arms in the Royal cause in 1642, and distinguished himself in several military affairs, but especially at Bradock Down, Stratton, where he obtained a decisive victory, and was in consequence created Baron Hopton 4th Sep., 1643. He went abroad during the Commonwealth, and died at Bruges in 1652. Of course Herrick inserted the later title on publishing his book.

Leprosie in houses.

WHEN to a House I come, and see
    The *Genius* wastefull, more then free :   [*than*
The servants *thumblesse*,[6] yet to eat,
With lawlesse tooth the floure of wheate :
The Sonnes to suck the milke of Kine,
More then the teats of Discipline :
The Daughters wild and loose in dresse ;
Their cheekes unstain'd with shamefac'tnesse :
The Husband drunke, the Wife to be
A Baud to incivility :[7]
I must confesse, I there descrie,
A House spred through with *Leprosie.*

Good Manners at meat.

THIS rule of manners I will teach my guests,
    To come with their own bellies unto feasts :
Not to eat equall portions ; but to rise
Farc't[8] with the food, that may themselves suffice.

[6] Qu—awkward, unhandy ? or from his former use of '*painful*
thumb' it may be negligent, idle.   See Glossarial Index s. v.

[7] = a harbourer and promoter of incivility or unmannerliness.

[8] = stuffed.

Drooping, I draw on to the vaults of death,
Or'e which you'l walk, when I am laid beneath.

The Begger.

SHALL I a daily Begger be,
   For loves sake asking almes of thee?
Still shall I crave, and never get
A hope of my desirèd bit?
Ah cruell maides! Ile goe my way,
Whereas (perchance) my fortunes may
Finde out a Threshold or a doore,
That may far sooner speed the poore :
Where thrice we knock, and none will heare,
Cold comfort still I'm sure lives there.

Bastards.

OUR Bastard-children are but like to Plate,
   Made by the Coyners illegitimate.

His change.

MY many cares and much distress,
   Has made me like a wilderness :
Or (discompos'd) I'm like a rude,
And all-confusèd multitude :
Out of my comely manners worne ;
And as in meanes, in minde all torne.

The Vision.

M E thought I saw (as I did dreame in bed)
  A crawling Vine about *Anacreon's* head :
Flusht was his face ; his haires with oyle did shine ;
And as he spake, his mouth ranne ore with wine.
Tipled he was ; and tipling lispt withall ;
And lisping reeld, and reeling like to fall.
A young *Enchantresse* close by him did stand
Tapping his plump thighes with a *mirtle* wand :
She smil'd ; he kist ; and kissing, cull'd⁵ her too ;
And being cup-shot,⁶ more he co'd not doe.
For which (me thought) in prittie anger she
Snatcht off his Crown, and gave the wreath to me :
Since when (me thinks) my braines about doe swim,
And I am wilde and wanton like to him.

A Vow to Venus.

H APPILY I had a sight
  Of my dearest deare last night ;
Make her this day smile on me,
And Ile Roses give to thee.

---

⁵ = embraced.   ⁶ As we speak of a gun-shot wound,
so a reeling tipsy, more or less helpless man, was said to be ' cup-
shot.' Halliwell gives ' cap-shotten.'

On his Booke.

THE bound (almost) now of my book I see,
   But yet no end of those therein or me :
Here we begin new life ; while thousands quite
Are lost, and theirs, in everlasting night.

A Sonnet of Perilla.

THEN did I live when I did see
   Perilla smile on none but me.
But (ah !) by starres malignant crost,
The life I got I quickly lost :
But yet a way there doth remaine,
For me embalm'd to live againe ;
And that's to love me ; in which state
Ile live as one *Regenerate.*

Bad may be better.

MAN may at first transgress, but next do well :
   Vice doth in some but lodge awhile, not dwell.

Posting to Printing.

LET others to the Printing Presse run fast,
   Since after death comes glory, *Ile not haste.*

Rapine brings Ruine.

WHAT'S got by Justice is establisht sure ;
   No Kingdomes got by Rapine long endure.

Comfort to a youth that had lost his Love.

WHAT needs complaints,
    When she a place
Has with the race
    Of Saints ?
In endlesse mirth,
She thinks not on
What's said or done
    In earth :
She sees no teares,
Or any tone
Of thy deep grone
    She heares :
Nor do's she minde,
Or think on't now,
That ever thou
    Wast kind.
But chang'd above,
She likes not there,
As she did here,
    Thy Love.
Forbeare therefore,
And lull asleepe
Thy woes, and weep
    No more.

Upon Boreman. *Epig.*

B*OREMAN* takes tole, cheats, flatters, lyes ; yet
   Boreman,
For all the Divell helps, will be a poore man.

Saint Distaffs day, or the morrow after
Twelth day.[7]

PARTLY worke and partly play
   Ye must on S. *Distaffs* day :
From the Plough soone free your teame ;
Then come home and fother[8] them.
If the Maides a-spinning goe,
Burne the flax, and fire the tow :
Scorch their plackets,[9] but beware
That ye singe no maiden-haire.
Bring in pailes of water then,
Let the Maides bewash the men.

---

[7] I have not hitherto met with any record of this saint, nor was I aware that such ever occurred in our calendar . . . . . . St. Distaff is perhaps only a coinage of our poets, to designate the day, when the Christmas vacation being over, good housewives, with others, resumed their usual employment N.   Good Dr. Nott is perhaps too absurdly matter-of-fact.   Probably St. Distaff was a piece of rustic witticism.   [8] = fodder.

[9] = a woman's pocket.

Give S. *Distaffe* all the right,
Then bid Christmas sport *good night ;*
And next morrow, every one
To his owne vocation.

Sufferance.

I N the hope of ease to come,
   Let's endure one Martyrdome.

His teares to Thamasis.

I SEND, I send here my supremest kiss
   To thee, my *silver-footed Thamasis.*
No more shall I reiterate [10] thy Strand,
Whereon so many Stately Structures stand :
Nor in the summers sweeter evenings go,
To bath in thee (as thousand others doe,)
No more shall I along thy christall glide,
In Barge (with boughes and rushes beautifi'd)
With soft-smooth Virgins (for our chast disport)
To *Richmond, Kingstone,* and to *Hampton-Court :*
Never againe shall I with Finnie-Ore
Put from, or draw unto the faithfull shore :
And Landing here, or safely Landing there,
Make way to my *Belovèd Westminster :*

[10] = pace and repace.

Or to the *Golden-cheap-side,* where the earth
Of *Julia Herrick* gave to me my Birth.
May all clean *Nimphs* and curious water Dames,
With Swan-like-state, flote up & down thy streams :
No drought upon thy wanton waters fall
To make them Leane, and languishing at all.
No ruffling winds come hither to discease [1]
Thy pure, and *Silver-wristed Naides.*
Keep up your state, ye streams ; and as ye spring,
Never make sick your Banks by surfeiting.
Grow young with Tydes, and though I see ye never,
Receive this vow, *so fare-ye-well for ever.*[2]

Pardons.

THOSE *ends in War the best contentment bring,*
  Whose Peace is made up with a Pardoning.

Peace not Permanent.

GREAT *Cities seldome rest : If there be none*
  T'invade from far ; They'l finde worse foes at home.

---

[1] =dis-ease, trouble or bring unrest. See Glossarial Index s. v.
[2] See Memorial-Introduction on this poem.

Truth and Errour.

T WIXT *Truth and Errour, there's this difference*
 known,
Errour is fruitfull,[3] *Truth is onely one.*

Things mortall, still mutable.

T HINGS *are uncertain, and the more we get,*
  The more on ycie pavements we are set.

Studies to be supported.

S TUDIES *themselves will languish and decay,*
  When either price, or praise is ta'ne away.

Wit punisht, prospers most.

D READ not the shackles : on with thine intent ;
  Good wits get more fame by their punishment.

Twelfe night, or King and Queene.

N OW, now the mirth comes
    With the cake full of plums,
  Where Beane's the *King* of the sport here ;
    Beside we must know,
    The Pea also
  Must revell, as *Queene,* in the Court here.

[3] —manifold, infinite.   Plato and Cicero.

Begin then to chuse,

(This night as ye use)

Who shall for the present delight here,

Be a *King* by the lot,

And who shall not

Be Twelfe-day *Queene* for the night here.

Which knowne, let us make

Joy-sops [4] with the cake;

And let not a man then be seen here,

Who unurg'd will not drinke

To the base from the brink

A health to the King and the Queene here.

Next crowne the bowle full

With gentle lambs-wooll; [5]

Adde sugar, nutmeg, and ginger,

With store of ale too;

And thus ye must doe

To make the wassaile a swinger. [6]

Give then to the King

And Queene wassailing:

And though with ale ye be whet here;

---

[4] = sops-of-joy.

[5] See the "Oxford Night-Cap" for a receipt for this drink mixture and Glossarial Index s. v.   [6] = large and full.

Yet part ye from hence,
As free from offence,
As when ye innocent met here.

His desire.

GIVE me a man that is not dull,
When all the world with rifts[7] is full :
But unamaz'd dares clearely sing,
Whenas the roof's a-tottering :
And, though it falls, continues still
Tickling the *Citterne*[8] with his quill.

Caution in Councell.

KNOW when to speake ; for many times it brings
Danger, to give the best advice to Kings.

Moderation.

LET moderation on thy passions waite
Who loves too much, too much the lov'd will
hate.

Advice the best actor.

STILL take advice ; though counsels, when they flye
At randome, sometimes hit most happily.

[7] = rents.   [8] = musical stringed instrument.

Conformity is comely.

CONFORMITY *gives comelinesse to things :*
And equall shares exclude all murmerings.

Lawes.

WHO violates the Customes, hurts the Health,
Not of one man, but all the Common-wealth.

The meane.[9]

TIS much among the filthy to be clean ;
Our heat of youth can hardly keep the mean.

Like loves his like.

LIKE will to like,[1] each Creature loves his kinde ;
Chaste words proceed still from a bashfull minde.

His Hope or sheat-Anchor.

AMONG these Tempests great and manifold
My Ship has here one only Anchor-hold ;
That is my hope ; which if that slip, I'm one
Wildred in this vast watry *Region.*

---

[9] = middle or medium. See Glossarial Index s. v.
[1] ὅμοιον ὁμοίῳ φίλον—a common-place of the Classics.

Comfort in Calamity.[2]

TIS no discomfort in the world to fall,
 When the great Crack[3] not Crushes one, but all.

Twilight.

THE Twi-light is no other thing (we say)
 Then Night now gone, and yet not sprung the
  Day.[4]

False Mourning.

HE who wears Blacks, and mournes not for the
 Dead,
Do's but deride the Party burièd.

The will makes the work, or consent
makes the Cure.

NO grief is grown so desperate, but the ill
 Is halfe way curèd, if the party will.

Diet.

IF wholsome Diet can re-cure[5] a man,
 What need of Physick, or Physitian?

---

[2] " Solamen misseris socios habuisse dolorum."
[3] So the ' crack of Doom.'   [4] See Glossarial Index s. v.
[5] Used (then) in one sense of cure.

Smart.

STRIPES justly given yerk[6] us (with their fall)
But causelesse whipping smarts the most of all.

The Tinkers Song.

ALONG, come along,
 Let's meet in a throng
  Here of Tinkers ;
And quaffe up a Bowle
As big as a Cowle
  To Beer Drinkers.
The pole of the Hop
Place in the Ale-shop
  To Bethwack us ;
If ever we think
So much as to drink
  Unto *Bacchus.*
Who frolick will be,
For little cost he
  Must not vary,
From Beer-broth at all,
So much as to call
  For Canary.[7]

---

[6] Yark, yerk, jerk, jirk = to lash or whip. Here the meaning is either to hurt as lashes do, or (more probably) make us kick as does a horse under the lash.   [7] Wine so named, from the Canary Isles.

His Comfort.

THE only comfort of my life
    Is, that I never yet had wife ;
Nor will hereafter ; since I know
Who Weds, ore-buyes his weal with woe.

Sincerity.

WASH clean the Vessell, lest ye soure
    Whatever Liquor in ye powre.[8]

To Anthea.

SICK is *Anthea*, sickly is the spring,
    The Primrose sick, and sickly every thing :
The while my deer *Anthea* do's but droop,
The *Tulips, Lillies, Daffadills* do *stoop ;*
But when again sh'as got her healthfull houre,
Each bending then, will rise a proper flower.

Nor buying or selling.

NOW, if you love me, tell me,
    For as I will not sell ye,
So not one cross to buy thee
Ile give, if thou deny me.

---

[8] " Sincerum est nisi vas, quodcunque infundis, acesit." Horace,
Epist. i. 2, 54.

To his peculiar friend M. Jo: Wicks.[9]

SINCE shed or Cottage I have none,
 I sing the more, that thou hast one ;
To whose glad threshold, and free door
I may a Poet come, though poor ;
And eat with thee a savory bit,
Paying but common thanks for it.
Yet sho'd I chance, (my *Wicks*) to see
An over-leven[1]-looke in thee,
To soure the Bread, and turn the Beer
To an exalted vineger ;
Or sho'dst thou prize me as a Dish
Of thrice-boyl'd-worts,[2] or third dayes fish ;
I'de rather hungry go and come,
Then to thy house be Burdensome ;   ⌊*than*
Yet, in my depth of grief, I'de be
One that sho'd drop his *Beads* for thee.

The more mighty, the more mercifull.

WHO *may do most, do's least : The bravest will*
 Shew mercy there, where they have power to kill.

---

[9] See Glossarial Index s. v.

[1] = sour, as barm or flour leavened with it, when it passes into
the further stage of acetous or vinegary fermentation.

[2] = cabbage.

After Autumne, Winter.

DIE ere long, I'm sure, I shall ;
　　After leaves, the tree must fall.

A good death.

FOR truth I may this sentence tell,
　　No man dies ill, that liveth well.[3]

Recompence.

WHO plants an Olive, but to eate the Oile ?
　　Reward, we know, is the chiefe end of toile.

On Fortune.

THIS is my comfort, when she's most unkind,
　　She can but spoile me of my Meanes, not Mind.

To Sir George Parrie, Doctor of the Civill Law.[4]

I HAVE my Laurel Chaplet on my head,
　　If 'mongst these many Numbers to be read,
But one by you be hug'd and cherishèd.

---

[3] See Memorial-Introduction for parallel later (in Pope).

[4] He was admitted to the College of Advocates, London, 3rd Nov., 1628; but almost nothing has been transmitted concerning him save that he married the d. and heir of Sir Giles Sweet, Dean of Arches.

Peruse my Measures thoroughly, and where
Your judgement finds a guilty Poem, there
Be you a Judge ; but not a Judge severe.

The meane passe by, or over, none contemne ;
The good applaud : the peccant lesse condemne,
Since *Absolution* you can give to them.

Stand forth Brave Man, here to the publique sight ;
And in my Booke now claim a two-fold right :
The first as *Doctor*, and the last as *Knight.*

Charmes.

THIS Ile tell ye by the way,
    Maidens when ye Leavens[5] lay,
Crosse your Dow,[6] and your dispatch,
Will be better for your Batch.[7]

Another.[8]

IN the morning when ye rise,
    Wash your hands, and cleanse your eyes.
Next be sure ye have a care,
To disperse the water farre.

---

[5] Also 'leavance'—the dough mingled with the barm or leavened: and though to lay leavance is explained by some as to mingle the two, it is more probably to lay it aside to rise or leaven.

[6] = dough.   [7] = the baking, or quantity or number baked.

[8] and [9] Folk-lore.

For as farre as that doth light,
So farre keepes the evill Spright.[9]

Another.

I F ye feare to be affrighted
  When ye are (by chance) benighted :
In your Pocket for a trust,
Carrie nothing but a Crust :
For that holy piece of Bread
Charmes the danger, and the dread.

Upon Gorgonius.[1]

U NTO *Pastillus* ranke *Gorgonius* came,
  To have a tooth twitcht out of's native frame.
Drawn was his tooth ; but stanke so, that some say,
The Barber stopt his Nose, and ranne away.

Gentlenesse.

T *HAT Prince must govern with a gentle hand,*
  Who will have love comply with his command.

---

[1] There is a slip here in the names : no doubt Herrick was think-
ing of Horace, Sat. i. 4, 92 : "Pastillos Rufillus olet, Gorgonius
hircum," and has made Pastillos into a man.

A Dialogue betwixt himselfe and Mistresse Eliza :
Wheeler, *under the name of* Amarillis.[2]

M Y dearest Love, since thou wilt go,
    And leave me here behind thee ;
For love or pitie let me know
    The place where I may find thee.

Amaril. In country Meadowes pearl'd with Dew,
    And set about with Lillies ;
There filling Maunds[3] with Cowslips, you
    May find your *Amarillis.*

Her.   What have the Meades to do with thee,
    Or with thy youthfull houres ?
Live thou at Court, where thou mayst be
    The *Queen* of men, not flowers.

Let Country wenches make 'em fine
    With Poesies,[4] since 'tis fitter
For thee with richest Jemmes to shine,
    And like the Starres to glitter.

Amaril. You set too high a rate upon
    A Shepheardess so homely ;
Her.   Believe it (dearest) ther's not one
    I'th' Court that's halfe so comly.

[2] See Glossarial Index s. v.
[3] = baskets. See Glossarial Index s. v.   [4] = posies.

I prithee stay. (*Am.*) I must away ;
　　　Lets kiss first, then we'l sever.
Ambo.　　And though we bid adieu to day,
　　　Wee shall not part for ever.

To Julia.

HELP me, *Julia*, for to pray,
　　　Mattens sing, or Mattens say :[5]
This I know, the Fiend will fly
Far away, if thou beest by.
Bring the Holy-water hither ;
Let us wash, and pray together :
When our Beads are thus united,
Then the Foe will fly affrighted.

To Roses in Julia's *Bosome.*

ROSES, you can never die,
　　　Since the place wherein ye lye,
Heat and moisture mixt are so,
As to make ye ever grow.

To the Honoured, Master Endimion Porter.[6]

WHEN to thy Porch I come, and (ravisht) see
The State of Poets there attending Thee :

[5] = matins.　　　　[6] See Glossarial Index s. v.

Those *Bardes* and I, all in a *Chorus* sing,
We are Thy *Prophets Porter; Thou our King.*

Speake in season.

WHEN times are troubled, then forbeare ; but
    speak,
When a cleare day, out of a Cloud do's break.

Obedience.

THE Power of Princes rests in the Consent
    Of onely those, who are obedient :
Which if away, proud Scepters then will lye
Low, and of Thrones the Ancient *Majesty.*

Another on the same.

N*O man so well a Kingdome Rules, as He,*
    Who hath himselfe obaid the Soveraignty.

Of Love.

1. INSTRUCT me now, what love will do ;
    2. 'Twill make a tongless man to wooe.
1. Inform me next, what love will do ;
2. 'Twill strangely make a one.of too.   [*two*
1. Teach me besides, what love wil do ;
2. 'Twill quickly mar, & make ye too.

1. Tell me, now last, what love will do;
2. 'Twill hurt and heal a heart pierc'd through.

Upon Trap.

TRAP, of a Player turn'd a Priest now is;
    Behold a suddaine *Metamorphosis*.
If Tythe-pigs faile, then will he shift the scean,
And, from a Priest, turne Player once again.

Upon Grubs.

GRUBS loves his Wife and Children, while that
       they
Can live by love, or else grow fat by Play:
But when they call or cry on *Grubs* for meat;
Instead of Bread, *Grubs* gives them stones to eat.
He raves, he rends, and while he thus doth tear,
His Wife and Children fast to death for fear.

Upon Dol.

NO question but *Dols* cheeks wo'd soon rost dry,
    Were they not basted by her either eye.

Upon Hog.

HOG has a place i'th' Kitchen, and his share
    The flimsie Livers, and blew Gizzards are.

The School or Perl of Putney, *the Mistress of all
singular manners, Mistresse* Portman.[7]

WHETHER I was my selfe, or else did see
    Out of my self that *Glorious Hierarchie !*
Or whether those (in orders rare) or these
Made up One State of *Sixtie Venuses ;*
Or whether *Fairies, Syrens, Nymphes* they were,
Or *Muses,* on their mountaine sitting there ;
Or some enchanted Place, I do not know
(Or *Sharon,* where eternall Roses grow.)
This I am sure ; I Ravisht stood, as one
Confus'd in utter Admiration.
Me thought I saw them stir, and gently move,
And look as all were capable of Love :
And in their motion smelt much like to flowers
Enspir'd by th' Sun-beams after dews & showers.
There did I see the *Reverend Rectresse* stand,
Who with her eyes-gleam, or a glance of hand,
Those spirits rais'd ; and with like precepts then,
(As with a *Magick*) laid them all agen :

[7] Mr. Henry Portman occurs frequently in the Putney Parish
Register during Herrick's period, and a Mrs. Mary Portman was
buried there 27th June, 1671. Apparently mistress of a finishing
school of deportment.

(A happy Realme ! When no compulsive Law,
Or fear of it, but Love keeps all in awe.)
Live you, *great Mistresse* of your Arts, and be
A nursing Mother so to Majesty ;
As those your Ladies may in time be seene,
For Grace and Carriage, every one a Queene.
One Birth their Parents gave them ; but their new,
And better Being, they receive from You.
Mans former Birth is grace-lesse ; but the state
Of life comes in, when he's Regenerate.

To Perenna.

THOU say'st I'm dull ; if edge-lesse so I be,
   Ile whet my lips, and sharpen Love on thee.

On himselfe.

LET me not live, if I not love,
   Since I as yet did never prove,
Where Pleasures met : at last, doe find,
All Pleasures meet in Woman-kind.

On Love.

THAT love 'twixt men do's ever longest last
   Where War and Peace the Dice by turns doe
cast.

Another on Love.

LOVE'S of it self, too sweet; the best of all
  Is, when loves hony has a dash of gall.

Upon Gut.

SCIENCE puffs up, sayes *Gut*, when either Pease
  Make him thus swell, or windy Cabbages.

Upon Chub.

WHEN *Chub* brings in his harvest, still he cries,
    Aha my boyes ! heres wheat for Christmas
        Pies !
Soone after, he for beere so scores [8] his wheat,
That at the tide, he has not bread to eate.

Pleasures Pernicious.

WHERE Pleasures rule a Kingdome, never there
  Is sober virtue seen to move her sphere.

On himself.

A WEARIED Pilgrim, I have wandred here
    Twice five and twenty (bate me but one yeer)
Long I have lasted in this world; ('tis true)
But yet those yeers that I have liv'd, but few.

---

[8] = runs up a score that is to be paid by his wheat, or by the price of it.

Who by his gray Haires, doth his lusters tell,
Lives not those yeers, but he that lives them well.
One man has reatch't his sixty yeers, but he
Of all those three-score, has not liv'd halfe three : [9]
He lives, who lives to virtue : men who cast
Their ends for Pleasure, do not live, but last.

To M. Laurence Swetnaham.[1]

READ thou my Lines, my *Swetnaham*, if there be
   A fault, 'tis hid, if it be voic't by thee.
Thy mouth will make the sourest numbers please ;
How will it drop pure hony, speaking these ?

His Covenant or Protestation to Julia.

WHY do'st thou wound, & break my heart,
   As if we sho'd for ever part ?

---

[9] Cf. Randolph and Herbert. See Memorial-Introduction.

[1] Baptisms of children of Lawrence Swettenham occur in the Parish Register of St. Margaret's, Westminster, as early as 1629, and in an Act Book of the Dean and Chapter of Westminster, 10th July, 1639, *Laurence Swetnam*, Gent., is mentioned as a church-warden of St. Margaret's. Thomas Swettenham, of Swettenham, co. Chester, Esq., who married, in 1602, Mary, d. of John Birtles, of Birtles Esquire, had a third son named Lawrence. Lawrence Sweatnam was buried in the East Cloister of Westminster Abbey, 2nd May, 1673. Cf. Col. Chester's "Westminster Abbey," s. n.

Hast thou not heard an Oath from me,
After a day, or two, or three,
I wo'd come back and live with thee?
Take, if thou do'st distrust that Vowe ;
This second Protestation now.
Upon thy cheeke that spangel'd Teare,
Which sits as Dew of Roses there :
That Teare shall scarce be dri'd before
Ile kisse the Threshold of thy dore.
Then weepe not, sweet ; but thus much know,
I'm halfe return'd before I go.

On himselfe.

I WILL no longer kiss,
   I can no longer stay ;
The way of all Flesh is,
   That I must go this day :
Since longer I can't live,
   My frolick Youths adieu ;
My Lamp to you Ile give,
   And all my troubles too.

To the most accomplisht Gentleman Master Michael Oulsworth.

NOR thinke that Thou in this my Booke art worst,
   Because not plac't here with the midst, or first.

Since Fame that sides with these, or goes before
Those, that must live with Thee for evermore.
That Fame, and Fames rear'd Pillar, thou shalt see
In the next sheet, *Brave Man*, to follow Thee.
Fix on that Columne then, and never fall ;
Held up by Fames *eternall Pedestall.*

To his Girles who would have him sportfull.

ALAS! I can't, for tell me how
   Can I be gamesome (agèd now :)
Besides, ye see me daily grow
Here, Winter-like, to Frost and Snow.
And I ere long, my Girles, shall see,
Ye quake for cold to looke on me.

Truth and falsehood.

TRUTH *by her own simplicity is known ;*
   Falsehood by Varnish and Vermillion.

His last request to Julia.

I HAVE been wanton, and too bold I feare,
   To chafe o'remuch the Virgins cheek or eare :
Beg for my Pardon, *Julia ; He doth winne*
Grace with the Gods, who's sorry for his sinne.
That done, my *Julia,* dearest *Julia,* come,
And go with me to chuse my Buriall roome :

My Fates are ended ; when thy *Herrick* dyes,
Claspe thou his Book, then close thou up his Eyes.

On himselfe.

ONE Eare tingles ;[2] some there be,
    That are snarling now at me :
Be they those that *Homer* bit,
I will give them thanks for it.

Upon Kings.

K*INGS must be dauntlesse : Subjects will contemne*
    Those, who want Hearts, and weare a Diadem.

To his Girles.

WANTON Wenches doe not bring
    For my haires black colouring :
For my Locks (Girles) let 'em be
Gray or white, all's one to me.

Upon Spur.

S*PUR* jingles now, and sweares by no meane
    oathes,
He's double honour'd, since h'as got gay cloathes :

---

[2] There seems to be a reference here to the classical notion, as in
Virgil: Bucol. It is of still living folk-lore.

Most like his Suite, and all commend the Trim ;
And thus they praise the Sumpter; but not him :
As to the Goddesse, people did conferre
Worship, and not to'th' Asse that carried her.[3]

To his *Brother* Nicolas Herrick.[4]

WHAT others have with cheapnesse seene, and
     ease,
In Varnisht Maps ; by'th' helpe of Compasses :
Or reade in Volumes, and those Bookes (with all
Their large Narrations, *Incanonicall*)[5]
Thou hast beheld those seas, and Countries farre ;
And tel'st to us, what once they were, and are.
So that with bold truth, thou canst now relate
This Kingdomes fortune, and that Empires fate :
Canst talke to us of *Sharon ;* where a spring
Of Roses have an endlesse flourishing.
Of *Sion, Sinai, Nebo,* and with them,
Make knowne to us the new *Jerusalem.*
The Mount of *Olives ; Calverie,* and where
Is (and hast seene) thy *Saviours Sepulcher.*

---

[3] —the ass carrying the mysteries: cf. Aristophanes' Frogs, 159.
[4] See Memorial-Introduction.
[5] —un-canonical, and therefore not to be wholly relied on.

So that the man that will but lay his eares,
As *Inapostate*,[6] to the thing he heares,
Shall by his hearing quickly come to see
The truth of Travails lesse in bookes then Thee.

                             [*than*

The Voice and Violl.

RARE is the voice itselfe ; but when we sing
    To'th' Lute or Violl, then 'tis ravishing.

Warre.

IF Kings and kingdomes, once distracted be,
    The sword of war must trie the Soveraignty.

A King and no King.

THAT Prince, who may doe nothing but what's just,
    Rules but by leave, and takes his Crowne on trust.

Plots not still prosperous.

ALL are not ill Plots, that doe sometimes faile ;
    Nor those false vows, which oft times don't
      prevaile.

---

[6] =a non-apostate—one who does not revolt or turn away. In next line 'by' is misprinted 'be.'

Flatterie.

WHAT is't that wasts a Prince ? example
     showes,
'Tis flatterie spends a King, more then his foes.   [*than*

Upon Rumpe.

RUMPE is a Turne-broach,[7] yet he seldome can
    Steale a swolne sop out of the Dripping pan.

Upon Shopter.

OLD Widow *Shopter*, whensoere she cryes,
    Lets drip a certain Gravie from her eyes.

Upon Deb.

IF felt and heard, (unseen) thou dost me please ;
    If seen, thou lik'st me, *Deb*, in none of these.

Excesse.

EXCESSE is sluttish : keepe the meane ; for why ?
    Vertue's clean Conclave is sobriety.

Upon Croot.

ONE silver spoon shines in the house of *Croot ;*
    Who cannot buie, or steale a second to't.

---

[7] =turn-spit.

The Soul is the salt.

THE body's salt, the soule is ; which when gon,
  The flesh soone sucks in putrifaction.

Upon Flood, or a thankfull man.

FLOOD, if he has for him and his a bit,
  He sayes his fore and after Grace for it :
If meate he wants, then Grace he sayes to see
His hungry belly borne by Legs *Jaile-free.*
Thus have, or have not, all alike is good,
To this our poore, yet ever patient *Flood.*

Upon Pimpe.

WHEN *Pimpes* feet sweat (as they doe often use)
  There springs a sope-like-lather in, his shoos.

Upon Luske.

IN Den'-shire Kerzie *Lusk* [8] (when he was dead)
  Wo'd shrouded be, and therewith buried.
When his Assignes askt him the reason why ?
He said, because he got his wealth thereby.

Foolishnesse.

IN'S *Tusc'lanes, Tullie* doth confesse,
  No plague ther's like to foolishnesse.

[8] Devonshire was in former times famous for manufactures..

Upon Rush.

RUSH saves his shooes, in wet and snowie wether ;
　　And feares in summer to weare out the lether :
This is strong thrift that warie *Rush* doth use
Summer and Winter still to save his shooes.

Abstinence.

AGAINST diseascs here the strongest fence
　　Is the defensive vertue, Abstinence.

No danger to men desperate.

WHEN feare admits no hope of safety, then
　　Necessity makes dastards valiant men.

Sauce for sorrowes.

ALTHOUGH our suffering meet with no relicfe,
　　An equall mind is the best sauce for griefe.[1]

To Cupid.

I HAVE a leaden, thou a shaft of gold ;
　　Thou kil'st with heate, and I strike dead with
　　　cold.

---

[1] "Æquam memento rebus in arduis
　　Servare mentem," &c.　Horace, Od. II. iii. ll. 1—2.

Let's trie of us who shall the first expire ;
Or thou by frost, or I by quenchlesse fire :
Extreames are fatall, where they once doe strike.
And bring to'th' heart destruction both alike.

Distrust.

WAT ever men for Loyalty pretend,
    Tis Wisdomes part to doubt a faithfull friend.[2]

The Hagg.

THE staffe is now greas'd :
    And very well pleas'd,
She cockes out her Arse at the parting,
    To an old Ram Goat,
    That rattles i'th' throat,
Halfe choakt with the stink of her farting.

    In a dirtie Haire-lace
    She leads on a brace
Of black-bore-cats [3] to attend her ;
    Who scratch at the Moone,
    And threaten at noone
Of night from Heaven for to rend her.

---

[2] From Aristotle onward, this has been a common-place.
[3] = male cats.

A-hunting she goes ;
A crackt horne she blowes ;
At which the hounds fall a-bounding ;
While th' Moone in her sphere
Peepes trembling for feare,
And night's afraid of the sounding.

The mount of the Muses.

AFTER thy labour take thine ease,
Here with the sweet *Pierides*.
But if so be that men will not
Give thee the Laurell Crowne for lot ;
Be yet assur'd, thou shalt have one
Not subject to corruption.

On Himselfe.

I L'E write no more of Love ; but now repent
Of all those times that I in it have spent.
Ile write no more of life ; but wish 'twas ended,
And that my dust was to the earth commended.

To his Booke.

GOE thou forth, my booke, though late ;
Yet be timely fortunate.

It may chance good-luck may send
Thee a kinsman, or a friend,
That may harbour thee, when I,
With my fates neglected lye.
If thou know'st not where to dwell,
See, the fier's by : *Farewell.*

The end of his worke.

PART of the worke remaines ; one part is past :
　And here my ship rides having Anchor cast.

To Crowne it.

MY wearied Barke, O let it now be Crown'd !
　The Haven reacht to which I first was bound.

On Himselfe.

THE worke is done : young men and maidens, set
　Upon my curles the *Mirtle Coronet*,
Washt with sweet ointments ; Thus at last I come
To suffer in the Muses *Martyrdome :*
But with this comfort, if my blood be shed,
The Muses will weare blackes, when I am dead.

The pillar of Fame.

FAMES pillar here, at last, we set,
 Out-during[4] *Marble, Brasse,* or *Jet,*
  Charm'd and enchanted so,
  As to withstand the blow,
   Of o v e r t h r o w,
   Nor shall the seas,
   Or O U T R A G E S
   Of storms orebear
   What we up-rear:
   Tho Kingdoms fal,
  This pillar never shall
  Decline or waste at all;
 But stand for ever by his owne
 Firme and well - fixt foundation.[5]

TO his Book's end this last line he'd have plac't,
 Jocond his Muse was; but his Life was chast.[6]

FINIS.

[4] = out-lasting.

[5] Horatian to the last is the bard Robert Herrick, concluding what
he terms his *Works Human* with an imitation of

  Exegi monumentum ære perennius, &c.

    Horat. Ode ult. Lib. 3. N.

[6] On this couplet see Cartwright's stinging allusion in our Memorial-Introduction.

II. GOLDEN APPLES.

NOTE.

The following Poems are gathered as so many fallen
'Golden Apples' of the Hesperides: hence my title. The
source of each is given in its place. To Mr. W. C. Hazlitt
belongs the credit of having been the first to print or re-
print the whole of these save the last (Vol. II. pp. 433-447);
but the first, "The Description of a Woman," is taken
from "Wit's Recreations" (1640), with additions and cor-
rections from the Ashmole MS. 38, page 88, Art. 109 (viz.
ll. 47-50, 57-8, 63-76, 79-84, 103-4, 109-112, and ll. 15-16
('shew' and 'growe' for 'shown' and 'grown.'). A colla-
tion of the Ashmole MSS. and of the original books has
corrected a great number of faulty readings, as well as
given accurate references to the several places in the
MSS. One poem (III) demanded very careful revision,
being a mass of errors. On these Poems see our Memorial-
Introduction, where it will be seen they are all-important
biographically. The various readings of I. are also therein
critically examined, along with others. Prefixed to it is
a fac-simile of 'the Woman' from 'Wit's Recreations.'
Instead of the "6 or 8" mentioned by Mr. Hazlitt, it will be
seen in our Memorial-Introduction that no fewer than 62 of
the poems of "Hesperides" appeared originally in "Wit's
Recreations," exclusive of "The Description of a Woman."
All this has hitherto been strangely overlooked by the
Editors of Herrick and Bibliographers, and equally so that
herein first appeared some of the choice poems of Crashaw,
Milton, &c., &c. G.

GOLDEN APPLES.

I. *The Discription of a Woman.*[1]

 HOSE head befringèd with be-scatterèd
tresses,   1

Shews like *Apolloes*, when the morn
he dresses :

[1] From " Wit's Recreations " (1640) as in Note on page 90 and
Ashmole M.S. 38, page 88, Art. 109.

Or like *Aurora* when with Pearle she sets
Her long disheveld Rose-crown'd Trammelets :[2]
Her forehead smooth, full polish'd, bright and high,
Bears in itself a gracefull Majesty;
Under the which, two crawling eye-brows twine
Like to the tendrills of a flatt'ring Vine :
Under whose shade, two starry sparkling eyes
Are beautifi'd with faire fringd Canopies.   10
Her comely nose with uniformall grace,
Like purest white, stands in the middle place,
Parting the paire, as wee may well suppose,
Each cheek resembling still a damaske Rose :
Which like a Garden manifestlye shew
How Roses, Lillies, and Carnations growe;
Which sweetly mixèd both with white and red,
Like Rose leaves, white and redd, seem minglèd.
Then nature, for a sweet allurement sets
Two smelling, swelling, bashfull Cherrylets;[3]   20
The which with ruby-rednesse being tip'd,
Do speake a Virgin, merry, Cherry-lip'd.
Over the which a neat sweet skin is drawne,
Which makes them shew like Roses under Lawne;

---

[2] = nets for the hair.   See Glossarial Index s. v.
[3] = diminutive of cherries.

These be the Ruby-portals, and divine,
Which ope themselues, to shew a holy shrine,
Whose breath is rich perfume, that to the sense
Smells like the burn'd *Sabean* Frankinsense ;
In which the tongue, though but a member small,
Stands guarded with a Rosie-hilly-wall ;   30
And her white teeth, which in her gums are set,
Like Pearl and Gold, make one rich Cabinet.
Next doth her chin, with dimpled beauty strive
For his white, plump, and smooth, prerogative ;
At whose faire top, to please the sight there grows
The fairest image of a blushing rose ;
Mou'd by the chin, whose motion causeth this,
That both her lips do part, do meet, do kiss,
Her ears, which like two labyrinths are plac'd
On eyther side, with rich rare Jewels grac'd :   40
Mouing a question, whether that by them,
The Jem is grac'd, or they grac'd by the Jem.
But the foundation of the Architect
Is the Swan-staining, faire, rare, stately neck,
Which with ambitious humblenesse stands under,
Bearing aloft this rich-round world of wounder.
Jn which the veynes jmplanted, seeme to lye
Lyke louing vines hidde vnder juorie ;
So full of clarrett, that whosoe prickes this vine
May see itt sprout forth streames lyke Muskadine. 50

Her breast, a place for beauties throne most fit,
Bears up two Globes, where love and pleasure sitt ;
Which, headed with two rich round Rubies, show
Like wanton Rose-buds growing out of Snow,
And in the milky valley that's between,
Sits *Cupid*, kissing of his mother Queen :
Ffingering the papps that feele like sleuèd[5] silke,
And prest a little, thay will weep pewr milke.
Then comes the belly, seated next below,
Like a faire mountain of *Riphean* snow ;   60
Whear Nature, in a whitenesse without spot,
Hath in the middle tide a Gordian knott ;
Or else that she in that white waxen hill
Hath seald the primrose [6] of her vttmost skill ;
But now my muse hath spied a darke descent
Ffrom this soe pretious pearly permanent,[7]
A milkye highe-way that direction yelds
Vnto the port-mouth of the Elizean feilds :
A place desired of all, but gott by these
Whom loue admitts to the Hesperides ;   70
Hers, goulden fruitt, that doth excede all price
Growing in this Loue-guarded parradice ;
Aboue the entrance, theire is wrighten this,
This is the portail to the bower of blisse,

---

[5] Soft changeable-coloured silk.
[6] See Glossarial Index s. v.   [7] Qu.—pavement ?

Through mid'st whearof, a christall streame there
    flowes
Passing the sweete-sweete of a muskie rose.
Now Loue invites me to survey hur thighes,
Swelling in likenesse like to Crystall skyes,
With plump softe flesh, of mettall pure and fine,
Resembling sheildes, both pure and christaline.   80
Hence rise those two ambitious hills, that looke
Jnto ye middle sweet sight-stealing crooke,
Which for the better bewtifing shrowds
Its humble selfe 'twixt two aspiring cloudes;
Which to the knees by nature fastned on,
Deriue their ever well 'greed motion.
Her legs with two clear calves, like siluer try'd,
Kindly swell up, with little pretty pride,
Leaving a distance for the comely small
To beautifie the leg and foot withall.   90
Then lowly, yet most lovely stand the feet,
Round, short and clear, lyke pounded Spices sweet :
And whatsoever thing they tread upon
They make it scent like bruisèd Cinnamon.
The lovely shoulders now allure the eye,
To see two Tablets of pure ivorie :
From which two arms like branches seem to spread,
With tender vein'd and siluer colouerèd ;

With little hands and fingers long and small,
To grace a Lute, a Violl, Virginall.   100
In length each finger doth his next excell,
Each richly headed with a pearly shell ;
Richer then that fayre, pretious, vertuous horne[8] [*than*
That armes the forehead of the unicorne.
Thus euery parte in contrariety
Meet in the whole and make an harmony ;
As divers strings do singly disagree,
But form'd by Number, make sweet melodie.
Vnto the jdoll of the worke deuine
J consecrate this louing life of myne,   110
Bowing my lipps vnto that stately roote
Wheare bewtye springs ; and thus j kiss (her) foote.[9]

II. *Mr. Hericke his Daughters Dowrye.*[1]

ERE J goe hence and bee noe more
    Seene to the world, J'le giue the skore
J owe vnto a female child,
And that is this, a uerse jnstylde

[8] The horn of the (mythical) unicorn was endowed with mystic curative virtues.

[9] ━ The MS. is signed " Finis.   Robt. Herrick."   [1] From the Ashmole MS. 38, p. 94, Art. 112.

My daughters dowrye ; haueing which,
J'le leaue thee then compleatly riche ;
Jnsteade of gould, pearle, rubies, bonds,
Longe forfaite pawnèd diamonds,
Or antique pledges, house or lande ;
J giue thee this that shall withstande   10
The blow of ruine and of chance :
Theis hurte not thyne jnheritance,
For 'tis ffee simple, and noe rent
Thou fortune ow'st for tenement ;
Howeuer after tymes will praise,
This portion, my prophetique bayes,
Cannot deliuer vpp to th' rust,
Yet J keepe peacefull in my dust.
As for thy birth, and better seeds
(Those which must growe to vertuous deeds :   20
Thou didst deriue from that old steem [2]
Loue and Mercie, cherish them),
Which, like a vestall virgine ply
With holye fier, least that itt dye.
Growe vpp with mylder lawes[3] to knowe
Att what tyme to say I [4] or noe ;

---

[2] —stem : I have placed l. 21 before l. 20 of the MS., which is here evidently in error.   [3] i. e. under milder laws than those of the vestals.   [4] —ay.

Lett manners teach thee whear to bee
More comely flowing, where les free :
Theis bringe thy husband, like to those
Old coynes and meddalls wee expose   30
To th' shew, but neuer part with ; next
As jn a more conspicuous text,
(Thy forehead) lett therin bee sign'd
The mayden candour [5] of thy mynde ;
And vnder it two chast-borne spyes
To barr out bolde adulteryes :
Ffor through these optickes, fly the dartes
Of lust, which sette on fier our hartes.
On eyther side of theis, quicke eares
Ther must bee plac'd, for seasoned feares,   40
Which sweeten loue, yett ne're come nighe
The plague of wilder jelousie.
Then lett each cheeke of thyne, intice
His soule as to a bedd of spice ;
Wheare hee may roule, and loose his sence
As in a bedd of frankensence :
A lipp jnkyndlèd with that coale,
With which Loue chafes and warmes the soule,
Bringe to hym next,[6] and in it shew
Loues cherries ; from such fyers growe   50

[5] whiteness, purity.
[6] The construction is ' Bring to him next a lip ' . . . .

And haue their haruest, which must stand
The gathering of the lipp, not hand ;
Then vnto theis, bee it thy care
To cloath thy words in gentle ayre,
That smooth as oyle, sweet, softe and cleane
As is the childish [7] bloome of beane,
They may fall downe and stroake (as the
Beames of the sunn the gracefull sea) :
With handes as smooth as mercies, bring
Hym for his better cherrishing.[8]   60
That when thou doest his necke jnsnare,
Or with thy wrist, or fluttering hayre,
Hee may (a prisoner) ther discrye
Bondage more loued then lybertye ;   [*than*
A nature, soe well form'd, soe wrought,
To [9] calme and tempest, lett bee brought
With thee, that should hee but jnclyne
To roughnes, claspe hym lyke a vine ;
Or lyke as woole meetes steele, giue way
Vnto the passion, not to stay ;[1]   70
Wrath yf resisted ouer-boyles,
Jff not, it dyes, or eles recoyles ;

[7] = just sprouting.
[8] There seems some omission after this, and also, judging from the confusion, after 'sea' preceding.
[9] Miswritten 'Too.'   [1] i. e. do not attempt to oppose its stay.

And lastly, see you bring to hym,
Somewhat peculiar to each lymm ;
And j charge thee to bee knowne
By n' other face, but by thyne owne.
Lett itt (in Loues name) bee keept sleeke
Yett to bee found when hee shall seeke
Jt, and not jnstead of [to] saint,
Giue vpp his worth vnto the painte ;   80
Ffor (trust me girle) shee ouer-does
Who by a double proxie woes ;
But least j should forgett his bedd,
Bee sure thou bringe a mayden-head,
That is a Margarite,[2] which lost,
Thou bring'st vnto his bedd a frost
Or a colde poyson, which his blood
Benummes like the forgettfull [3] floode.
Now for some jewells to supplye
The wante of eare-rings brauerye,   90
Ffor publike eyes ; take onlye theis,
Ne're broughte far beyonde the seas ;
Theyre nobly-home-breed, yett haue price
Beyound the fare-fetch [4] marchandize.
Obedience, wise-distrust, peace, shey[5]
Distance, and sweet vrbanitie :

---

[2] = pearl.   [3] = of Lethe.   [4] Miswritten 'fetch.'   [5] = shy.

Safe modestie, lou'd patience, feare
Of offending, temperance, deare
Constancie, bashfullnes, and all
The vertues lesse, or cardinall,   100
Take with my blessinge ; and goe forth
Jnjewelld with thy natiue worthe.
And now yf ther a man bee founde,
That lookes for such preparèd grownd,
Lett hym, but with indifferent skill,
Soe good a soile bee-stocke and till ;
Hee may ere longe haue such a wyfe,
Nourish in's breast, a Tree of Life.

Finis. ROBT. HERICKE.

III. *Mr. Robert Hericke his Farwell vnto Poetrie.*[6]

I HAUE behelde two louers, in a night
Hatcht [7] o're with moone-shine, from their stolen
  delight,—
When this to that, and that to this, had giuen
A kisse to such a jewell of the heuen :

---

[6] From the Ashmole MS. 38, p. 108, Art. 121. The MS. is a chaos of mispunctuation, and it is not improved by Mr. Hazlitt. An attempt has been made to rectify wrong words, and improving punctuation. See Memorial-Introduction specially.

[7] —engraved, inlaid.

Or while that each from other's breath did drincke
Healthes to the rose, the violet, or pinke,—
Call'd [8] on the suddayne by the jealouse mother,
Some strickter Mrs. or suspitious other,
Vrging diuorcement (woorse then death to theis) [*than*
By the soone gingling of some sleepy keyes,
Parte with a hastye kisse ; and in that shew
How stay thay would, yet forc't thay are to goe.
Euen such are wee : and in our parting, doe
Noe otherwise then as those former two ;   [*than*
Natures like ours, wee who haue spent our tyme
Both from the morning to the euening chyme ;
Nay, till [9] the bell-man [1] of the night had tould
Past noone of night, yett weare [2] the howers not old,
Nor dull'd with yron sleeps, but haue out-worne
The fresh and fayrest flourish of the morne
With flame, and rapture ; drincking to the ode [3]
Number of wyne, which makes vs full with God,
And yn that misticke frenzie, wee haue hurl'de,
(As with a tempeste) nature [4] through the worlde,
And yn a whirl-wynd twirl'd her home, agast
Att that which in her extasie had past ;

---

[8] The construction is Called &c. (l. 7) from their stolen delight.
[9] Miswritten 'tell.'   [1] See Glossarial Index s. v.   [2] = were.
[3] = odd.—οἶνος and *vinum* both give 5 the number of perfection.
[4] i. e. our nature, our spirit.

Thus crownd with rose-budds, sacke, thou mad'st
    mee flye
Like fier-drakes,[5] yett didst mee no harme therby.
O thou allmightye nature, who did'st giue
True heate, whearwith humanitie doth liue
Beyond its stinted[6] circle ; giueing foode
White fame,[7] and resurrection to the good ;
Soaring them vpp, boue ruyne, till the doome
The generall Aprill[8] of the worlde dothe come,
That makes all æquall. Manye thowsands should
(Wert not for thee) haue crumbled ynto mould,
And with thayr ceareclothes rotted, not to shew[9]
Whether the world such sperritts had or noe,
Whearas by thee, those, and a million since,
Nor fate, nor enuye, cann theyr fames conuince.[1]
Homer, Musæus, Ouid, Maro, more,
Of those god-full prophetts longe before
Helde[2] there[3] eternall fiers ; and ours of late
(Thy mercie helping) shall resist stronge fate,
Nor stoope to th' center, but suruiue as longe
As fame or rumour, hath or trumpe or tongue ;

---

[5] The ignis fatuus (plural).

[6] = stopped, i. e. confined.   [7] See Glossarial Index s. v. = good
or happy, fame.   [8] See Glossarial Index s. v.   [9] = so as not
(or never) to shew.   [1] = overcome.

[2] Miswritten 'Holde.'   [3] = their.

But vnto mee, bee onlye hoarse, since now
(Heauen and my soule beare record of my vowe)
I, my desires screw from thee, and directe
Them and my thoughts to that sublim'd respecte
And conscience vnto priesthood ; tis not need
(The skarcrow vnto mankinde) that doth breed
Wiser conclusions in mee, since I knowe
I've more to beare my chardges,[4] then way to goe; [*than*
Or had I not, I'de stopp the spreading itch .
Off craueing more : soe yn conceipt bee ritch ;   [*of*
But tis the god of nature who yntends,
And shaps my function for more glorious ends :
Kisse,[5] soe departe; yett stay awhile to [6] see
The lines of sorrowe, that lye drawne in mee
Yn speach, in picture; noe otherwise then when, [*than*
(Judgment and death, denounc'd gainst guilty men),
Each takes a weeping farewell, rackt in mynde
With joyes before, and pleasures left behind :
Shakeing the head, whilst each to each dothe mourne
With thought thay goe, whence thay must ner
          returne.
Soe with like lookes, as once the ministrell
Cast, leading his Euredice through hell,

---

[4] Miswritten 'I am . . . . . chardge:'—I have more [money] to bear my chardges than I have road to travel.   [5] Miswritten 'Guesse.'   [6] Again miswritten 'too.'

I stricke thy loues, and greedyly persue
Thee, with myne eyes, or in, or out, of view.
Soe look't the Grecian oratour when sent
Ffroms natiue cuntrye, into banishment,
Throwing his eye-balls backward to suruaye
The smoake of his beloue`d Attica :[7]
Soe Tullye [8] look't, when from the brooks of Rome
The sad soule went, not with his loue, but doome :
Shooting his eye-darts 'gainst it, to surprise
Yt, or to drawe the cittie to his eyes.
Such is my parting with thee ; and to proue
Ther was not varnish (only) in my loue,
But substance, lo ! receaue this pearlye teare
Ffrozen with greife, and place it in thyne eare,
Then parte in name of peace ; and softely on
With numerous [9] feete to Hoofy [1] Helicon ;
And when thou art vppon that sacred hill
Amongest the thrice three sacred virgins, fill
A full brimm'd bowle of furye and of rage,
And quafe it to the prophets of our age ;
When drunck with rapture, curse the blind and lame
Base ballad-mongers, who vsurpe thy name
And fowle thy altar ; charme some ynto froggs,
Some to bee ratts, and others to bee hoggs ;

[7] Demosthenes.   [8] Cicero.
[9] ▬ rythmical.   [1] ▬ alluding to Pegasus.

Ynto the loathsoms ['t] shapps thou canst deuise
To make ffooles hate them, onlye by disguise ;
Thus with a kisse of warmth, and loue, I parte
Not soe, but that some relique yn my harte
Shall stand for euer, though I doe addresse
Chiefelye my selfe to what I must proffess :
Knowe yet (rare soule) when my diuiner muse
Shall want a hand-mayde (as she ofte will vse),[2]
Bee readye, thou for mee, to wayte vppon her,
Thoughe as a seruant, yet a mayde of honor.
The crowne of dutye is our dutye : well
Doing's, the fruite of doinge well.   Farewell.

              Fimis.   MR. ROBT. HERRICKE.

IV. *A Charroll presented to Dr.* Williams, *Bp. of
Lincolne, as a Newyears Guift.*[3]

H YE hence, pale Care, noe more remember
    Past sorrowes with the fled December,
But let each plesant cheeke appeare
Smooth as the childhood of the yeare,
    And sing a carroll here.

   [2] =use to want.   [3] From Ashmole MS. 36, 298.   See Memorial-Introduction and also poem to this Bishop, Vol. I. p. 88.

'Twas braue, 'twas braue could we comand the hand
Of Youths swift watch to stand
As you haue done your day ;
Then should we not decay,
But all we wither, & our light
Is spilt in euerlasting night,
When as your sight
Shewes like the heavens aboue ye moone
Like an eternall noone,
That sees no setting sunn.

Keepe vp those flames, & though you shroud
Awhile your forehead in a cloude,
Doe it like the sun to write
I'th ayre, a greater text of light ;
Welcome to all our vowes,
And since you pay
To vs the day
Soe longe desir'd,
See we haue fyr'd
Our holy spicknard, and ther's none
But brings his stick of cynamon,
His eager eye, or smoother smyle ;
And layes it gently on the pyle,
Which thus enkindled, we invoke
Your name amidst the sacred smoke.

Chorus. Come then, greate Lord,
    And see our Alter burne
    With love of your returne,
And not a man here but consumes
His soule to glad you in perfumes.

        Rob : Herrick.

 V. *Song.*   *His Mistris to him at his Farwell.*[4]

YOU may vow Ile not forgett
    To pay the debt,
Which to thy Memorie stands as due
    As faith can seale It you :
Take then tribute of my teares,
    So long as I haue feares
    To prompt mee, I shall euer
Languiſh and looke, but thy returne see neuer :
    Oh then to leſsen my diſpaire,
    Print thy lips Into the ayre,
    So by this
Meanes, I may kiſse thy kiſse,
    whenas some kinde
     winde
shall hither waft it ; and In leiw,
My lipps shall send a 1000 back to you.

        Ro : HERRICK.

 [4] From Additional MS. Br. Mus. 11,811, fol. 37.

VI. *Vpon Parting.*[5]

GOE hence away, and in thy parting know
    'tis not my voice, but heauens that bidds thee
       goe;
Spring hence thy faith, nor thinke it ill desart
I finde in thee, that makes me thus to part.
But voice of fame, and voice of heauen haue thunderd
we both were lost, if both of us not sunderd:
fould now thine armes, and in thy last looke reare
one Sighe of loue, and coole it with a teare:
since part we must, let's kisse; that done, retire
with as cold frost, as erst we mett with fire;
with such white vowes as fate can nere difsever
but truth knitt fast; and so farewell for euer.

                R : HERRICK.

VII. *Upon Master Fletchers Incomparable Playes*[6].

APOLLO sings, his harpe refounds: give roome,
    For now behold the golden Pompe is come,
Thy Pompe of playes, which thoufands come to fee,
With admiration both of them and thee.

---

[5] From Harleian MS. 6,917, fol. 82 back.
[6] From Beaumont and Fletcher's Works, 1647: and in Beaumont's poems, 1653. See Dyce, Vol. l. p. xlvii. In the original all in italic: names of the Plays Roman except *Love lyes a Bleeding*, which is in italic.

O Volume worthy, leafe by leafe, and cover,
To be with juice of Cedar [7] wafh't all over ;
Here's words with lines, and lines with fcenes confent,
To raife an Act to full aftonifhment ;
Here melting numbers, words of power to move
Young men to fwoone, and Maides to dye for love.
Love lyes a bleeding here, Evadne, there
Swells with brave rage, yet comely every where ;
Here's a *mad lover*, there that high defigne
Of *King and no King*, (and the rare Plott thine.)
So that whene'ere wee circumvolve [8] our Eyes,
Such rich, fuch frefh, fuch fweet varietyes,
Ravifh our fpirits, that entranc't wee see
None writes lov's paffion in the world, like thee.

　　　　　　　　　　　　ROBERT HERRICK.

VIII. *THE NEW CHARON,*

Upon the Death of Henry *Lord* Hastings.[9]

The Mufical part being fet by M. Henry Lawes.

　　　　　‘　　The Speakers,
　　　　Charon and *Eucofmeia.*

Euc. CHARON, O Charon, draw thy Boat to th' Shore,
　　　And to thy many, take in one foul more.

---

[7] See Glossarial Index s. v.　　　[8] See Glossarial Index s. v.
[9] From " Lachrymæ Musarum. The Tears of the Muses : ex-
preft in Elegies written by divers persons of Nobility and Worth.

Cha. Who calls? who calls? *Euc.* One overwhelm'd
    with ruth ;

Have pity either on my tears or Youth,

And take me in, who am in deep Distress ;

But firſt caſt off thy wonted Churliſhneſs.

Cha. I will be gentle as that Air which yeelds

A breath of Balm along th' *Elizean* fields.

Speak, what art thou ? *Euc.* Onc, once that
    had a lover,   [*than*

Then which, thy ſelf ne'er waſtcd ſweeter over.

He was—— *Cha.* Say what. *Eu.* Ay me, my
    woes are deep.

Cha. Prethee relate, while I give ear and weep.

Euc. He was an *Hastings;* and that one Name has

In it all good, that is, and ever was.

He was my Life, my Love, my Joy ; but di'd

Some hours before I shou'd have been his Bride.

Chorus. *Thus, thus the gods celeſtial still decree,*

    For Humane Joy, Contingent Misery.

Euc. The *hallowed Tapers* all preparèd were,

And *Hymen* call'd to bleſs the Rites. *Cha.* Stop
    there.

upon the death of the most hopefull Henry, Lord Hastings," &c.
Collected and set forth by R[ıchard] B[rome]. Lond. 1649, 8vo.
pp. 38-9. See Memorial-Introduction on this in (probable) relation
to his " Charon and Nightingale." As being printed (not MS.) the
Roman and Italic intermixture of types has not been reproduced.

Euc. Great are my woes.   *Cha.* And great muſt that
        Grief be,
        That makes grim *Charon* thus to pity thee.
        But now come in.   *Euc.* More let me yet relate.
Cha. I cannot ſtay; more ſouls for waftage wait,
        And I muſt hence.   *Euc.* Yet let me thus much
        know,
        Departing hence, where Good and Bad ſouls go.
Cha. Thoſe ſouls which ne'er were drencht in plea-
        ſures ſtream,
        The Fields of *Pluto* are reſerv'd for them ;
        Where, dreſt with garlands, there they walk
        the ground,
        Whose blessèd Youth with endleſs flow'rs is
        crown'd.
        But ſuch as have been drown'd in this wilde ſea,
        For thoſe is kept the Gulf of Hecatè ;
        Where, with their own contagion they are fed ;
        And there do puniſh, and are puniſhèd.
        This known, the reſt of thy ſad ſtory tell,
        When on the Flood that nine times circles Hell.
Chorus. *We ſail along, to viſit mortals never ;*
        But there to live, where Love ſhall laſt for ever.
                                ROB. HERRICKE.

IX. *Epitaph on the Tomb of Sir* Edward Giles
& his wife in the South Aisle of Dean
Prior Church, Devon.[10]

NO truſt to Metalſ nor to Marbleſ, when
Theſe have their Fate, and wear away aſ Men ,
Timeſ, Titleſ, Trophieſ, may be loſt and Spent ;
But Vertue Rearſ the eternal Monument.   [Pay?
What more than theſe can Tombſ or Tomb-ſtoneſ
But here'ſ the Sun-ſet of a Tediouſ day :
Theſe Two aſleep are : I'll but be Vndreſt
And ſo to Bed : Pray wiſh uſ all Good Reſt.

[10] See Memorial-Introduction on this hitherto inedited Epitaph.

III. NOBLE NUMBERS.

NOTE.

It will be observed that the 'Noble Numbers' is dated
1647, which was doubtless 1647-8; and from the close of
the 'Hesperides' it would seem Herrick intended 'Noble
Numbers' to be prefixed, not affixed, thereto. See Memorial-Introduction for more on this. G.

HIS
NOBLE NUMBERS:

OR,

HIS PIOUS PIECES,

Wherein (amongſt other things)
He ſings the Birth of his CHRIST:
and ſighes for his *Saviours* ſuffe-
ring on the *Croſſe*.

HESIOD.

Ἴδμεν ψεύδεα πολλὰ λέγειν ἐτύμοισιν ὁμοῖα.
Ἴδμεν δ᾽ εὖτ᾽ ἐθέλωμεν, ἀληθέα μυθήσασθαι.

LONDON.
Printed for *John Williams*, and *Francis Eglesfield.*
1647.

HIS

NOBLE NUMBERS:

OR,

HIS PIOUS PIECES.

His Confession.

OOK how our foule Dayes do exceed
    our faire ;
And as our bad, more then our good
    Works are,   [than
Ev'n so those Lines, pen'd by my wanton Wit,
Treble the number of these good I've writ.
Things precious are least num'rous : Men are prone
To do ten Bad, for one Good Action.

His Prayer for Absolution.

FOR Those my unbaptizèd Rhimes,
    Writ in my wild unhallowéd Times ; [1]

[1] See Memorial-Introduction ; but ' unhallowed ' here is simply =
lay as opposed to clerical.

For every sentence, clause, and word,
That's not inlaid with Thee, (my Lord)
Forgive me, God, and blot each Line
Out of my Book, that is not Thine.
But if, 'mongst all, Thou find'st here one
Worthy thy Benediction ;
That One of all the rest, shall be
The Glory of my Work, and Me.

To finde God.

WEIGH me the Fire ; or canst thou find
    A way to measure out the Wind ;
Distinguish all those Floods that are
Mixt in the watrie Theater ;
And tast thou them as saltlesse there,
As in their Channell first they were.
Tell me the People that do keep
Within the Kingdomes of the Deep ;
Or fetch me back that Cloud againe,
·Beshiver'd [2] into seeds of Raine ;
Tell me the motes, dust, sands, and speares [3]
Of Corn, when Summer shakes his eares ;

---

[2] ═ all or wholly shivered.   [3] ═ spires or heads.

Shew me that world of Starres, and whence
They noiselesse spill their Influence :
This if thou canst ; then shew me Him
That rides the glorious *Cherubim.*[4]

What God is.

GOD is above the sphere of our esteem,
 And is the best known, not defining Him.

Upon God.

GOD is not onely said to be
 An *Ens*, but *Supraentitie.*[5]

Mercy and Love.

GOD hath two wings, which He doth ever move,
 The one is Mercy, and the next is Love :
Under the first the Sinners ever trust ;
And with the last he still directs the Just.

Gods Anger without Affection.

GOD when He's angry here with any one,
 His wrath is free from perturbation ;
And when we think His looks are sowre and grim,
The alteration is in us, not Him.

---

[4] Psalm lxviii. 4, 33. [5] = above Being.

God not to be comprehended.

'TIS hard to finde God, but to comprehend
   Him, as He is, is labour without end.

Gods part.

PRAYERS and Praises are those spotlesse two
   Lambs, by the Law, which God requires as due.[6]

Affliction.

GOD n'ere afflicts us more then our desert,   [*than*
   Though He may seem to over-act His part :
Somtimes He strikes us more then flesh can beare ;
But yet still lesse then Grace can suffer here.

Three fatall Sisters.

THREE fatall Sisters wait upon each sin ;
   First, Fear and Shame without, then Guilt within.

Silence.

SUFFER thy legs, but not thy tongue to walk :
   God, the most Wise, is sparing of His talk.

---

[6] The cleansing sacrifice.   Cf. Numbers xxviii. 3 and 9, with
Leviticus xiv. 10.

Mirth.

TRUE mirth resides not in the smiling skin :
    The sweetest solace is to act no sin.

Loading and unloading.

GOD loads, and unloads, (thus His work begins)
    To load with blessings, and unload from sins.

Gods Mercy.

GODS boundlesse mercy is (to sinfull man)
    Like to the ever-wealthy Ocean :
Which though it sends forth thousand streams, 'tis
        ne're
Known, or els seen to be the emptier ;
And though it takes all in, 'tis yet no more
Full, and fild-full,[7] then when full-fild before.   [than

Prayers must have Poise.

GOD He rejects all Prayers that are sleight,
    And want their Poise : words ought to have
    their weight.

[7] See Glossarial Index s. v.

To God : an Anthem, sung in the Chappell at
White-Hall, before the King.

Verse.   MY God, I'm wounded by my sin,
                    And sore without, and sick within :
Ver. Chor. I come to Thee, in hope to find
                    Salve for my body, and my mind.
Verse.   In *Gilead* though no Balme be found,
                    To ease this smart, or cure this wound ;
Ver. Chor. Yet, Lord, I know there is with Thee
                    All saving health, and help for me.
Verse.   Then reach Thou forth that hand of
                    Thine,
                    That powres in oyle, as well as wine.
Ver. Chor. And let it work, for I'le endure
                    The utmost smart, so Thou wilt cure.

Upon God.

GOD is all fore-part ; for, we never see
    Any part backward in the Deitie.

Calling, and correcting.

GOD is not onely mercifull, to call,
    Men to repent, but when He strikes withall.

No Escaping the scourging.

GOD scourgeth some severely, some He spares ;
    But all in smart have lesse, or greater shares.

The Rod.

GODS Rod doth watch while men do sleep, &
  then
The Rod doth sleep, while vigilant are men.

God has a twofold part.

GOD when for sin He makes His Children smart,
  His own He acts not, but anothers part :
But when by stripes He saves them, then 'tis known,
He comes to play the part that is His own.

God is One.

GOD, as He is most Holy knowne ;
  So He is said to be most One.

Persecutions profitable.

AFFLICTIONS they most profitable are
  To the beholder, and the sufferer :
Bettering them both, but by a double straine,
The first by patience, and the last by paine.

To God.

DO with me, God ! as Thou didst deal with *Iohn*,
  (Who writ that heavenly *Revelation*) ;

Let me (like him) first cracks of thunder heare;
Then let the Harps inchantments strike mine eare;
Here give me thornes; there, in thy Kingdome, set
Upon my head the golden coronet;
There give me day; but here my dreadfull night:
My sackcloth here; but there my *Stole* of white.

Whips.

GOD has His whips here to a twofold end,
   The bad to punish, and the good t'amend.

Gods Providence.

IF all transgressions here should have their pay,
   What need there then be of a reckning day?
If God should punish no sin, here, of men,
His Providence who would not question then?

Temptation.

THOSE Saints, which God loves best,
   The Devill tempts not least.

His Ejaculation to God.

MY God! looke on me with Thine eye
   Of pittie, not of scrutinie;
For if Thou dost, Thou then shalt see
Nothing but loathsome sores in mee.

O then ! for mercies sake, behold
These my irruptions[8] manifold ;
And heale me with Thy looke, or touch :
But if Thou wilt not deigne so much,
Because I'm odious in Thy sight,
Speak but the word, and cure me quite.

Gods gifts not soone granted.

GOD heares us when we pray, but yet defers
    His gifts, to exercise Petitioners :
And though awhile He makes Requesters stay,
With Princely hand He'l recompence delay.

Persecutions purifie.

GOD strikes His Church, but 'tis to this intent,
    To make, not marre her, by this punishment :
So where He gives the bitter Pills, be sure,
'Tis not to poyson, but to make thee pure.

Pardon.

GOD pardons those, who do through frailty sin ;
    But never those that persevere therein.

---

8 —eruptions.

An Ode of the Birth of our Saviour.

1. IN Numbers, and but these few,
     I sing Thy Birth, Oh JESU !
    Thou prettie Babie, borne here,
    With sup'rabundant scorn here :
    Who for Thy Princely Port here,
             Hadst for Thy place
             Of Birth, a base
    Out-stable for thy Court here.

2. Instead of neat Inclosures
    Of inter-woven Osiers ;[9]
    Instead of fragrant Posies
    Of Daffadills, and Roses ;
    Thy cradle, Kingly Stranger,
             As Gospell tells,
             Was nothing els,
    But, here, a homely manger.

3. But we with Silks, (not Cruells,[10])
    With sundry precious Jewells,
    And Lilly-work will dresse Thee ;
    And as we dispossesse Thee

---

[9] = cradles.   [10] = worsted used for fancy needle-work.

Of clouts, wee'l make a chamber,
   Sweet Babe, for Thee,
   Of Ivorie,
And plaister'd round with Amber.

4. The Jewes they did disdaine Thee,
  But we will entertaine Thee
  With Glories to await here
  Upon Thy Princely State here,
  And more for love, then pittie.   [*than*
   From yeere to yeere
   Wee'l make Thee, here,
  A Free-born of our Citie.

Lip-labour.

I N the old Scripture I have often read,
  The calfe without meale n'ere was offerèd ;
To figure to us, nothing more then this, [*than*
Without the heart, lip-labour nothing is.

The Heart.

I N Prayer the Lips ne're act the winning part,
  Without the sweet concurrence of the Heart.

Eare-rings.

WHY wore th' Egyptians Jewells in the Eare?
But for to teach us, all the grace is there,
When we obey, by acting what we heare.

Sin seen.

WHEN once the sin has fully acted been,
Then is the horror of the trespasse seen.

Upon Time.

TIME was upon
The wing, to flie away;
And I cal'd on
Him but awhile to stay;
But he'd be gone,
For ought that I could say.

He held out then,
A Writing, as he went;
And askt me, when
False man would be content
To pay agen,
What God and Nature lent.

An houre-glasse,
In which were sands but few,
As he did passe,
He shew'd and told me too,
Mine end near was,
And so away he flew.

His Petition.

IF warre, or want shall make me grow so poore,
  As for to beg my bread from doore to doore ;
Lord ! let me never act that beggars part,
Who hath Thee in his mouth, not in his heart.[1]
He who asks almes in that so sacred Name,
Without due reverence, playes the cheaters game.

To God.

THOU hast promis'd, Lord, to be
    With me in my miserie ;
Suffer me to be so bold,
As to speak, Lord, say and hold.[2]

---

[1] Cf. Ezekiel xxxiii. 31.
[2] Apparently a known and proverbial phrase—say and hold to it,
i. e. perform thy promise.

His Letanie, to the Holy Spirit.

1. IN the houre of my distresse,
       When temptations me oppresse,
    And when I my sins confesse,
           Sweet Spirit comfort me !

2. When I lie within my bed,
    Sick in heart and sick in head,
    And with doubts discomforted,
           Sweet Spirit comfort me !

3. When the house doth sigh and weep,
    And the world is drown'd in sleep,
    Yet mine eyes the watch do keep ;
           Sweet Spirit comfort me !

4. When the artlesse[3] Doctor sees
    No one hope, but of his Fees,
    And his skill runs on the lees ;
           Sweet Spirit comfort me !

5. When his Potion and his Pill,
    Has, or none, or little skill,
    Meet for nothing, but to kill ;
           Sweet Spirit comfort me !

---

³ unskilful. See Memorial-Introduction on this (II. Critical).

6. When the passing-bell doth tole,
   And the Furies in a shole
   Come to fright a parting soule ;
       Sweet Spirit comfort me !

7. When the tapers now burne blew,
   And the comforters are few,
   And that number more then true ;[4]   [*than*
       Sweet Spirit comfort me !

8. When the Priest his last hath praid,
   And I nod to what is said,
   'Cause my speech is now decaid ;
       Sweet Spirit comfort me !

9. When (God knowes) I'm tost about,
   Either with despaire, or doubt ;
   Yet before the glasse be out,
       Sweet Spirit comfort me !

10. When the Tempter me pursu'th
    With the sins of all my youth,
    And halfe damns me with untruth ;
        Sweet Spirit comfort me !

[4] = and when the few that gather around me are not all true friends or comforters.

11. When the flames and hellish cries
    Fright mine eares, and fright mine eyes,
    And all terrors me surprize ;
        Sweet Spirit comfort me !

12. When the Judgment is reveal'd,
    And that open'd which was seal'd,
    When to Thee I have appeal'd ;
        Sweet Spirit comfort me ! .

Thanksgiving.

THANKSGIVING for a former, doth invite
God to bestow a second benefit.

Cock-crow.

BELL-MAN of Night,[5] if I about shall go
For to denie my Master, do thou crow.
Thou stop'st S. *Peter* in the midst of sin ;
Stay me, by crowing, ere I do begin ;
Better it is, premonish'd, for to shun
A sin, then fall to weeping when 'tis done.   [*than*

---

[5] The cock. So Spenser :
        ———— " Bell-man of the night,
        The bird that warnèd Peter of his fall." Fairy Queen.

All Things run well for the Righteous.

ADVERSE and prosperous Fortunes both work on
 Here, for the righteous mans salvation :
Be he oppos'd, or be he not withstood,
All serve to th' Augmentation of his good.

Paine ends in Pleasure.

AFFLICTIONS bring us joy in times to come,
 When sins, by stripes, to us grow wearisome.

To God.

I'LE come, I'le creep, (though Thou dost threat,)
 Humbly unto Thy Mercy-seat :
When I am there, this then I'le do,
Give Thee a Dart, and Dagger too ;
Next, when I have my faults confest,
Naked I'le shew a sighing brest ;
Which if that can't Thy pittie wooe,
Then let Thy Justice do the rest,
   And strike it through.

A Thanksgiving to God, for His House.

LORD, Thou hast given me a cell
  Wherein to dwell ;

A little house, whose humble Roof
    Is weather-proof;
Under the sparres of which I lie
    Both soft, and drie;
Where Thou my chamber for to ward
    Hast set a Guard
Of harmlesse thoughts, to watch and keep
    Me, while I sleep.
Low is my porch, as is my Fate,
    Both void of state;
And yet the threshold of my doore
    Is worn by th' poore,
Who thither come, and freely get
    Good words, or meat:
Likeas my Parlour, so my Hall
    And Kitchin's small:
A little Butterie, and therein
    A little Byn,
Which keeps my little loafe of Bread
    Unchipt, unflead:[6]
Some brittle sticks of Thorne or Briar
    Make me a fire,
Close by whose living coale I sit,
    And glow like it.

[6] Probably = good, undamaged by mould, &c.   Halliwell has
' fled ' as a Shropshire word.

Lord, I confesse too, when I dine,
    The Pulse is Thine,
And all those other Bits, that bee
    There plac'd by Thee ;
The Worts,[7] the Purslain,[8] and the Messe
    Of water-cresse,
Which of Thy kindnesse Thou hast sent ;
    And my content
Makes those, and my belovèd Beet,
    To be more sweet.
'Tis Thou that crown'st my glittering Hearth
    With guiltlesse mirth ;
And giv'st me Wassaile Bowles to drink,
    Spic'd to the brink.
Lord, 'tis Thy plenty-dropping hand,
    That soiles[9] my land ;
And giv'st me, for my Bushell sowne,
    Twice ten for one :
Thou mak'st my teeming Hen to lay
    Her egg each day :
Besides my healthfull Ewes to beare
    Me twins each yeare :
The while the conduits of my Kine
    Run Creame, (for Wine.)

---

[7] = cabbage.   [8] A kind of sallad.   See Glossarial Index s. v.
[9] = manures.

All these, and better Thou dost send
      Me, to this end,
That I should render, for my part,
      A thankfull heart;
Which, fir'd with incense, I resigne,
      As wholly Thine;
But the acceptance, that must be,
      My Christ, by Thee.

To God.

MAKE, make me Thine, my gracious God,
    Or with Thy staffe, or with Thy rod;
And be the blow too what it will,
Lord, I will kisse it, though it kill:
Beat me, bruise me, rack me, rend me,
Yet, in torments, I'le commend Thee:
Examine me with fire, and prove me
To the full, yet I will love Thee:
Nor shalt Thou give so deep a wound,
But I as patient will be found.

Another, to God.

LORD, do not beat me,
    Since I do sob and crie,
And swowne away to die,

Ere Thou dost threat me.
Lord, do not scourge me,
If I by lies and oaths
Have soil'd my selfe, or cloaths,
But rather purge me.

None truly happy here.

HAPPY'S that man, to whom God gives
A stock of Goods, whereby he lives
Neer to the wishes of his heart :
No man is blest through ev'ry part.

To his ever-loving God.

CAN I not come to Thee, my God, for these
So very-many-meeting hindrances,
That slack my pace ; but yet not make me stay ?
Who slowly goes, rids[1] (in the end) his way.
Cleere Thou my paths, or shorten Thou my miles,
Remove the barrs, or lift me o're the stiles :
Since rough the way is, help me when I call,
And take me up ; or els prevent the fall.
I kenn[2] my home ; and it affords some ease,
To see far off the smoaking Villages.

[1] = gets rid or clear of his way, i. e. finishes his journey.
[2] = know.

Fain would I rest ; yet covet not to die,
For feare of future-biting penurie :
No, no, (my God) Thou know'st my wishes be
To leave this life, not loving it, but Thee.

Another.

THOU bidst me come ; I cannot come ; for why,
    Thou dwel'st aloft, and I want wings to flie.
To mount my Soule, she must have pineons given ;
For, 'tis no easie way from Earth to Heaven.

To Death.

THOU bidst me come away,
    And I'le no longer stay,
Then for to shed some teares   [*than*
For faults of former yeares ;
And to repent some crimes,
Done in the present times :
And next, to take a bit
Of Bread, and Wine with it :
To d'on my robes of love,
Fit for the place above ;
To gird my loynes about
With charity throughout ;

And so to travaile hence
With feet of innocence :
These done, I'le onely crie
God mercy ; and so die.

Neutrality loathsome.

GOD will have all, or none ; serve Him, or fall
   Down before *Baal, Bel,* or *Belial :*
Either be hot, or cold : God doth despise,
Abhorre, and spew out all Neutralities.[3]

Welcome what comes.

WHATEVER comes, let's be content withall :
   Among God's Blessings, there is no one small.

To his angrie God.

THROUGH all the night
   Thou dost me fright,
And hold'st mine eyes from sleeping ;
   And day, by day,
   My Cup can say,
My wine is mixt with weeping.

Thou dost my bread
   With ashes knead,
Each evening and each morrow :

[3] Revelation, c. iii. v. 16.

Mine eye and eare
Do see, and heare
The coming in of sorrow.

Thy scourge of steele,
(Ay me !) I feele,
Upon me beating ever :
While my sick heart
With dismall smart
Is disacquainted never.

Long, long, I'm sure,
This can't endure ;
But in short time 'twill please Thee,
My gentle God,
To burn the rod,
Or strike so as to ease me.

Patience, or Comforts in Crosses.

ABUNDANT plagues I late have had,
  Yet none of these have made me sad :
For why, my Saviour, with the sense
Of suffring gives me patience.

Eternitie.

1. O YEARES ! and Age ! Farewell :
      Behold I go,

Where I do know
Infinitie to dwell.

2. And these mine eyes shall see
All times, how they
Are lost i' th' Sea
Of vast Eternitie.

3. Where never Moone shall sway
The Starres ; but she,
And Night, shall be
Drown'd in one endlesse Day.

To his Saviour, a Child ; a Present, by a child.

GO prettie child, and beare this Flower
Unto thy little Saviour ;
And tell Him, by that Bud now blown,
He is the *Rose of Sharon* known :
When thou hast said so, stick it there
Upon His Bibb, or Stomacher :
And tell Him, (for good handsell [4] too)
That thou hast brought a Whistle new,
Made of a clean strait oaten reed,
To charme His cries, (at time of need :)

[4] See Glossarial Index s. v.

Tell Him, for Corall, thou hast none ;
But if thou hadst, He sho'd have one ;
But poore thou art, and knowne to be
Even as monilesse, as He.
Lastly, if thou canst win a kisse
From those mellifluous lips of His ;
Then never take a second on,
To spoile the first impression.

The New-yeeres Gift.

LET others looke for Pearle and Gold,
    Tissues, or Tabbies [5] manifold :
One onely lock of that sweet Hay
Whereon the blessed Babie lay,
Or one poore Swadling-clout, shall be
The richest New-yeeres Gift to me.

To God.

IF any thing delight me for to print
    My Book, 'tis this ; that, *Thou, my God, art in't.*

God, and the King.

HOW am I bound to Two ! God, who doth give
    The mind ; the King, the meanes whereby I live.

---

[5] =kind of thick-threaded silk watered by presses. See Glossarial Index s. v : cloth, called ' tabby : ' and we still have ' tabinet : ' qu. —as resembling the smooth coat of a cat ' Tabby.'

Gods mirth, Mans mourning.

WHERE God is merry, there write down thy
  fears :
What He with laughter speaks, heare thou with tears.

Honours are hindrances.

GIVE me Honours ! what are these,
  But the pleasing hindrances ?
Stiles, and stops, and stayes, that come
In the way 'twixt me, and home :
Cleer the walk, and then shall I
To my heaven lesse run, then flie.   ⌊*than*

The Parasceve, or Preparation.

TO a Love-Feast we both invited are :
  The figur'd Damask, or pure Diaper,[6]
Over the golden Altar now is spread,
With Bread, and Wine, and Vessells furnishèd ;
The *sacred Towell*, and the *holy Eure*[7]
Are ready by, to make the Guests all pure :
Let's go (my *Alma*)[8] yet, e're we receive,
Fit, fit it is, we have our *Parasceve*.[9]
Who to that *sweet Bread* unprepar'd doth come,
Better he starv'd, then but to tast one crumme. [*than*

[6] = figured linen. See Glossarial Index s. v.
[7] = flagon.   [8] = pure one, virgin.   [9] = preparation.

To God.

GOD gives not onely corne, for need,
  But likewise sup'rabundant seed ;
Bread for our service, bread for shew ;
Meat for our meales, and fragments too :
He gives not poorly, taking some
Between the finger, and the thumb ;
But, for our glut, and for our store,
Fine flowre prest down, and running o're.

A will to be working.

ALTHOUGH we cannot turne the fervent fit
  Of sin, we must strive 'gainst the streame of it :
And howsoe're we have the conquest mist ;
'Tis for our glory, that we did resist.

Christs part.

CHRIST, He requires still, wheresoere He comes,
  To feed, or lodge, to have the best of Roomes :
Give Him the choice ; grant Him the nobler part
Of all the House : the best of all's the Heart.

Riches and Poverty.

GOD co'd have made all rich, or all men poore ;
  But why He did not, let me tell wherefore :

Had all been rich, where then had Patience been ?
Had all been poore, who had His Bounty seen ?

Sobriety in Search.

TO seek of God [1] more then we well can find, [*than*
    Argues a strong distemper of the mind.

Almes.

GIVE, if thou canst, an Almes ; if not, afford,
    Instead of that, a sweet and gentle word :
God crowns our goodnesse, wheresoere He sees,
On our part, wanting all abilities.

To his Conscience.

CAN I not sin, but thou wilt be
    My private *Protonotarie ?*[2]
Can I not wooe thee to passe by
A short and sweet iniquity ?
I'le cast a mist and cloud, upon
My delicate transgression,
So utter dark, as that no eye
Shall see the hug'd [3] impietie :

---

[1] i.e. to seek into the nature and acts of God.

[2] = prothonotary, or chief recording scribe, as in the courts of law.

[3] = hugged. See similarly Glossarial Index under ' rag'd ' for ' ragged.'

Gifts blind the wise, and bribes do please,
And winde all other witnesses :
And wilt not thou, with gold, be ti'd
To lay thy pen and ink aside ?
That in the mirk[4] and tonguelesse night,
Wanton I may, and thou not write ?
It will not be : And, therefore, now,
For times to come, I'le make this Vow,
From aberrations to live free ;
So I'le not feare the Judge, or thee.

To his Saviour.

LORD, I confesse, that Thou alone art able
　To purifie this my *Augean* stable :
Be the Seas water, and the Land all Sope,
Yet if Thy Bloud not wash me, there's no hope.

To God.

GOD is all-sufferance here ; here He doth show
　No Arrow nockt,[5] onely a stringlesse Bow :
His Arrowes flie, and all his stones are hurl'd
Against the wicked, in another world.

His Dreame.

I DREAMT, last night, Thou didst transfuse
　Oyle from Thy Jarre, into my creuze ;

---

[4] = dark.   [5] = The nock or noch of the arrow set in the bow-string.

And powring still, Thy wealthy store,
The vessell full, did then run ore :
Me thought, I did Thy bounty chide,
To see the waste ; but 'twas repli'd
By Thee, Deare God, God gives man seed
Oft-times for wast, as for his need.
Then I co'd say, that house is bare,
That has not bread, and some to spare.[6]

Gods Bounty.

GODS Bounty, that ebbs lesse and lesse,
  As men do wane in thankfulnesse.

To his sweet Saviour.

NIGHT hath no wings, to him that cannot sleep ;
  And Time seems then, not for to flie, but creep ;
Slowly her chariot drives, as if that she
Had broke her wheele, or crackt her axeltree.
Just so it is with me, who list'ning, pray
The winds, to blow the tedious night away ;
That I might see the cheerfull peeping day.
Sick is my heart ! O Saviour ! do Thou please
To make my bed soft in my sicknesses:

[6] A reference to " Exilis domus est, ubi non et multa supersunt,
&c. Horace, Ep. I. vi. l. 45.

Lighten my candle, so that I beneath
Sleep not for ever in the vaults of death :
Let me Thy voice betimes i' th' morning heare ;
Call, and I'le come ; say Thou, the when, and where
Draw me but first, and after Thee I'le run,
And make no one stop, till my race be done.

His Creed.

I DO believe, that die I must,
   And be return'd from out my dust :
I do believe, that when I rise,
Christ I shall see, with these same eyes :
I do believe, that I must come,
With others, to the dreadfull Doome : [7]
I do believe, the bad must goe
From thence, to everlasting woe :
I do believe, the good, and I,
Shall live with Him eternally :
I do believe, I shall inherit
Heaven, by Christs mercies, not my merit :
I do believe, the One in Three,
And Three in perfect Unitie :
Lastly, that JESUS is a Deed
Of Gift from God : *And heres my Creed.*

[7] See Glossarial Index s. v.

Temptations.

TEMPTATIONS hurt not, though they have
    accesse :
Satan o'ercomes none, but by willingnesse.

The Lamp.

WHEN a man's Faith is frozen up, as dead ;
    Then is the Lamp and oyle extinguishèd.

Sorrowes.

SORROWES our portion are : Ere hence we goe,
    Crosses wc must have ; or, hereafter woe.

Penitencie.

A MANS transgression God do's then remit,
    When man he makes a Penitent for it.

The Dirge of Jephthahs *Daughter : sung by the Virgins.*

1. O THOU, the wonder of all dayes !
      O Paragon,[8] and Pearle of praise !
    O Virgin-martyr, ever blest
            Above the rest

---

[8] The highest or most precious, chief among virgins. See quotation from Gough in Nares s. v. The origin of the phrase may be doubtful, but probably it is from the eye being so bright and precious a part of the body.

Of all the Maiden-Traine !   We come,
And bring fresh strewings to thy Tombe.

2. Thus, thus, and thus we compasse round
    Thy harmlesse and unhaunted Ground ;
    And as we sing thy Dirge, we will
                        The Daffadill,
    And other flowers, lay upon
    (The Altar of our love) thy Stone.

3. Thou wonder of all Maids, li'st here,
    Of Daughters all, the Deerest Deere ;
    The eye of Virgins ;[9] nay, the Queen,
                        Of this smooth Green,
    And all sweet Meades ; from whence we get
    The Primrose, and the Violet.

4. Too soon, too deere did *Jephthah* buy,
    By thy sad losse, our liberty :
    His was the Bond and Cov'nant, yet
                        Thou paid'st the debt :
    Lamented Maid ! he won the day,
    But for the conquest thou didst pay.

[9] See Glossarial Index s. v.

5. Thy Father brought with him along
    The Olive branch, and Victors Song :
    He slew the Ammonites,[1] we know,

                    But to thy woe ;

    And in the purchase of our Peace,
    The Cure was worse then the Disease.   [*than*

6. For which obedient zeale of thine,
    We offer here, before thy Shrine,
    Our sighs for Storax, teares for Wine ;

                    And to make fine,

    And fresh thy Herse-cloth,[2] we will, here,
    Foure times bestrew thee ev'ry yeere.

7. Receive, for this thy praise, our teares :
    Receive this offering of our Haires :[3]
    Receive these Christall Vialls fil'd

                    With teares, distil'd

    From teeming eyes ; to these we bring,
    Each Maid, her silver Filleting,

---

[1] Cf. Judges xi. 1—33.

[2] Here metaphorical for the turf or tomb covering her.

[3] Referring to the Eastern custom of shaving or cutting the hair in token of grief.   Cf. Job. i. 30 : Jer. vii. 29.

8. To guild thy Tombe ; besides, these Caules,[4]
These Laces, Ribbands, and these Faules,
These Veiles, wherewith we use to hide
                    The Bashfull Bride,
When we conduct her to her Groome :
And, all we lay upon thy Tombe.

9. No more, no more, since thou art dead,
Shall we ere bring coy Brides to bed ;
No more, at yeerly Festivalls
                    We Cowslip balls,
Or chaines of Columbines [5] shall make,
For this, or that occasions sake.

10. No, no ; our Maiden-pleasures be
Wrapt in the winding-sheet, with thee :
'Tis we are dead, though not i' th' grave :
                    Or, if we have
One seed of life left, 'tis to keep
A Lent for thee, to fast and weep.

11. Sleep in thy peace, thy bed of Spice ;
And make this place all Paradise :
May Sweets grow here ! & smoke from hence,
                    Fat Frankincense :

---

[4] =curls or head-dresses.   [5] Flowers so named.

Let Balme and Cassia, send their scent
From out thy Maiden-Monument.

12. May no Wolfe howle, or Screech-Owle stir
A wing about thy Sepulcher!
No boysterous winds, or stormes, come hither,
                    To starve, or wither
Thy soft sweet Earth! but (like a spring)
Love keep it ever flourishing.

13. May all shie Maids, at wonted hours,
Come forth, to strew thy Tombe with flow'rs:
May Virgins, when they come to mourn,
                    Male-Incense burn[6]
Upon thine Altar! then return,
And leave thee sleeping in thy Urn.

To God, on his sicknesse.

WHAT though my Harp, and Violl be
        Both hung upon the Willow-tree?
What though my bed be now my grave,
And for my house I darknesse have?
What though my healthfull dayes are fled,
And I lie numbred with the dead?
Yet I have hope, by Thy great power,
To spring; though now a wither'd flower.

[6] See Glossarial Index s. v.

Sins loath'd, and yet lov'd.

SHAME *checks our first attempts;* but then 'tis
    prov'd,
Sins first dislik'd, are after that belov'd.[7]

Sin.

SIN leads the way, but as it goes, it feels
    The following plague still treading on his heels.

Upon God.

GOD when He takes my goods and chattels hence,
    Gives me a portion, giving patience :
What is in God is God ; if so it be,
He patience gives ; He gives himselfe to me.

Faith.

WHAT here we hope for, we shall once[8] inherit :
    By Faith we all walk here, not by the Spirit.

Humility.

HUMBLE we must be, if to Heaven we go :
    High is the roof there ; but the gate is low :
When e're thou speak'st, look with a lowly eye :
Grace is increasèd by humility.

---

[7] See Memorial-Introduction for a parallel later (in Pope).
[8] = at some future time and continuously, once and for aye.

Teares.

OUR present Teares here (not our present laughter)
Are but the handsells of our joyes[9] hereafter.

Sin and Strife.

AFTER true sorrow for our sinnes, our strife
Must last with Satan, to the end of life.

An Ode, or Psalme, to God.

DEER God,
   If thy smart Rod
Here did not make me sorrie,
   I sho'd not be
   With Thine, or Thee,
In Thy eternall Glorie.

   But since
   Thou didst convince
My sinnes, by gently striking;
   Add still to those
   First stripes, new blowes,
According to Thy liking.

---

[9] Cf. Herbert: (Vol. i. p. 65, l. 13, F. W. Library edn.) " Thou
art Joye's handsell."

Feare me,[1]
Or scourging teare me ;
That thus from vices driven,
I may from Hell
Flie up, to dwell
With Thee, and Thine in Heaven.

Graces for Children.

WHAT God gives, and what we take,
    'Tis a gift for Christ His sake :
Be the meale of Beanes and Pease,
God be thank'd for those, and these :
Have we flesh, or have we fish,
All are Fragments from His dish.
He His Church save, and the King,
And our Peace here, like a Spring,
Make it ever flourishing.

God to be first serv'd.

HONOUR thy Parents ; but good manners call
    Thee to adore thy God, the first of all.

Another Grace for a Child.

HERE a little child I stand,
    Heaving up my either hand ;

[1] ― make me afraid.

Cold as Paddocks[2] though they be,
Here I lift them up to Thee,
For a Benizon[3] to fall
On our meat, and on us all.   *Amen.*

A Christmas Caroll, *sung to the King in the Presence at* White-Hall.[4]

Chor. WHAT sweeter musick can we bring,
        Then a Caroll, for to sing   [*than*
The Birth of this our heavenly King?
Awake the Voice ! awake the String !
Heart, Eare, and Eye, and every thing
Awake ! the while the active Finger
Runs division with the Singer.

From the Flourish they came to the Song.

1. Dark and dull night, flie hence away,
   And give the honour to this Day,
   That sees *December* turn'd to *May.*

2. If we may ask the reason, say;
   The why, and wherefore all things here
   Seem like the Spring-time of the yeere ?

---

[2] = frogs.   [3] = benison, benediction.
[4] See Memorial-Introduction.

3. Why do's the chilling Winters morne
   Smile, like a field beset with corne?
   Or smell, like to a Meade new-shorne,
   Thus, on the sudden?   4. Come and see
   The cause, why things thus fragrant be :
   'Tis He is borne, whose quickning Birth
   Gives life and luster, publike mirth,
   To Heaven, and the under-Earth.

Chor. We see Him come, and know him ours,
   Who, with His Sun-shine, and His showers,
   Turnes all the patient ground to flowers.

1. The Darling of the world is come,
   And fit it is, we finde a roome
   To welcome Him.   2. The nobler part
   Of all the house here, is the heart,

Chor. Which we will give Him ; and bequeath
   This Hollie, and this Ivie Wreath,
   To do Him honour ; who's our King,
   And Lord of all this Revelling.

> *The Musicall Part was composed by*
> M. Henry Lawes.

The New-yeeres Gift, or Circumcisions Song,
sung to the King in the Presence at
White-Hall.[5]

1. PREPARE for Songs ; He's come, He's
    come ;
    And be it sin here to be dumb,
    And not with Lutes to fill the roome.

2. Cast Holy Water all about,
    And have a care no fire gos out,
    But 'cense the porch and place, throughout.

3. The Altars all on fier be ;
    The Storax fries ; and ye may see,
    How heart and hand do all agree,
    To make things sweet. *Chor.* Yet all less sweet
    then He.   [*than*

4. Bring Him along, most pious Priest,
    And tell us then, whenas thou seest
    His gently-gliding, Dove-like eyes,
    And hear'st His whimp'ring, and His cries ;
    How canst thou this Babe circumcise ?

[5] Ibid.

5. Ye must not be more pitifull then wise ;   [*than*
   For, now unlesse ye see Him bleed,
   Which makes the Bapti'me ;[6] 'tis decreed,
The Birth is fruitlesse : *Chor.* Then the *work God
      speed.*

1. Touch gently, gently touch ; and here
   Spring Tulips up through all the yeere ;
   And from His sacred Bloud, here shed,
May Roses grow, to crown His own deare Head.

Chor. Back, back again ; each thing is done
   With zeale alike, as 'twas begun ;
   Now singing, homeward let us carrie
   The Babe unto His Mother *Marie ;*
   And when we have the Child commended
To her warm bosome, then our Rites are ended.

   Composed by M. Henry Lawes.

*Another New-yeeres Gift, or Song for
      the Circumcision.*

1. HENCE, hence prophane, and none appeare
   With any thing unhallowed, here :

No jot of Leven must be found
Conceal'd in this most holy Ground :[7]

2. What is corrupt, or sowr'd with sin,
Leave that without, then enter in ;

Chor. But let no Christmas mirth begin
Before ye purge, and circumcise
Your hearts, and hands, lips, eares, and eyes.

3. Then, like a perfum'd Altar, see
That all things sweet, and clean may be :
For, here's a Babe, that (like a *Bride*)
Will *blush to death,* if ought be spi'd
Ill-scenting, or unpurifi'd.

Chor. The room is cens'd :[8] help, help t'invoke
Heaven to come down, the while we choke
The Temple, with a cloud of smoke.

4. Come then, and gently touch the Birth
Of Him, Who's Lord of Heav'n and Earth ;

5. And softly handle Him : y'ad need,
Because the *prettie Babe* do's bleed.
Poore-pittied Child ! Who from Thy Stall

---

[7] **Exodus xxxiv. 25.**   [8] **See Glossarial Index s. v.**

Bring'st, in Thy Blood, a Balm, that shall
Be the best New-yeares Gift to all.

1. Let's blesse the Babe : And, as we sing
His praise ; so let us blesse the King :

Chor. Long may He live, till He hath told
His New-yeeres trebled to His old :
And, when that's done, to re-aspire
A new-borne *Phœnix* from His own chast fire.

Gods Pardon.

WHEN I shall sin, pardon my trespasse here ;
For, once in hell, none knowes Remission there.

Sin.

SIN once reacht up to Gods eternall Sphere,[9]
And was committed, not remitted there.

Evill.

EVILL no Nature hath ; the losse of good
Is that which gives to sin a livelihood.

---

[9] Referring to Satan's rebellion.

The Star-Song: a Caroll to the King;
sung at White-Hall.[1]

The Flourish of Musick: then followed the Song.

1. TELL us, thou cleere and heavenly Tongue,
    Where is the Babe but lately sprung?
Lies He the Lillie-banks among?

2. Or say, if this new Birth of ours
Sleeps, laid within some Ark of Flowers,
Spangled with deaw-light; thou canst cleere
All doubts, and manifest the where.

3. Declare to us, bright Star, if we shall seek
Him in the Mornings blushing cheek,
Or search the beds of Spices through,
To find him out?

Star. No, this ye need not do;
But only come, and see Him rest
A Princely Babe in's Mothers Brest.

Chor. He's seen, He's seen, why then a Round,[2]
Let's kisse the sweet and holy ground;
And all rejoyce, that we have found
A King, before conception crown'd.

---

[1] See Memorial-Introduction.   [2] = a dance.

4. Come then, come then, and let us bring
　　Unto our prettie *Twelfth-Tide King*,[3]
　　Each one his severall offering;

Chor. And when night comes, wee'l give Him
　　　　　wassailing;
And that His treble Honours may be seen,
Wee'l chuse Him King, and make His Mother Queen.

To God.

WITH golden Censers, and with Incense, here,
　　Before Thy Virgin-Altar I appeare,
To pay Thee that I owe, since what I see
In, or without; all, all belongs to Thee:
Where shall I now begin to make, for one
Least loane of Thine, half Restitution?
Alas! I cannot pay a jot; therefore
I'le kisse the Tally,[4] and confesse the score.[5]
Ten thousand Talents lent me, Thou dost write:
'Tis true, my God; *but I can't pay one mite.*

To his deere God.

I'LE hope no more,
　　　For things that will not come:
And, if they do, they prove but cumbersome;

---

[3] The 'Holy Child' Jesus.
[4] ▬ the notched stick for marking of debts.　　　[5] ▬ debts.

Wealth brings much woe :
And, since it fortunes so ;
'Tis better to be poore,
Than so t'abound,
As to be drown'd,
Or overwhelm'd with store.

Pale care, avant,
I'le learn to be content
With that small stock, Thy Bounty gave or lent.
What may conduce
To my most healthfull use,
Almighty God me grant ;
But that, or this,
That hurtfull is,
Denie Thy suppliant.

To God, his good will.

GOLD I have none, but I present my need,
   O Thou, that crown'st the will, where wants
      the deed.
Where Rams are wanting, or large Bullocks thighs,
There a poor Lamb's a plenteous sacrifice.
Take then his Vowes, who, if he had it, would
Devote to Thee, both incense, myrrhe, and gold,
Upon an Altar rear'd by Him, and crown'd
Both with the *Rubie, Pearle,* and *Diamond.*

On Heaven.

PERMIT mine eyes to see
    Part, or the whole of Thee,
    O happy place !
    Where all have Grace,
    And Garlands shar'd,
    For their reward ;
    Where each chast Soule
    In long white stole,
    And Palmes in hand,
    Do ravisht stand ;
    So in a ring,
    The praises sing
    Of Three in One,
    That fill the Throne ;
    While Harps, and Violls then
    To Voices, say, *Amen.*

The Summe, and the Satisfaction.

LAST night I drew up mine Account,
    And found my Debits to amount
To such a height, as for to tell
How I sho'd pay, 's impossible :
Well, this I'le do ; my mighty score
Thy mercy-seat I'le lay before ;

But therewithall I'le bring the Band,
Which, in full force, did daring[6] stand,
Till my Redeemer (on the Tree)
Made void for millions, as for me.
Then, if Thou bidst me pay, or go
Unto the prison, I'le say, no;
Christ having paid, I nothing owe :
For, this is sure, the Debt is dead
By Law, the Bond once *cancellèd*.

Good men afflicted most.

GOD makes not good men wantons, but doth
    bring
Them to the field, and, there, to skirmishing ;
With trialls those, with terrors these He proves,
And hazards those most, whom the most He loves ;
For *Sceva*, darts ; for *Cocles*, dangers ; thus
He finds a fire for mighty *Mutius ;*
Death for stout *Cato ;* and besides all these,
A poyson too He has for *Socrates ;*
Torments for high *Attilius ;* and, with want,
Brings in *Fabricius* for a Combatant :[7]

---

[6] = frightening, causing fear—a hawking and bird-catching term.
[7] All the names herein are classical commonplaces, and need no
annotation.

But, bastard-slips, and such as He dislikes,
He never brings them once to th' push of Pikes.[8]

Good Christians.

PLAY their offensive and defensive parts,
　　Till they be hid o're with a wood of darts.

The Will the cause of Woe.

WHEN man is punisht, he is plaguèd still,
　　Not for the fault of Nature, but of will.

To Heaven.

OPEN thy gates
　　To him, who weeping waits,
　　　And might come in,
But that held back by sin.
　　Let mercy be
So kind, to set me free,
　　And I will strait
Come in, or force the gate.

The Recompence.

ALL I have lost, that co'd be rapt from me ;
　　And fare it well : yet *Herrick*, if so be

[b] Hebrews xii. 8 — danger or affliction.

Thy Deerest Saviour renders thee but one
Smile, that one smile's full restitution.

To God.

PARDON me God, (once more I Thee intreat)
　　That I have plac'd Thee in so meane a seat,
Where round about Thou seest but all things vaine,
Uncircumcis'd, unseason'd, and prophane.
But as Heavens publike and immortall Eye
Looks on the filth, but is not soil'd thereby;
So Thou, my God, may'st on this impure, look,
But take no tincture from my sinfull Book:
Let but one beame of Glory on it shine,
And that will make me, and my Work divine.[9]

To God.

LORD, I am like to *Misletoe*,
　　Which has no root, and cannot grow,
Or prosper, but by that same tree
It clings about; so I by Thee.
What need I then to feare at all,
So long as I about Thee craule?
But if that Tree sho'd fall, and die,
Tumble shall heav'n, and down will I.

[9] Cf. Cowper (end of " Task ")
　　" Whose approbation prospers even mine."

His wish to God.

I WOULD to God, that mine old age might have
    Before my last, but here a living grave,
Some one poore Almes-house ; there to lie, or stir,
Ghost-like, as in my meaner sepulcher ;
A little piggin,[1] and a pipkin[2] by,
To hold things fitting my necessity ;
Which, rightly us'd, both in their time and place,
Might me excite to fore and after-grace.
Thy Crosse, my *Christ*, fixt 'fore mine eyes sho'd be,
Not to adore that, but to worship Thee.
So, here the remnant of my dayes I'd spend,
Reading Thy Bible, and my Book ;[3] *so end.*

Satan.

WHEN we 'gainst Satan stoutly fight, the more
    He teares and tugs us, then he did before ; [*than*
Neglecting once to cast a frown on those
Whom ease makes his, without the help of blowes.

[1] = earthenware dish = a little pig—still its name : = also a wooden half-barrel pail having one stave longer than the rest to serve as handle.
[2] = a little tiny earthen pot with handle of same. See Glossarial Index.   [3] i. e. the Bible, which is my book.

Hell.

HELL is no other, but a soundlesse[4] pit,
   Where no one beame of comfort peeps in it.

The way.

WHEN I a ship see on the Seas,
   Cuft with those watrie savages,
And therewithall, behold, it hath
In all that way no beaten path ;
Then, with a wonder, I confesse,
Thou art our way i'th wildernesse :
And while we blunder in the dark,
Thou art our candle there, or spark.

Great grief, great glory.

THE lesse our sorrowes here and suffrings cease,
   The more our Crownes of Glory there increase.

Hell.

HELL is the place where whipping-cheer abounds,
   But no one Jailor there to wash the wounds.[5]

---

[4] = fathomless.
[5] Cf. Acts of the Apostles of the jailor at Philippi : c. xvi. 33.

The Bell-man.

ALONG the dark, and silent night,
   With my Lantern, and my Light,
And the tinkling of my Bell,
Thus I walk, and this I tell :
Death and dreadfulnesse call on,
To the gen'rall Session ;
To whose dismall Barre, we there
All accompts must come to cleere :
Scores of sins w'ave made here many,
Wip't out few, (God knowes) if any.
Rise, ye Debters, then, and fall
To make paiment, while I call.
Ponder this, when I am gone ;
By the clock 'tis almost *One.*

The goodnesse of his God.

WHEN Winds and Seas do rage,
   And threaten to undo me,
Thou dost their wrath asswage,
   If I but call unto Thee.

A mighty storm last night
   Did seek my soule to swallow,
But by the peep of light
   A gentle calme did follow.

What need I then despaire,
    Though ills stand round about me ;
Since mischiefs neither dare
    To bark, or bite, without Thee ?

The Widdowes teares: or, Dirge of Dorcas.

1. COME pitie us, all ye, who see
        Our Harps hung on the Willow-tree :
    Come pitie us, ye Passers by,
    Who see, or heare poor Widdowes crie :
    Come pitie us; and bring your eares,
    And eyes, to pitie Widdowes teares.
        Chor. And when you are come hither ;
                Then we will keep
                A Fast, and weep
            Our eyes out all together.

2. For *Tabitha*, who dead lies here,
    Clean washt, and laid out for the Beere ;
    O modest Matrons, weep and waile !
    For now the Corne and Wine must faile :
    The Basket and the Bynn of Bread,
    Wherewith so many soules were fed
        Chor. Stand empty here for ever :
                And ah ! the Poore,
                At thy worne Doore,
            Shall be releevèd never.

3. Woe worth the Time, woe worth the day,
    That reav'd us of thee *Tabitha !*
    For we have lost, with thee, the Meale,
    The Bits, the Morsells, and the deale[6]
    Of gentle Paste, and yeelding Dow,
    That Thou on Widdowes didst bestow.
    Chor. All's gone, and Death hath taken
            Away from us
            Our Maundie ;[7] thus,
            Thy Widdowes stand forsaken.

4. Ah *Dorcas, Dorcas !* now adieu
    We bid the Creuse and Pannier too :
    I and the flesh, for and[8] the fish,
    Dol'd to us in That Lordly dish.
    We take our leaves now of the Loome,
    From whence the house-wives cloth did come
    Chor. The web affords now nothing ;
            Thou being dead,
            The woosted[9] thred
            Is cut, that made us clothing.

---

[6] = the portion dealt out.   [7] See Glossarial Index s. v.

[8] ' for and ' : an old and originally perhaps intransitive form of ' and ' or ' also,' but sometimes, as here, used simply as ' and.'

[9] = worsted.

5. Farewell the Flax and Reaming[1] wooll,
   With which thy house was plentifull.
   Farewell the Coats, the Garments, and
   The Sheets, the Rugs, made by thy hand.
   Farewell thy Fier and thy Light,
   That ne're went out by Day or Night :
      Chor. No, or thy zeale so speedy,
             That found a way
             By peep of day,
         To feed and cloth the Needy.

6. But, ah, alas ! the Almond Bough,
   And Olive Branch is wither'd now.
   The Wine Presse now is ta'ne from us,
   The Saffron and the Calamus.[2]
   The Spice and Spiknard hence is gone,
   The Storax and the Cynamon,
      Chor. The Caroll of our gladnesse
             Ha's taken wing,
             And our late spring
         Of mirth is turn'd to sadnesse.[3]

[1] = *mantling*, or like wine poured out: hence here picturesquely applied to wool carded into long locks ready for thread making.

[2] = a gum from the calamus odoratus or aromaticus.

[3] Exodus xxx. 23.

7. How wise wast thou in all thy waies!

How worthy of respect and praise!

How Matron-like didst thou go drest!

How soberly above the rest

Of those that prank[4] it with their Plumes;

And jet[5] it with their choice purfumes.

    Chor. Thy vestures were not flowing:

            Nor did the street

            Accuse thy feet

       Of mincing[6] in their going.

8. And though thou here li'st dead, we see

A deale[7] of beauty yet in thee.

How sweetly shewes thy smiling face,

Thy lips with all diffusèd grace!

Thy hands (though cold) yet spotlesse, white,

And comely as the Chrysolite.

    Chor. Thy belly like a hill is,

            Or as a neat

            Cleane heap of wheat,

       All set about with Lillies.

---

[4] = adorn: but generally used in an ill sense as over-adorn, or adorn ostentatiously and fantastically. [5] = to throw one's body or one's self forward, i. e. to strut proudly. Cf. Glossarial Index s. v.

[6] = walking in a proud fantastic or affected manner. See Isaiah iii. 16, where margin has 'walking nicely' (i. e. delicately).

[7] See Glossarial Index under 'deale.'

9. Sleep with thy beauties here, while we
   Will shew these garments made by thee ;
   These were the Coats, in these are read
   The monuments of *Dorcas* dead.
   These were thy Acts, and thou shalt have
   These hung, as honours o're thy Grave :
     Chor. And after us (distressèd)
       Sho'd fame be dumb ;
       Thy very Tomb
       Would cry out, *Thou art blessèd.*

To God, in time of plundering.

RAPINE has yet tooke nought from me ;
  But if it please my God, I be
Brought at the last to th' utmost bit,
God make me thankfull still for it.
I have been gratefull for my store :
Let me say grace when there's no more.

To his Saviour. The New-yeers gift.

THAT little prettie bleeding part
  Of Foreskin send to me :
And Ile returne a bleeding Heart ;.
  For New-yeers gift to Thee.

Rich is the Jemme that Thou did'st send,
  Mine's faulty too, and small :
But yet this Gift Thou wilt commend,
  Because I send Thee *all*.

Doomes-Day.

LET not that Day Gods Friends and Servants scare :
  The Bench is then their place ; and not the Barre.

The Poores Portion.

THE sup'rabundance of my store,
  That is the portion of the poore :
Wheat, Barley, Rie, or Oats ; what is't
But he takes tole of? all the Griest.[8]
Two raiments have I : *Christ* then makes
This Law ; that He and I part stakes.
Or have I two loaves ; then I use
The poore to cut, and I to chuse.

The White Island : or place of the Blest.

IN this world (the *Isle of Dreames*)
  While we sit by sorrowes streames,
Teares and terrors are our theames
                Reciting :

[8] = grist.

But when once from hence we flie,
More and more approaching nigh
Unto young Eternitie
              Uniting :

In that *whiter Island*, where
Things are evermore sincere ;[9]
Candor[10] here, and lustre there
              Delighting :

There no monstrous fancies shall
Out of hell an horrour call,
To create (or cause at all)
              Affrighting.

There in calm and cooling sleep
We our eyes shall never steep ;
But eternall watch shall keep,
              Attending

Pleasures, such as shall pursue
Me immortaliz'd, and you ;
And fresh joyes, as never too
              Have ending.

[9] See Glossarial Index s. v.   [10] = whiteness.

To Christ.

I CRAWLE, I creep ; my *Christ*, I come
　　To Thee, for curing *Balsamum :*
Thou hast, nay more, Thou art the Tree,
Affording salve of Soveraigntie.
My mouth I'le lay unto Thy wound
Bleeding, that no Blood touch the ground :
For, rather then one drop shall fall　　　*[than*
To wast, my JESU, I'le take all.

To God.

GOD ! to my little meale and oyle,
　　Add but a bit of flesh, to boyle :
And Thou my Pipkinnet[1] shalt see,
Give a *wave-offring* unto Thee.

Free Welcome.

GOD He refuseth no man ; but makes way
　　For All that now come, or hereafter may.

Gods Grace.

GODS Grace deserves here to be daily fed,
　　That, thus increast, it might be perfected.

---

[1] Diminutive of ' pipkln.'

Coming to Christ.

TO him, who longs unto his CHRIST to go,
  Celerity even it self is slow.

Correction.

GOD had but one Son free from sin ; but none
  Of all His sonnes free from correction.[2]

Gods Bounty.

GOD, as He's potent, so He's likewise known,
  To give us more then Hope can fix upon. [*than*

Knowledge.

SCIENCE in God, is known to be
  A Substance, not a Qualitie.

Salutation.

CHRIST, I have read, did to His Chaplains say,
  Sending them forth, *Salute no man by th' way :*[3]
Not, that He taught His Ministers to be
Unsmooth, or sowre, to all civilitie ;

---

[2] A favorite saying with the old Puritan Preachers.
[3] The elaborateness of Eastern salutations, wherein much time was consumed, explains the injunction.

But to instruct them, to avoid all snares
Of tardidation[4] in the Lords Affaires.
Manners are good : but till his errand ends,
Salute we must, nor Strangers, Kin, or Friends.

Lasciviousnesse.

LASCIVIOUSNESSE is known to be
The sister to saturitie.[5]

Teares.

GOD from our eyes all teares hereafter wipes,
And gives His Children kisses then, not stripes.

Gods Blessing.

IN vain our labours are, whatsoe're they be,
Unlesse God gives the *Benedicite.*

God, and Lord.

GOD, is His Name of Nature ; but that word
Implies His Power, *when He's cal'd the LORD.*

The Judgment-Day.

GOD hides from man the reck'ning Day, that He
May feare it ever for uncertaintie :

---

[4] =delaying.   [5] Probably used with the double sense of the Latin *saturitas* =excess and ordure.

That being ignorant of that one, he may
Expect the coming of it ev'ry day.

Angells.

ANGELLS are call'd Gods; yet of them, none
   Are Gods, but by *participation :*
As just Men are intitled Gods, yet none
Are Gods, of them, but by Adoption.

Long life.

THE longer thred of life we spin,
   The more occasion still to sin.

Teares.

THE teares of Saints more sweet by farre,
   Then all the songs of sinners are.   [*than*

Manna.

THAT Manna, which God on His people cast,
   Fitted it self to ev'ry Feeders tast.

Reverence.

TRUE rev'rence is (as *Cassiodore*[6] doth prove)
   The feare of God, commixt with cleanly love.

[6] Reverentia est enim Domini timor cum amore permixtus : (Cassiodor. Expos. in Psalt. xxxiv. 30. p. 118.)

Mercy.

MERCY, the wise Athenians held to be
  Not an Affection, but a *Deitie.*

Wages.

AFTER this life, the wages shall
  Not shar'd alike be unto all.

Temptation.

GOD tempteth no one (as S. *Aug'stine* saith)[7]
  For any ill ; but, for the proof of Faith :
Unto temptation God exposeth some ;
But none, of purpose, to be overcome.

Gods hands.

GODS hands are round, & smooth, that gifts
   may fall
Freely from them, and hold none back at all.

Labour.

LABOUR we must, and labour hard
  I'th *Forum* here, or *Vineyard.*

---

[7] Cf. Serm. ii De tentatione Abrahamae a Deo—"Deus tentat ut aperiat homini," and again, "Deus tentat ut doceat:" (Op. v. pp. 5, 7, *et alibi.*

Mora Sponsi, *the stay of the Bridegroome.*

THE time the Bridegroom stayes from hence,
    Is but the time of penitence.

Roaring.

ROARING is nothing but a weeping part,
    Forc'd from the mighty dolour of the heart.

The Eucharist.

HE *that is hurt seeks help:* sin is the wound ;
    The salve for this i'th Eucharist is found.

Sin severely punisht.

GOD in His own Day will be then severe,
    To punish great sins, who small faults whipt
    here.

Montes Scripturarum, *the Mounts of the*
Scriptures.

THE Mountains of the Scriptures are (some say)
    Moses, and *Iesus,* callèd *Joshua :*
The *Prophets,* Mountains of the Old are meant ;
The *Apostles,* Mounts of the *New Testament.*

Prayer.

A PRAYER, that is said alone,
    Starves, having no companion.
Great things ask for, when thou dost pray,
And those great are, which ne're decay.
Pray not for silver, rust eats this ;
Ask not for gold, which metall is :
Nor yet for houses, which are here
But earth : *such vowes nere reach Gods eare.*

Christs sadnesse.

CHRIST was not sad, i'th garden, for His own
    Passion, but for His sheeps dispersion.

God heares us.

GOD, who's in Heav'n, will hear from thence ;
    If not to'th sound, yet, to the sense.

God.

GOD (as the learnèd *Damascen*[8] doth write)
    A *Sea of Substance* is, *Indefinite.*

[8] Ioann. Damasc. de Fide Orthod. i. 9 : (Op. i. p. 142 Lequier.)

Clouds.

HE that ascended in a cloud, shall come
In clouds, descending to the publike *Doome.*⁹

Comforts in contentions.

THE same, who crownes the Conquerour, will be
A Coadjutor in the Agonie.

Heaven.

HEAV'N is most faire; but fairer He
That made that fairest Canopie.

God.

IN God there's nothing, but 'tis known to be
Ev'n God Himself, in perfect *Entitie.*

His Power.

GOD can do all things, save but what are known
For to imply a contradiction.

Christs words on the Crosse, My God, My God.

CHRIST, when He hung the dreadfull Crosse
upon,
Had (as it were) a *Dereliction* ;

⁹ See Glossarial Index s. v.

In this regard, in those great terrors He
Had no one *Beame* from Gods sweet Majestie.

Jehovah.

JEHOVAH, as *Boëtius*[1] saith,
No number of the *Plurall* hath.

Confusion of face.

GOD then confounds mans face, when He not
hears
The Vowes of those, who are Petitioners.

Another.

THE shame of mans face is no more
Then prayers repel'd, (sayes *Cassiodore*.)[2] [*than*

Beggars.

JACOB Gods Beggar was ; and so we wait
(Though ne're so rich) all beggars at His Gate.

[1] Nulla est omnino pluralitas, quare nec numerus (Boetius de Trin. ii. p. 1251 : Migne.)

[2] Fideles *non erubescunt*, quoniam impetrant. *Erubescere* enim decepti est, qui ad sua desideria non valet pervenire : (Cassiod : Expos. in Psalt. xxxiii. 5, p. 110).

Good, and bad.

THE Bad among the Good are here mixt ever :
The Good without the Bad are here plac'd never.

Sin.

SIN *no existence; Nature none it hath,*
Or Good at all, (as learn'd *Aquinas* saith.)[3]

Martha, Martha.

THE repetition of the name made known
No other, then *Christs* full Affection.   [*than*

Youth, and Age.

GOD on our Youth bestowes but little ease ;
But on our Age most sweet *Indulgences.*

Gods Power.

GOD is so potent, as His Power can
Draw out of *bad* a soveraigne *good* to man.

Paradise.

PARADISE is (as from the Learn'd I gather)
A quire of blest Soules circling in the Father.

---

[3] See St. Thomas contra Gentes, l. iii, c. 7, and De Malo Q. i. a.
1. u. 20.

Observation.

THE Jewes, when they built Houses (I have read)
    One part thereof left still unfinishèd :
To make them, thereby, mindfull of their own
Cities most sad and dire destruction.[4]

The Asse.

GOD did forbid the Israelites, to bring
    An Asse unto Him, for an *offering :*
Onely, by this dull creature, to expresse
His detestation to all slothfulnesse.

Observation.

THE Virgin-Mother stood at distance (there)
    From her Sonnes Crosse, not shedding once a
      teare :
Because the Law forbad to sit and crie
For those, who did as malefactors die.

---

[4] " The Jews at this day, when they build a house, they are, say the Rabbins, to leave one part of it unfinished, and lying rude, in remembrance that Jerusalem and the temple are, at present, desolate (Hist. of Rites of Jews, by Leo Moden). At least they used to leave about a yard square of the house unplastered, on which they write in great letters that of the Psalmist, If I forget Jerusalem, then let my right hand forget her cunning (Ps. cxxxvii.) or else these words, Zecher Lechorbon, The Memory of the Desolation." (TRAPP on Nehemiah ii. 3 : 1656).

So she, to keep her mighty woes in awe,
Tortur'd her love, not to transgresse the Law.
Observe we may, how *Mary Joses* then,
And th' other *Mary (Mary Magdalen)*
Sate by the Grave ; and sadly sitting there,
Shed for their Master many a bitter teare :
But 'twas not till their *dearest Lord* was dead ;
And then to weep they both were licensèd.

Tapers.

THOSE Tapers, which we set upon the grave,
    In fun'rall pomp, but this importance[5] have ;
That soules departed are not put out quite ;
But, as they walk't here in their *vestures* white,
So live in Heaven, in everlasting light.

Christs Birth.

ONE Birth our Saviour had ; the like none yet
    Was, or will be a *second* like to it.

The Virgin Mary.

TO work a *wonder*, God would have her shown,
    At once, a Bud, and yet a *Rose full-blowne.*

[5] Apparently used in sense of ' import.'

Another.

AS sun-beames pierce the glasse, and streaming in,
  No crack or Schisme leave i'th subtill skin :
So the Divine Hand work't, and brake no thred,
But, in a *Mother*, kept a *maiden-head.*

God.

GOD, in the *holy Tongue*, they call
  The Place that filleth *All in all.*

Another of God.

GOD'S said to leave this place, and for to come
  Nearer to that place, then to other some :
Of locall motion, in no least respect,
But only by impression of effect.

Another.

GOD is *Jehovah* cal'd ; which name of His
  Implies or *Essence*, or the *He* that Is.

Gods presence.

GOD'S evident, and may be said to be
  Present with just men, to the veritie :

But with the wicked if He doth comply,
'Tis (as S. *Bernard* saith)[6] but seemingly.

Gods Dwelling.

GOD'S said to dwell there, wheresoever He
    Puts down some prints of His high Majestie :
As when to man He comes, and there doth place
His *holy Spirit*, or doth plant His *Grace.*

The Virgin Mary.

THE *Virgin Marie* was (as I have read)
    The House of God, by *Christ* inhabited ;
Into the which He enter'd : but, the Doore
Once shut, was never to be open'd more.[7]

---

[6] 'Comply' : probably in sense of French complaire, conform, or apply Himself to the humours of. The thought is frequent in St. Bernard. See under Balaam, etc.

[7] The reference is to Ezekiel xliv. 2, which is applied to the Virgin Mary in the Roman Breviary. Off. Conc. See St. Bernard (Op. iii. p. 813 : Venet : 1727), or rather Bernard (of Toledo) to whom the work belongs, though it was formerly attributed to Bernard of Clairvaux—"Tu es castellum in quod Iesus intravit, habens turrim humilitatis, &c.

To God.

GOD'S undivided, *One* in *Persons Three ;*
    And *Three* in *Inconfusèd Unity :*
Originall of Essence there is none,
'Twixt God the *Father, Holy Ghost,* and *Sonne .*
And though the *Father* be the first of *Three,*
'Tis but by *Order,* not by *Entitie.*

Upon Woman and Mary.

SO long (it seem'd) as *Maries* Faith was small,
    Christ did her *Woman,* not her *Mary* call :
But no more *Woman,* being strong in Faith ;
But *Mary* cal'd then (as S. *Ambrose* saith.)[8]

North and South.

THE *Jewes* their beds, and offices of ease,
    Plac't *North* and *South,* for these cleane pur-
        poses ;
That mans uncomely froth might not molest
Gods wayes and walks, which lie still East and West.

---

[a] See Expos. in. Luc. Lib. x. 161 sq: (Op. i. p. 1539 edn. Bened.
Paris 1686.)

Sabbaths.

SABBATHS are threefold, (as S. *Austine* sayes :)[9]
    The first of Time, or Sabbath here of Dayes ;
The second is a Conscience trespasse-free ;
The last the *Sabbath of Eternitie.*

The Fast, or Lent.

NOAH the first was (as Tradition sayes)
    That did ordaine the Fast of forty Dayes.[1]

Sin.

THERE is no evill that we do commit,
    But hath th' extraction of some good from it :
As when we sin ; God, the great *Chymist*, thence
Drawes out th' *Elixar*[2] of true penitence.

God.

GOD is more here, then in another place,   [*than*
    Not by His *Essence*, but commerce of *Grace.*

---

[9] See *de Civitate Dei,* xxii. 30 : (Op. vii. p. 701) : also on the 'conscience trespasse free' Enarr. in Ps. xci. 1, and St. Jerome in Ezech. xlvi. 1, apud a-Lapide *in locum.*

[1] St. Augustine (Serm. 69) compares together Lent and the Deluge. So, too, St. Ambrose (*de Jejunio*) and Origen.

[2] = elixir.

This, and the next World.

GOD hath this world for many made; 'tis true:
　　But He hath made the world to come for few.[3]

Ease.

GOD gives to none so absolute an Ease,
　　As not to know, or feel some *Grievances.*

Beginnings and Endings.

P*AUL*, he began ill, but he ended well;
　　Judas began well, but he foulely fell:
In godlinesse, not the beginnings, so
Much as the ends are to be lookt unto.

Temporall Goods.

THESE temp'rall goods God (the most Wise)
　　commends
To th' good and bad, in common, for two ends:
First, that these goods none here may o're esteem,
Because the wicked do partake of them:

---

[3] One must take every opportunity of protesting against this perversion of Divine Truth. The vision of the Apocalypse—1900 years ago—was not of ' few ' but of an unreckonable multitude.

Next, that these ills none cowardly may shun ;
Being, oft here, the just mans portion.

Hell fire.

THE fire of Hell this strange condition hath,
    To burn, not shine (as learnèd *Basil* saith.)[4]

Abels *Bloud.*

SPEAK, did the Bloud of *Abel* cry
    To God for vengeance ; yes, say I ;
Ev'n as the sprinkled bloud cal'd on
God, for an expiation.

Another.

THE bloud of *Abel* was a thing
    Of such a rev'rend reckoning,
As that the old World thought it fit,
Especially to sweare by it.

A Position in the Hebrew Divinity.

ONE man repentant is of more esteem
    With God, then one, that never sin'd 'gainst
    Him. [5]   [*than*

---

[4] See a very striking passage in St. Basil Hom. on Psalm xxviii :
(Op. i. p. 121, edn. Garnier).

[5] Questionable exegesis of (I suppose) Talmudic origin.

Penitence.

THE Doctors, in the Talmud, say,
      That in this world, one onely day
In true repentance spent, will be
More worth, then Heav'ns Eternitie.   [*than*

God's presence.

GOD'S present ev'ry where; but most of all
      Present by Union *Hypostaticall:* [6]
God, He is there, where's nothing else (Schooles say)
And nothing else is there, *where He's away.*

The Resurrection possible, and probable.

FOR each one Body, that i'th earth is sowne,
      There's an up-rising but of one for one :
But for each Graine, that in the ground is thrown,
Threescore or fourescore spring up thence for one :
So that the wonder is not halfe so great,
Of ours, as is the rising of the wheat.

Christs Suffering.

JUSTLY our *dearest Saviour* may abhorre us,
      Who hath more suffer'd by us farre, then for us.
                                              [*than*

------

[6] = substantially.

Sinners.

SINNERS confounded are a twofold way,
    Either as when (the learnèd Schoolemen say)
Mens sins destroyed are, when they repent;
Or when, for sins, men suffer punishment.

Temptations.

NO man is tempted so, but may o'recome,
    If that he has a will to Masterdome.

Pittie, and punishment.

GOD doth embrace the good with love; & gaines
    The good by mercy, as the bad by paines.

Gods price, and mans price.

GOD bought man here with his hearts blood
      expence;
And man sold God here for base *thirty pence.*

Christs Action.

CHRIST never did so great a work, but there
    His humane Nature did, in part, appeare:
Or, ne're so meane a peece, but men might see
Therein some beames of His Divinitie:

So that, in all He did, there did combine
His Humane Nature, and His Part Divine.

Predestination.

PREDESTINATION is the Cause alone
Of many standing, but of fall to none.

Another.

ART thou not destin'd? then, with hast, go on
To make thy faire *Predestination:*
If thou canst change thy life, God then will please
To change, or call back, His past *Sentences.*

Sin.

SIN never slew a soule, unlesse there went
Along with it some tempting blandishment.

Another.

SIN is an act so free, that if we shall
Say,[7] 'tis not free, 'tis then no sin at all.

---

[7] Not to ' *say* ' but actually to be ' not free.' The meaning perhaps
is that sin is so free that we are never constrained to it, but if we say
that is believe of a thing that we are constrained to it or commanded
to do it, then is it no sin.

Another.

SIN is the cause of death; and sin's alone
    The cause of Gods *Predestination :*
And from Gods *Prescience* of mans sin doth flow
Our *Destination* to eternall woe.

Prescience.

GODS *Prescience makes none sinfull ;* but th'
    offence
Of man's the chief cause of Gods *Prescience.*

Christ.

TO all our wounds, here, whatsoe're they be,
    Christ is the one sufficient *Remedie.*

Christs Incarnation.

CHRIST took our Nature on Him, not that He
    'Bove all things lov'd it, for the puritie :
No, but He drest Him with our humane Trim,
Because our flesh stood most in need of Him.

Heaven.

HEAVEN is not given for our good works here :
    Yet it is given to the *Labourer.*

Gods keyes.

GOD has *foure keyes*, which He reserves alone;
    The first of *Raine*, the key of *Hell* next known
With the third key He opes and shuts the wombe;
And with the *fourth key* He unlocks the tombe.[8]

Sin.

THERE'S no constraint to do amisse,
    Whereas but one enforcement is.

Almes.

GIVE unto all, lest he, whom thou deni'st,
    May chance to be no other man, but *Christ.*

Hell fire.

ONE onely fire has Hell; but yet it shall,
    Not after one sort, there excruciate all:
But look, how each transgressor onward went
Boldly in sin, shall feel more punishment.

To keep a true Lent.

1. IS this a Fast, to keep
          The Larder leane?
              And cleane
    From fat of Veales, and Sheep?

[8] Rabbinical lore.

2. Is it to quit the dish
>   Of Flesh, yet still
>   To fill
> The platter high with Fish?

3. Is it to fast an houre,
>   Or rag'd[9] to go,
>   Or show
> A down-cast look, and sowre?

4. No : 'tis a Fast, to dole
>   Thy sheaf of wheat,
>   And meat,
> Unto the hungry Soule.

5. It is to fast from strife,
>   From old debate,
>   And hate ;
> To circumcise thy life.

6. To shew a heart grief-rent ;
>   To sterve thy sin,
>   Not Bin ;
> And that's to keep thy Lent.

[9] = ragged.

No time in Eternitie.

BY houres we all live here, in Heaven is known
　　No spring of Time, or Times succession.

His Meditation upon Death.

BE those few hours, which I have yet to spend,
　　Blest with the Meditation of my end :
Though they be few in number, I'm content ;
If otherwise, I stand indifferent :
Nor makes it matter, *Nestors* yeers to tell,
If man lives long, and if he live not well.
A multitude of dayes still heapèd on,
Seldome brings order, but confusion.
Might I make choice, long life sho'd be withstood ;
Nor wo'd I care how short it were, if good :
Which to effect, let ev'ry passing Bell
Possesse my thoughts,[1] next comes my dolefull knell :
And when the night perswades me to my bed,
I'le thinke I'm going to be buried :
So shall the Blankets which come over me,
Present those Turfs, which once[2] must cover me :

---

[1] i. e. Possesse my thoughts [that] next, &c.
[2] See Glossarial Index s. v.

And with as firme behaviour I will meet
The sheet I sleep in, as my Winding-sheet.
When sleep shall bath his body in mine eyes,
I will believe, that then my body dies :
And if I chance to wake, and rise thereon,
I'le have in mind my Resurrection,
Which must produce[3] me to that *Gen'rall Doome*,
To which the Pesant,[4] so the Prince must come,
To heare the Judge give sentence on the Throne,
Without the least hope of affection.[5]
Teares, at that day, shall make but weake defence ;
When Hell and Horrour fright the Conscience.
Let me, though late, yet at the last, begin
To shun the least Temptation to a sin ;
Though to be tempted be no sin, untill
Man to th' alluring object gives his will.
Such let my life assure me, when my breath
Goes theeving from me, I am safe in death ;
Which is the height of comfort, when I fall,
I rise triumphant in my Funerall.

Cloaths for Continuance.

THOSE Garments lasting evermore,
    Are works of mercy to the poore,

---

[3] = lead me forth.   [4] = peasant.   [5] = partiality.

Which neither Tettar,[6] Time, or Moth
Shall fray that silke, or fret this cloth.

To God.

COME to me God; but do not come
   To me, as to the gen'rall Doome,
In power; or come Thou in that state,
When Thou Thy Lawes didst promulgate,
Whenas the Mountains quak'd for dread,
And sullen clouds bound up his head.
No, lay thy stately terrours by,
To talke with me familiarly;
For if Thy thunder-claps I heare,
I shall lesse swoone, then die for feare.   [*than*
Speake Thou of love and I'le reply
By way of *Epithalamie*,
Or sing of *mercy*, and I'le suit
To it my Violl and my Lute:
Thus let Thy lips but love distill,
Then come my God, and hap what will.

The Soule.

WHEN once the Soule has lost her way,
   O then, how restlesse do's she stray!

[6] — worms that eat away cloth, for skin tetter (ringworm) was
supposed to be due to a worm.

And having not her God for light,
How do's she erre[6] in endlesse night !

The Judgement-day.

I N doing justice, God shall then be known,
Who shewing mercy here, few priz'd, or none.

Sufferings.

W E merit all we suffer, and by far
More stripes, then God layes on the sufferer.

[*than*

Paine and pleasure.

G OD suffers not His Saints, and Servants deere,
To have continuall paine, or pleasure here :
But look how night succeeds the day, so He
Gives them by turnes their grief and jollitie.

Gods presence.

G OD is *all-present* to whate're we do,
And as *all-present*, so *all-filling* too.

Another.

T HAT there's a God, we all do know,
But what God is, we cannot show.

[6] =wander.

The poore mans part.

TELL me rich man, for what intent
   Thou load'st with gold thy vestiment?
Whenas the poore crie out, to us
Belongs all gold superfluous.

The right hand.

GOD has a Right Hand, but is quite bereft
   Of that, which we do nominate the Left.

The Staffe and Rod.

TWO instruments belong unto our God;
   The one a *Staffe* is, and the next a *Rod* :
That if the twig sho'd chance too much to smart,
The staffe might come to play the friendly part.

God sparing in scourging.

GOD still rewards us more then our desert : [*than*
   But when He strikes, He quarter-acts[7] His part.

Confession.

CONFESSION twofold is (as *Austine* sayes) [8]
   The first of *sin* is, and the next of *praise* :

---

[7] = diminishes his blow by three-fourths = strikes gently.
[8] *Confessions,* et alibi, frequenter.

If ill it goes with thee, thy faults confesse :
If well, then chant Gods praise with cheerfulnesse.

Gods descent.

GOD is then said for to descend, when He
    Doth, here on earth, some thing of novitie ;[9]
As when, in humane nature He works more
Then ever, yet, the like was done before.   [*than*

No coming to God without Christ.

GOOD and great God ! how sho'd I feare
    To come to Thee, if *Christ* not there !
Co'd I but think, He would not be
Present, to plead my cause for me ;
To Hell I'd rather run, then I   [*than*
Wo'd see Thy Face, and He not by.

Another, to God.

THOUGH Thou beest all that *Active Love,*
    Which heats those ravisht Soules above ;
And though all joyes spring from the glance
Of Thy most winning countenance ;
Yet sowre and grim Thou'dst seem to me ;
If through my *Christ* I saw not Thee.

[9] —newness or novelty (novitas).

The Resurrection.

THAT *Christ* did die, the *Pagan* saith ;
    But that He rose, that's *Christians* Faith.

Coheires.

WE are Coheires with *Christ;* nor shall His own
    Heire-ship be lesse, by our adoption :
The number here of Heires, shall from the state
Of His great *Birth-right* nothing derogate.

The number of two.

GOD hates the *Duall Number ;* being known
    The lucklesse number of division :
And when He blest each sev'rall Day, whereon
He did His *curious operation;*
'Tis never read there (as the Fathers say)[1]
God blest His work done on the *second day :*
Wherefore two prayers ought not to be said,
Or by our selves, or from the Pulpit read.

Hardning of hearts.

GOD'S said our hearts to harden then,
    Whenas His grace not supples men.

---

[1] Origen, St. Augustine, St. Jerome and others on Genesis c. i.

The Rose.

BEFORE Mans fall, the Rose was born,
(S. *Ambrose* says)[2] without the Thorn :
But, for Mans fault, then was the Thorn,
Without the fragrant Rose-bud, born ;
But ne're the Rose without the Thorn.

Gods time must end our trouble.

GOD doth not promise here to man, that He
Will free him quickly from his miserie ;
But in His own time, and when He thinks fit,
Then He will give a happy end to it.

Baptisme.

THE strength of *Baptisme*, that's within ;
It saves the soule, by drowning sin.

Gold and Frankincense.

GOLD serves for Tribute to the King ;
The *Frankincense* for Gods Offring.[3]

---

[2] See Hexaem iii. 11 : (I. p. 51) " Surrexerat ante floribus im-
mixta, &c.
[3] i. e. offering to God.

To God.

GOD, who me gives a will for to repent ;
  Will add a power, to keep me innocent ;
That I shall ne're that trespasse recommit,
When I have done true Penance here for it.

The chewing the Cud.

WHEN well we speak, & nothing do that's good,
  We not divide the *Hoof*, but chew the *Cud :*
But when good words, by good works, have their
  proof,
We then both chew the *Cud*, and cleave the *Hoof.*[4]

Christs twofold coming.

THY former coming was to cure
  My soules most desp'rate *Calenture ;*[5]
Thy second *Advent*, that must be
To heale my Earths infirmitie.

---

[4] Unclean in the first instance, clean in the second. Cf. Leviticus xi. 4.

[5] =a heat-fever among sailors in hot climates, attended with the fancy that the sea is the green fields of home, and in this sense peculiarly applicable here.

To God, his gift.

AS my little Pot doth boyle,
    We will keep this *Levell-Coyle ;*[6]
That a *Wave*, and I will bring
To my God, a *Heave-offering.*

Gods Anger.

GOD can't be wrathfull ; but we may conclude,
    Wrathfull He may be, by similitude :
God's wrathfull said to be, when He doth do
That without *wrath*, which wrath doth *force us* to.

Gods Commands.

IN Gods commands, ne're ask the reason why ;
    Let thy *obedience* be the best Reply.

To God.

IF I have plaid the *Truant*, or have here
    Fail'd in my part ; Oh ! Thou that art my *deare.*
My *mild*, my *loving Tutor, Lord and God !*
Correct my errors gently with Thy Rod.
I know, that faults will many here be found,
But where sin swells, there let Thy grace abound.

[6] See Glossarial Index s. v.

To God.

THE work is done; now let my *Lawrell* be
    Given by none, but by Thy selfe, to me :
That done, with Honour Thou dost me create
Thy *Poet*, and Thy *Prophet Lawreat.*

Good Friday: Rex Tragicus, *or Christ going to His Crosse.*

PUT off Thy Robe of *Purple*, then go on
    To the sad place of execution :
Thine houre is come ; and the Tormentor stands
Ready, to pierce Thy tender Feet, and Hands.
Long before this, the base, the dull, the rude,
Th' inconstant, and unpurgèd Multitude
Yawne for Thy coming ; some e're this time crie,
How He deferres, how loath He is to die !
Amongst this scumme, the Souldier, with his speare,
And that sowre Fellow, with his *vineger*,
His *spunge*, and *stick*, do ask why Thou dost stay?
So do the *Skurfe*[7] and *Bran*[8] too : Go Thy way,

---

[7] To accuse any of skin disease was a common reproach, and constantly applied to the lower classes as putting them in the same rank with the lowest of the low, with whom these diseases were common. Thus we have ' scab ' and ' scroyles ' (Les escronëlles, the King's evil) and as adjectives scald and scurvy.   [8] = thin bark.

Thy way, Thou guiltlesse man, and satisfie
By Thine approach, each their beholding eye.
Not as a thief, shalt Thou ascend the mount,
But like a Person of some high account :
The *Crosse* shall be Thy *Stage;* and Thou shalt there
The spacious field have for Thy *Theater.*
Thou art that *Roscius*,[9] and that markt-out man,
That must this day act the Tragedian,
To wonder and affrightment : Thou art He,
Whom all the flux[1] of Nations comes to see;
Not those poor Theeves that act their parts with
     Thee :
Those act without regard, when once a *King*,
And *God*, as Thou art, comes to suffering.
No, No, this *Scene* from Thee takes life and sense,
And soule and spirit, plot and excellence.
Why then begin, great King ! ascend Thy Throne,
And thence proceed, to act Thy Passion
To such an height, to such a period rais'd,
As Hell, and Earth, and Heav'n may stand amaz'd.
God, and good Angells guide Thee; and so blesse
Thee in Thy severall parts of bitternesse;

Singular use of the player-name.   [1] = flow or flood.

That those, who see Thee nail'd unto the Tree,
May (though they scorn Thee) praise and pitie Thee.
And we (Thy Lovers) while we see Thee keep
The Lawes of Action, will both sigh, and weep ;
And bring our Spices, to embalm Thee dead ;
That done, wee'l see Thee sweetly burièd.

His words to Christ, going to the Crosse.

WHEN Thou wast taken, Lord, I oft have read,
    All Thy Disciples Thee forsook, and fled.[2]
Let their example not a pattern be
For me to flie, but now to follow Thee.

Another, to his Saviour.

IF Thou beest taken, *God* forbid,
    I flie from Thee, as others did :
But if Thou wilt so honour me,
As to accept my companie,
I'le follow Thee, hap hap what shall,[3]
Both to the *Judge*, and *Judgment-Hall :*

[2] St. Matthew xxvi. 56.
[3] I delete comma (,) after ' hap '—the first is a verb, the second its substantive ━ happen what hap shall.

And, if I see Thee posted there,
To be all-flayd with whipping-cheere,[4]
I'le take my share ; or els, my God,
Thy stripes I'le kisse, or burn the *Rod.*

His Saviours words, going to the Crosse.

HAVE, have ye no regard, all ye
    Who passe this way, to pitie me,
Who am a man of miserie ![5]

A man both bruis'd, and broke, and one
Who suffers not here for mine own,
But for my friends *transgression !*

Ah ! *Sions Daughters*, do not feare
The *Crosse*, the *Cords*, the *Nailes*, the *Speare*,
The *Myrrhe*, the *Gall*, the *Vineger*

For *Christ*, your loving Saviour, hath
Drunk up the wine of Gods fierce wrath ;
Onely, there's left a little froth,

---

[4] See Glossarial Index s. v.
[5] See Memorial-Introduction for parallel in George Herbert.

Lesse for to tast, then for to shew,   [*than*
What bitter cups had been your due,
Had He not drank them up for *you*.

His Anthem, to Christ on the Crosse.

WHEN I behold Thee, almost slain,
    With one, and all parts, full of
        pain :
When I Thy gentle Heart do see
Pierc't through, and dropping bloud, for
        me,
I'le call, and cry out, Thanks to Thee.

Vers. But yet it wounds my soule, to think,
    That for my sin, Thou, Thou must drink,
    Even Thou alone, the *bitter cup*
    Of *furie*, and of *vengeance* up.

Chor. Lord, I'le not see Thee to drink all
    The *Vineger*, the *Myrrhe*, the *Gall :*

Ver. Chor. But I will sip a little wine ;
    Which done, Lord say, *The rest is mine.*

This Crosse-Tree here
Doth JESUS *beare,*
Who sweet'ned first,
The Death accurs't.

HERE all things ready are, make hast, make hast away;
For long this work wil be, & very short this Day.
Why then, go on to act : Here's wonders to be done,
Before the last least sand of Thy ninth houre be run;
Or e're dark Clouds do dull, or dead the Mid-dayes Sun.

Act when Thou wilt,
Bloud will be spilt;
Pure Balm, that shall
Bring Health to All.
Why then, Begin
To powre first in
Some Drops of Wine,
In stead of Brine,
To search the Wound,
So long unsound :
And, when that's done,
Let Oyle, next, run,
To cure the Sore
Sinne made before.
And O! Deare Christ,
E'en as Thou di'st,
Look down, and see
Us weepe for Thee.
And tho (Love knows)
Thy dreadfull Woes
Wee cannot ease;
Yet doe Thou please,
Who Mercie art,
T'accept each Heart,
That gladly would
Helpe, if it could.
Meane while, let mee,
Beneath this Tree,
This Honour have,
To make my grave.

To his Saviours Sepulcher: his Devotion.

HAILE holy, and all-honour'd Tomb,
  By no ill haunted ; here I come,
With shoes put off, to tread thy Roome.
I'le not prophane, by soile of sin,
Thy Doore, as I do enter in :
For I have washt both hand and heart,
This, that, and ev'ry other part ;
So that I dare, with farre lesse feare,
Then full affection, enter here.   [*than*
Thus, thus I come to kisse Thy Stone
With a warm lip, and solemne one :
And as I kisse, I'le here and there
Dresse Thee with flowrie Diaper.
How sweet this place is ! as from hence
Flow'd all *Panchaia's*[6] Frankincense ;
Or rich *Arabia* did commix,
Here, all her rare *Aromaticks.*
Let me live ever here, and stir
No one step from this *Sepulcher.*
Ravisht I am ! and down I lie,
Confus'd, in this brave Extasie.

[6] See Glossarial Index s. v.

Here let me rest ; and let me have
This for my *Heaven*, that was Thy *Grave :*
And, coveting no higher sphere,
I'le my Eternitie spend here.

His Offering, with the rest, at the Sepulcher.

TO joyn with them who here confer[7]
  Gifts to my Saviours Sepulcher ;
Devotion bids me hither bring
Somewhat for my Thank-Offering.
Loe ! thus I bring a Virgin-Flower,
To dresse my Maiden-Saviour.

His coming to the Sepulcher.

HENCE they have born my Lord ; behold ! the
  Stone
Is rowl'd away, and my sweet Saviour's gone.
Tell me, white[8] Angell, what is now become
Of Him we lately seal'd up in this Tombe ?
Is He, from hence, gone to the shades beneath,
To vanquish Hell, as here he conquer'd Death ?

---

[7] = bring together or in union.
[8] See Glossarial Index s. v.

If so, I'le thither follow, without feare,
And live in Hell, if that my *Christ* stayes there.

O F all the good things whatsoe're we do,
      God is the ΑΡΧΗ,[9] and the ΤΕΛΟΣ[10] too.

[9] = beginning.   [10] = end.

ALPHABETICAL INDEX OF

FIRST LINES.

ALPHABETICAL INDEX OF

FIRST LINES.

C.

H.

J.

K.

M.

N.

25

O.

FIRST LINES.

GLOSSARIAL INDEX

AND

INDEX OF NAMES.

GLOSSARIAL INDEX.

As a rule, the references given will guide to explanations or illustrations of the word or thing in the place or places. A few additions are made in the Index itself *s. v.* Nouns and verbs and other forms are placed together; also words occasionally different though spelled alike, e. g. neat=oxen, and elegant, but in the places the meaning will in each case be found. An earnest effort has been made to include every word in any way noticeable.

A.

Abby-Lubbers, i. 161.
Aches, ii. 51.
Action, i. 76.
Adulce, ii. 218.
Affection, iii. 207.
Ale-dy'd, ii. 196.
Alma, iii. 145.
Altar, hallowed, ii. 77.
All, and some, i. 132.
All-filling, iii. 209.
Allay, ii. 180.
Amber, i. 37, ii. 67.
Amber-greece, i. 8, 33 : ii. 172.
And, i. 103: iii. 176.
Apostate, ii. 15.*
Aprill day, ii. 259: iii. 103.

* Cf. Shirley :—
  " And can thy proud apostate eyes
    Court her again, with hope t' entice
    One gentle language, or a smile
    Upon a renegade so vile."
                    (Poems by Dyce, p. 146.)

† So too later Cleveland (1669 p. 3) :—
    " Hark how the sprightly Chanticlere
    That Baron Tell clock of the night."

Bice, i. 65.

Bin, ii. 128, 246.

Bishop't i. 109.

Black-bore, iii. 85.

Blacks = mourning gar-
ments, iii. 10, 62, 87.

Blaze, ii. 20.

Blew-ruler, ii. 123.

Blithefull, ii. 209.

Blouze, ii. 264.

Blush-guiltinesse, ii. 288.

Bodies, ii. 91.

'Bove, i. 77.

Bonnet, ii. 89.

Bo-peep, ii. 153.

Bousing, ii. 159.

Box, ii. 183: iii. 4.

Bran, iii. 216.

Brand, iii. 5.

Brasse, i. 50.

Brave, i. 173.

Bridgeman, i. 65.

Briefs, i. 66.

Bristle, ii. 18.

Broke heart, ii. 26.

Bruckel'd, i. 159.

Brusle, ii. 18.

Buck, ii. 126-7.‡

Buckittings, i. 35.

Buckram, ii. 23, 167.

Bucksome, ii. 38.

Bulging, i. 39.

Burle, ii. 182.

Burling, i. 65.

Burr, ii. 205.

Bussing, ii. 145.

Button'd-staffe, ii. 71, 190.

C.

Calamus, iii. 177.

Calenture, iii. 214.

Call, ii. 11.

Canary, ii. 75 : iii. 63.

Candid, ii. 110, 159, iii. 7.

Candidate, ii. 2, 280.

Candour, i. 10 : ii. 249 : iii. 98, 181.*

Candle-light, ii. 107.

‡ "Send me to the conduit with the water-tankard : I'll beat linen bucks, or anything to redeem my negligence." (T. Heywood's 2nd Part of "If you know not me, &c. Act I. i. 1606). See Merry Wives of Windsor iii. 5.

* Cf Landor in our own day, thus :—
"Negligent as the blossoms of the field,
Array'd in candour and simplicity." (Count Julian.)

Capring, iii. 45.

Carbage, iii. 34.

Carkanet, i. 23, 50 : ii. 44, 118, 150, 217.

Carrionere, ii. 184.

Casques, i. 26.

Caule, ii. 108 : iii. 154.

Cecubum, ii. 178.

Cedar, i. 77, 108, 155 : iii. 110.

Cense, ii. 106.

Cens'd, iii. 163.

Ceremonies, iii. 4, 5, 38.

Cess, i. 55.

Ceston, ii. 106.

Chamlets, i. 81.

Chardges, iii. 104.

Charme, ii. 160.

Charmes, iii. 2, 3.

Cherrylets, iii. 92.

Cherrypit, i. 32.

Chesnuts, fired, ii. 38.

Chev'rell, i. 123.

Chine, ii. 52.

Chips, ii. 169.

Childish, iii. 99.

Chirring, ii. 25.

Chit, ii. 202.

Chives, i. 163 : ii. 46, 221.

Christal, i. 129.

Chop-cherry, ii. 64.

Circular, ii. 50.

Circumbends, i. 159.

Circumcrost, ii. 208.

Circumcision, ii. 217.

Circumflankt, ii. 251.

Circumfused, i. 119.

Circummortal, i. 168 : ii. 110.

Circumspacious, iii. 31.

Circumspangle, ii. 277.

Circumgyration, iii. 32.

Circumstants, i. 137.

Circumvolving, iii. 110.

Cirque, ii. 78.

Citterne, iii. 60.

Civil, ii. 162, 216.

Civilly, ii. 155.

Civility, i. 47, 154 : ii. 168.

Cleanly-Watonnesse, i. 7.

Closet-gods, i. 24.

Coats, i. 8.

Cob-web, i. 13.

Cockall, i. 159.

Cockes, i. 59.

Cock-rood, ii. 215.

Cockring, ii. 63.

Codlins, i. 159.

Codled, ii. 15.

Codpiece, i. 162 : ii. 24.

Columbine, ii. 190 : iii. 154.

Comming, ii. 149.

Commutual, i. 121.

Companie, ii. 101.

Compartlement, ii. 208.

Compost, ii. 263.

Comply, ii. 108, 175 : iii. 195.

Compulsive, iii. 74.

Confer, iii. 223.

Congesting, ii. 238.†

Consonant, ii. 181.

· Contemnes, ii. 231.

Continent, ii. 142, 249.

Convinces, i. 133 : iii. 103.

Coorse, ii. 25.

Coosning, ii. 211.

Cornish, i. 157.

Corrols, ii. 191.

Counter, ii. 106.

Counter-changed, ii. 176.

Counter-feit, ii. 281.

Coveting, iii. 223.

Cowle=cowl, iii. 63.

Crack, iii. 62.

Creame=froth, i. 14.

Creeking, ii. 240.

Crosse and pile, ii. 145.

Crosse-line, i. 109.

Cruells, iii. 128.

Cuckoes spittle, ii. 25.

Cull'd, iii. 52.

Cunctation, ii. 250 : iii. 16.

Cup-shot, iii. 52.

Cure, ii. 289.

Curious-comely, ii. 208.

D.

Dampish, ii. 126.

Dandillions, ii. 108.

Daphne=laurel, ii. 65.

Dardanum, i. 50.

Daring, iii. 169.

Dead, ii. 271.

Deaf, ii. 217.

Deale, i. 42, 118 : iii. 176, 178.‡

Decent, ii. 243.

Decurted, iii. 7.

Denounc'd, i. 78.

Dereliction, iii. 189.

Descrie, iii. 50.

Deservelesse=undeserving. i. 132.

Designments, iii. 17.

Determines, ii. 176.

Devote, i. 46.

Dew, i. 99.

---

† Instead of quotation intended for the Memorial-Introduction, I must content myself with reference to my edition of Southwell. *s.v.*

‡ here ⚊ a good deal, considerable : in I. 118 ⚊ a goodly number.

F.

Factours, ii. 69.

Fan, i. 77.

Fairies, i. 177.

Farc't, iii. 48.

Farcing, ii. 169.

Fardell, ii. 253.

Farre-fetch, iii. 100.

Fat-fed, ii. 71.

Fatts, i. 177.

Feare, iii. 158.

Female, ii. 294.

Feel, ii. 94.

Fellon, ii. 131.

Fetuous, i. 160.

Fier-drakes, iii. 103.

Filcher, i. 121, 122.

Fil'de, ii. 61.

Filitings, i. 19.

Fild-full, iii. 123.

Fill-horse, i. 176.

Firstling, i. 25.

Flagonet, ii. 269.

Flax, ii. 109.

Flitches=buttocks, ii. 264.

Flock, ii. 94.

Float, ii. 247.

Flosculet, ii. 36.

Flux, iii. 217.

Fly-blow, ii. 201.

Footmanship, ii. 92.

Fond, ii. 244.

Fondling, i. 19.

For and, iii. 176.*

Fore-fend, ii. 95.

Fore-right, ii. 32.

Fore-sounds, ii. 38.

Forgetfull, iii. 100.

Forked-Fee, ii. 167.

Forme, ii. 145.

Forum, Holy, ii. 2.

Fother, iii. 55.

Four-square, iii. 17.

Four-leav'd grasse=sham-rock, ii. 106.

Fox i' th' hole, ii. 37, 214.

Foxe-furre, ii. 218.†

Frantick, ii. 160.

* "The lyght of the body is the eye. Wherfore yf thyne eye be single, all thy body shal be ful of lyght. *But and yf* thyne eye be wycked, all thy body shalbe full of darknesse."—The Great Bible, (Cranmer's, 1541)), Matthew vi., 22-3.

Also the same in Edmund Becke's, printed by Day and Serres. 1540.

† See note in this Glossary under (sagge).

Fresh-quilted, i. 116.

Frie, i. 68, 85, 106 : ii. 87, 170 : iii. 13.

From, ii. 175.

Froth, ii. 81.

Frumentie, i. 177.

Fulfill, ii. 239 : iii. 39.

Ful-filling, i. 165.

Full-stop, ii. 195.

Furre, i. 78.

Furr'd, ii. 9.

Fuz-ball, ii. 25, 202.

G.

Gall'd, i. 89.

Gamesome, iii. 40.

Gelli-flours, i. 128.

Gemmal ring, i. 112.

Gemmes, ii. 204.

Gentle-licking, i. 166.

Gentlenes, ii. 16.

Gentle-heart, ii. 17.

Genius, i. 168 : ii. 268.

Giblets, ii. 72.

Give, ii. 245.

Glade, ii. 215.

Gleab, ii. 263.

Globe, of radiant fire, ii. 176.*

Gloves, ii. 245.

Glut, iii. 145.

Gospel-tree, i. 34.

Gotiere, i. 67.

Gotwit, ii. 74.

Granges, ii. 117, 240.

Green-gown, i. 118.

Greenie-Kalendar, ii. 112.

Great-blew-ruler, ii. 123.

Griefs, small, i. 26.

Griest, iii. 180.

Grutch, ii. 19.

Guest-rite, ii. 72.

Guild, i. 88.

Guilded, ii. 131.

H.

Haires, iii. 153.

Hair-less, ii. 59.

Halcions, i. 156.

Hap, iii. 218.

Handsell, iii. 143, 157.

Handsome-handed, ii. 137.

Hat, ii. 68.

Hatcht, i. 161 : iii. 101.

Hay in's horn, ii. 104.

Hearce-cloth, i. 180 : iii. 153.

Heraldic terms, iii. 21.

Heyes, ii. 151.

* The promised quotations were crushed out. See my Memorial-Introduction to Giles Fletcher in this Series.

Just, ii. 295.
Justments, i. 45.

K.

Karkanet, i. 23.
Kathern, ii. 278.
Kenn, iii. 139.
Kerzie, iii. 83.
Kidney-lipt, i. 107.
Kisse, iii. 104.
Kitling and kitlings, i. 138 :
  ii. 25, 54, 107.
Knap, ii. 40.
Knot, ii. 298.

L.

Lace, i. 23.
Lachrimæ, ii, 67.
Lake, i. 65.
Ladanum, ii, 133.
Lambs-wool, iii. 59.
Larr, i. 62 : ii. 41, 46, 53, 71,
  83, 99, 269.
Lares, i. 24 : ii. 129, 221.
Larded, ii. 269.

Lations, i. 81.
Launders, i. 170.
Laureat, ii. 63.
Laurell, i. 11.
Lautitious, ii. 269.
Lawne, i. 13.
Least, i. 179.
Lends, ii. 16.
Lemster Ore, ii. 105.*
Lesse, of heart, i. 169.
Leavens, iii. 67.
Levell-Coyle, iii. 50, 215.
Leven, ii. 162 : iii. 26, 41.
Lictors, iii. 16.
Lie, ii. 126.
Like, iii. 61.
Lillie-center, ii. 102.
Lilly-wristed, ii. 212.
Lip-labour, iii. 129.
Lively-hood, ii. 82.
Lobster, lady of the, i. 162.
Logomachie, iii. 8.
Love-lies-bleeding, i. 22.
Loving-lucklesse, i. 25.

---

* " As for the Wooll in this County, [Herefordshire,] it is best known to the honour thereof by the name of *Lempster Ore*, being absolutely the finest in this County and indeed in all England."— Fuller's Worthies, p. 33.

    Similarly we read of an arm of the Zuyder Zee, as follows :— " In many places a very rich alluvion, forming a most valuable manure, is found at the bottom of these shallows; hence the name of Mer d' Or, or golden sea, the inhabitants deriving a golden harvest of hay from its employment on these meadows." (" The Dead Cities of the Zuyder Zee," by Havard, p. 29 : 1875.)

Lullaby, i. 149.

Lusters, i. 45 : ii. 216.

Lustie-gellie, iii. 29.

M.

Maidenhead, i. 59.*

Maids, ii. 157, 247.

Maidens-blush, ii. 17, 269.

Maiden-haire, i. 31, 89.

Male, ii. 294.

Male-incense, iii. 155.

Man, ii. 118.

Manchet, ii. 128.

Mantle, ii. 269.

Mantle-tree, ii. 46.

Mare, shooe the, ii. 37.

Margarite, iii. 100.

Margents, ii. 173.

Marjoram, ii. 12.

Marmelet, ii. 208.

Maronian, ii. 220.

Masterdom, iii. 201.

Mashes, ii. 303.

Mask, ii. 244.

Mattens, i. 150 : iii. 70.

Maukin, i. 175.

Maund, ii. 268 : iii. 69.

Maundie, iii. 176.

Maying, i. 116.

Meane, iii. 21, 61.

Meddow-verse, ii. 62.

Mell, ii. 67.

Merited, i. 21,—an odd misprint for 'invited' in footnote.

Mew, ii. 68.

Mew'd, ii. 217.

Miching, ii. 241.

Mincing, iii. 178.

Mickle, ii. 202.

Mirk, iii. 148.

Monilesse, iii. 144.

Mop-ey'd, i. 170.

* Cf. Shirley :—

> "For him to whom your heart is tied
> Keep it still virgin, and a bride,
> That often as you go to bed
> You give or take a maidenhead."
> (Poems by Dyce, p. 434.)

Or as in Rawlinson MS. :—

> "May your husbands' love renew
> Every day their marriage vow,
> And yourselves, as newly wed,
> Give each night a maidenhead."

Moonlesse, i. 44.
Moon-tann'd, ii. 108.
Morris-dance, ii. 257.
Mosse-like, ii. 106.
Mothering, ii. 224.
Mowes, ii. 129.
Much-more, i. 127.
Mummeries, ii. 214.
Mute, iii. 36.

N.

Narde, i. 125.
Nature, iii. 102.
Nay's. ii. 247.
Neat, i. 9, 59, 177 : ii. 204,
　213 : iii. 13.
Neat-herds, ii. 235.
Neat-herdesse, ii. 236: iii. 39.
Nectarell, i. 33.
Neech, i. 157.
Nerv'lits, i. 28.

Neere, ii. 129.
Newt's, ii. 26.
Nine-bones, ii. 131.
Nine-holes, ii. 84.
Niplet, ii. 102.
Nits, i. 162.
Nockt, iii. 148.
Nominate, iii. 210.
Nose, i. 139.
Novitie, iii. 211.
Num'rous, ii. 105 : iii. 105.
Nutts, i. 97.

O.

Oathes and lyes, ii. 135.*
Oate, ii. 136, 172, 235, 237.
Ode, iii. 102.
Offring, iii. 213.
Oke, i. 43.
One, i. 111.
Onely, ii. 143.

* Hooke in his Amanda says—"I will not
　——Wrack my fancie for a kisse ;
　Fool to your laughing *Ladyship,*
　To get a smile, or touch your lip ;
　Protest with oathes high and mighty,
　That your spittle is, *aqua vitæ.*

　Amongst the gallants swear and rant.
　And of your kindnesse boast and vant ;
　Then drink diseases down, and wave
　All thoughts of sicknesse or the graue."
　　　　　　　　　　　　　Amanda, p. 60.

Plaudite, i. 164.*

Poesies, iii. 69.

Poetresse, ii. 5.

Poise, iii. 123.

Points, ii. 16.

Poking-sticks, ii. 302.

Pomander, i. 22-3 : ii. 133.

Poore, ii. 180.

Postern-bribe, ii. 167.

Post and Paire, ii. 228.†

Posts, i. 95.

Pounc't, i. 114.

Prank, i. 176 : iii. 178.

Pre-compos'd, ii. 208.

Predestination, ii. 86.

Predicant, ii. 80.

Preportions, ii. 232.

President, ii. 60.

Pression, ii. 248.

Prevaricate, i. 137.

Priestresse, ii. 158.

Pricelesse, i. 36.

---

* Erasmus, in his Apophth. says of Augustus Cæsar :—

When he perceiued and feled his diyng houre to approche, he enquired of his familiares, beyng let into his chamber to come and see him, whether it semed to them, that he had any thing handsomely enough played his parte in passyng his life.

" Meanyng of the trade and course of his presente life, which many writers doen resemble and compare vnto plaiyng a parte in an Enterlude. And then pronounced he this Greke verse folowing, customablie vsed to be soungen at the last end of Comedies, exhibited, and plaied to an ende.

δότε κρότον καὶ πάντες ἡμῖν μετὰ χαρᾶς κτυπήσατε.
"That is,

" Clappe hands, in signe of contentacion,
And with good harte, allow this our accion."
[Reprint Apoph. Erasmus, by Mr. Robert Roberts, Boston.]

† In Jonson's Christmas his Masque as it was presented at Court 1616, among the children is " Post and Paire. With a paire-Royall of Aces in his Hat; his Garment all done over with Payres and Purrs; his Squier carrying a Box, Cards and Counter." There is also " Wassall. Like a neat Sempster or Songster; her Page bearing a browne bowle drest with Ribbands and Rosemarie before her."

Pricket, i. 24.

Prick-madam, ii. 17.

Prince, ii. 62.

Primme, iii. 94.

Produce, iii. 207.

Profuser, ii. 226.

Progermination, ii. 251.

Propulsive, ii. 111.

Proscenium, ii. 57.

Prospective, ii. 220.

Protestant, ii. 6.

Prove, i. 109.

Protonotarie, iii. 145.

Prove, i. 109.

Ptsick, ii. 50.

Purfling, ii. 173.

Purls, ii. 136, 235.

Purslain, iii. 137.

Push, of pikes, iii. 170.

Push-pin, i. 29 : ii. 223.

Pushes, ii. 182.

Put = pusht, i. 29.

Pyramides, i. 147.

Q.

Quarelets, i. 41.

Quarter-acts, iii. 210.

Quick, ii. 140.

Quintell, ii. 93, 214 : iii. 41.

Quorum, iii. 36

R.

Rag'd, iii. 205.

Raile, ii. 74.

Reaching, ii. 13.

Reaks, i. 96.

Reaming, iii. 176.

Reconverse, iii. 33.

Recollect, ii. 239.

Recure, iii. 62.

Recommit, iii. 214.

Rector, ii. 41.

Rectresse, iii. 73.

Redeem, ii. 105.

Regredience, ii. 210.

Regression, ii. 252.

Reiterate, iii. 56.

Religious, i. 14.

Re-meeting, ii. 61.

Remora, i. 24.

Rents, ii. 133.

Reeve, ii. 74.

Repullulate, ii. 48.

Repullulation, ii. 273.

Repleat, ii. 128.

Repurgation, ii. 144.

Residenciarie, ii. 206.

Resident, ii. 149.

Resigne, i. 125.

Respasses, ii. 70.

Retorted, i. 139.

Retract, ii. 75.
Revolve, ii. 274.
Ribanings, iii. 40.
Rids, iii. 139.
Rifts, iii. 60.
Ropes, ii. 217.
Round, i. 12 : ii. 9, 161, 214 : iii. 165.
Roundelay, ii. 94.
Rosemarie, ii. 217.
Rowle=roll, iii. 21.
Rubelet, ii. 208.
Ruffe, ii. 74.

S.

Sack, i. 132.
Sack posset, ii. 19.
Sacietie, iii, 25.
Sad, ii. 287.
Sagge, ii. 25-6.†
Salt, i. 134, ii. 245.
Saints-bells, ii. 262.

Salute, iii. 183.
Salvages, i. 48 : ii. 10.
Sampler, i. 17, 180.
Saturitie, iii. 184.
Say, iii. 20, 29.
Say, and hold, iii. 181.
Scar-fire, i. 35 : ii. 28.
Scarre-crow-like, ii. 222.
Sceanes, i. 132 : ii. 253 : iii. 27.
Scene, ii. 244.
Schisme, ii. 131.
Sciography, ii. 59.
Scrip, i. 123 : ii. 116.
Scores, iii. 75, 166.
Sea-horse, i. 51.
Seldome, i. 64.
Sement, ii. 193.
Sere, i. 101.
Servility, iii. 2.
Severe, ii. 263.
Shagg'd, i. 76.

† The following are apposite examples of this word in Nash's *Pierce Pennilesse* :—" vpstarts that out-face towne and countrey in their veluets when Sir Rowland Russet-coat, their dad, goes *sagging* euerie day in his round gascoynes of white cotton, and hath much adoe (poore pennie-falter) to keep his vnthrift elbowes in reparation " (p. 8). " At length (as Fortune serude) I lighted vppon an old straddling usurer, clad in a damaske cassocke, edged with fox-furre; a pair of trunke slops, *sagging* down like a shoomaker's wallet," &c., (p. 11). (See under fox-furre in this Index.)

* " Near House of Law by *Temple*-Bar,
Now man of Mace cares not how far,
In stockings Blew he marcheth on,
With Velvet Cape his Cloack upon ;
In Girdle, Scrowles, where names of some,
Are written down' whom touch of Thumbe
On Shoulder left must safe convoy,
Anoying Wights with name of Roy.
Poor Pris'ners friend that sees the touch,
Cries out, aloud, I thought as much."
                         Davenant, p. 291.

Smutch, ii. 176.

Snugging, i. 42.

Sociate, iii. 8.

Sodden, iii. 23.

Sodders, iii. 23.

Soiles, iii. 137.

Sold, ii. 250.

Sometimes, ii. 105.

Souce, ii. 202, 269.

Soundlesse, iii. 173.

Soyl'd, ii. 213.

Spell, ii. 262.

Sperrables, ii. 207.

Speares, iii. 120.

Sphere, iii. 164.

Sphering=revolving, ii. 54.

Spinners, ii. 103, 109.

Sports, i. 10.

Sporting, i. 60.

Spring, i. 14.

Springall, i. 25.

Square, i. 62.

Stamp, i. 100.

Staffe, i. 124.

Starre-led, ii. 187.*

State, i. 13, ii. 280.

Staited, ii. 153.

State-like, i. 38.

St.=Saints, i. 157.

Stay, iii. 99.

Stench, ii. 285.

Steem, iii. 97.

Steerling, ii. 237.

Steletto, i. 30.

Still, ii. 122.

Stint, i. 58.

Stinted, iii. 103.

Stocks, ii. 129.

Stool-ball, ii. 226.

Stones, ii. 245.

Storax, ii. 45, 90.

Streakes, ii. 37.

Stringlesse, iii. 148.

Strutt, ii. 219.

Strutting, ii. 25-6, 219.

Suger'd, ii. 236.

Summer-birds, ii. 80.

Summer-friends, ii. 80.

Sunck, ii. 109.

Superlast, ii. 87.

Supervive, ii. 163.

Supraentitie, iii. 121.

Swadling-clout, iii. 144.

Sweating-closet, ii. 76.

* The pseudo-phenomenon was earlier and later employed by the Royalists to glorify "our most religious King," especially at the "glorious" Restoration.

Sweet, i. 93.

Sweets, ii. 57.

Sweet-breath, ii. 61.

Sweetling, ii. 198.

Sweet-sad, ii. 94.

Swerved, i. 44.

Swinger, iii. 59.

Sybells, ii. 234.

T.

Tabbies, ii. 176, iii. 144.

Tally, iii. 166.

Tanner, farting, ii. 86.*

Tansie, ii. 227.

Tardidation, iii. 184.

Teases, ii. 287.

Tearmly, iii. 35.

Teaster, ii. 84.

Tearce, iii. 15.

Tearcely, i. 59.

Tedious, ii. 23.

Telling, ii. 16.

Teemd, i. 181.

Teen, ii. 271.

Teend, iii. 6.

Teending, ii. 269.

Tελοσ, iii. 224.

Temper, ii. 78 : iii. 11.

Tent, i. 30.

Ternarie, ii. 246.

Terce, i. 140.

Tettar, iii. 208

The, ii. 293

Theeving = slipping away, iii. 207

Then = than, i. 19, and throughout

There, iii. 103

Threshold, i. 95

Thumb, i. 50, 60 : ii. 198

Thumblesse, iii. 48

Thyrse, i. 12 : ii. 160

Thrumme, i. 132

Thronclet, ii. 281

Tiffanie, i. 13, 56 : ii. 18

Till, iii. 102

* There was a Tanner whose unsavory exploits have been variously chronicled. He appears to have beaten the Miller of Mansfield, of Percy's Reliques' ballad, in the vigour of his 'cracks,' and to have immortalized himself by letting-fly point-blank in the king's face as he was giving him a leg up on his horse. This and much more will be found in " King Edward II. and the Tanner of Tamworth." Shirley in his " Fairies " remembers " The men of ginger-bread."

Tincture, i. 19, 129 : iii. 171

Tingles, iii. 79

Tinseld, ii. 105

Tinselling, i. 57 : ii. 173

Title, ii. 236

Tittyries, ii. 36

Toadstones, ii. 107*

Tods, ii. 260

Tonguelesse, i. 100.

Toning, ii. 113.

Too, ii. 88 : iii. 99, 104.

Too-too, ii. 144.

Took, i. 21.

Topick, ii. 116.

Top-gallant, ii. 168.

Toucht, ii. 223.

Trammell net, ii. 214.

Trammelets, iii. 92.

Tramplers, ii. 31.

Trasy, ii. 241 : iii. 33.

Trebius, ii. 74.

Trencher-creature, ii. 73.

Trentall, i. 154: ii. 179, 211,
    225 : iii. 37.

Troule, ii. 221.

True-love-knots, ii. 112.

Tucker, ii. 182.

True, iii. 133.

True-pac'd, ii. 77.

Truss, iii. 33.

Turne-broach, iii. 82.

Turbant, i. 163.

Turfe, i. 137.

Twelfth-tide King, iii. 166.

Twilight, ii. 295 : iii. 62.

Two, ii. 20.

U.

Umber, i. 65.

Unrude, ii. 72.

Unsluce, i. 24.

Unshorne, i. 116 : ii. 300.

Unchipt, iii. 136.

Unflead, iii. 136.

Unhallowed, iii. 119.

Under-dead, i. 180.

Under-lies, i. 180.

Underpropt, iii. 35.

Unperplext, ii. 187.

Unsmooth, ii. 171 : iii. 184.

Unsober, ii. 181.

Unsoft, ii. 251.

Uptailes, ii. 242.

Untruths, ii. 303.

Use, iii. 106.

---

* By a singular blunder the foot-note here is = infants. On
'Toadstones' see Bailey *s. v.*

V.

Vaile, yellow, i. 94.
Valentine, i. 52-3, 96.
Veales, ii. 74 : iii. 204.
Velome, ii. 110.
Venter, ii. 186.
Vestiments, iii. 34, 50.
Vesterie, i. 161 : ii. 91.
Vigil, ii. 71.
Vineger, ii. 298.
Virtue, ii. 16, 76.
Vizard, ii. 73.
Vultures, ii. 296.

W.

Wafer, ii. 59.
Wakes, i. 7 : ii. 256.
Warden, ii. 70.
Waste, i. 68 : ii. 86.
Watched, i. 160 : ii. 20.
Warpt, ii. 71.
Washt, or's, ii. 51.
Wassaile, i. 7 : ii. 271.*
Wassell boule, ii. 37.
Wassailing, ii. 271.
Weary, i. 101.
Weare, iii. 102.
Were, ii. 114.

Weed, ii. 30.
Weres, ii. 85.
We'l, ii. 105.
Weekly-strewings, i. 15.
Wheales, ii. 287.
Whelk, ii. 287.
Whimpering, ii. 130.
Whipping-cheere, iii. 173, 219.
Whorry, ii. 91.
Whit-flaw, i. 113 : ii. 107.
White, i. 42: ii. 86, 114, 139,
    158, 162, 255: iii. 103, 223.
Wimbling, ii. 302.
Wood, corrupted, ii. 107.
Wool, whitest, i. 99, 149.
Woolie-bubbles, ii. 108.
Wort, ii. 164 : iii. 65, 137.
Woosted, iii. 176.
Wrapt, i. 23.
Wrie-nosed, ii. 171.
Writhing, i. 28.

Y.

Yerk, iii. 63.
Yirkt, ii. 72.
Yet, ii. 222.
Yonker, i. 111.

* See note in this Glossarial-Index under ' Post and Paire.'

Younglings, ii. 71, 201.

You, ii. 72.

Z.

Zeallesse, ii. 294.

Zonulet, i. 68.

INDEX OF NAMES.

In order not to over-burden the Glossarial-Index, the proper names—persons, and a few places—are given here by themselves. Under several will be found supplementary information overlooked in the Memorial-Introduction and Essay—because promised in foot-notes.

Bethlehem, i. 149.*

Biancha, i. 49, 54 : iii. 6, 43.

Bice, ii. 273.

Blanch, i. 55 : ii. 172.

Blinks, ii. 287.

Blisse, iii. 22.

Boëtius, iii. 190.

Bold, Henry (H. B.), i. 52.

Boreman, iii. 55.

Bran, ii. 196.

Brand, i. 14, 15, 34, 53.

Bradshaw, Mrs. Katherine,
i. 163.

Braithwaite, ii. 265.

Bridgeman, i. 65.

Bridget, ii. 92.

Brock, ii. 9.

Broomsted, ii. 165.

Brugel, ii. 79.

Brutus, i. 10.

Buckingham, i. 173.

Buggins, iii. 50.

Bunce, i. 144.

Bungie, ii. 30.

Burns, i. 66 : iii. 35.

Burr, iii. 22.

Byron, i. 51.

C.

Carew, ii. 3.

Carlile, Countess of, i. 110.

Cartwright, William, iii. 88.

Cassius, Iatrosophista, or
Cassius Felix, i. 135.

Cassiodorus, iii. 185, 190.

Cato, i. 10.

Catullus, i. 40, 49, 86, 94,
97, 119, 124, 140, 141,
164 : ii. 253, 291 : iii. 13.

Center, ii. 85.

Chapman, i. 161.

Charles I, i. 41, 43, 105: ii.
4, 93, 224, 283 : iii. 30,
124, 159, 161, 165.

Charles, Prince of Wales
(= Charles II.), i. 5, 148 :
ii. 187, 254.

Chaucer, i. 53.

Chipperfield, ii. 86.

Chub, iii. 75.

Churton, i. 23.

Cicero, ii. 232 : iii. 58, 105.

Cleopatra, ii. 231, 281.

Clunn, iii. 21.

Cob, ii. 207.

* The 'star' that appeared on the birthday of our "most religious king," Charles II., shines in all the contemporary verse and
on The Restoration ('glorious!') it reappears with shocking ful-
someness.

* Simon Cowne and Edward, Richard and Lawrence occur in the Dean Prior register—same as Coone.

† Did Randolph in his " Complaint against Cupid, that he never made him in love," intend Herrick in these lines ?

" This on his Cloris spends his thoughts and time ;
That chaunts Corinna in his amorous rhyme."

‡ In II. 98 the passing quarrel may be compared with Herrick's words to the Bp. of Lincoln. He was placable and genial.

* Dundridges occur frequently in the Dean Prior register. Marie, the d. of Christopher Dundridge, was buried the 9th of October, 1643, and Christopher, sonne of John Dundridge, the 18th of January, 1643.

† The 'Satires' of Hall and other Poems could not but form a bond of union with Herrick.

* No trace remains of the ' painter' Herrick.

* Further research has failed to shed light on the 'fair lady's' history. I have an impression that she is elsewhere celebrated.

* Robert, Bartholomew and Richard Mudge, are in the Dean Prior Register—a common Devonshire name.
† Doubtless Herrick became acquainted with this Knight through his contributions to " Wit's Recreations," fully noticed in Memorial-Introduction.

O.

Oberon, ii. 24, 104, 203, *et passim*.

Oenone, ii. 111, 272, 286.

Oulsworth, iii. 77.

Origen, iii. 197, 212.

Orpheus, ii. 274.

Ovid, i. 17, 26, 89, 139 : ii. 189, 295, 300 : iii. 25.

P.

Pagget, i. 111.

Panchaia, i. 98 : iii. 222.

Parson, Sir Thomas, i. 160.

Parsons, Mrs. Dorothy, ii. 141.

Parsons, T'omasin iii. 38.

Parrat, ii. 141.

Parrie, Sir George, iii. 66.

Paske, ii. 64.

Pastillos, iii. 68

Patrick, ii. 92.

Paul, ii. 245.

Pelops, i. 59.

Peapes, ii. 287.

Pearch, ii. 276.

Peason, ii. 290.

Pemberton, Sir Lewis, ii. 71.

Pembroke, Earl of, ii. 62.

Pennie, iii. 45.

Perenna, i. 16, 155, 179 : ii. 125 : iii. 37, 74.

Perilla i. 14, 101 : iii. 53.

Persius, i. 97 : ii. 51, 253, 291.

Petrarch, i. 8.

Phillis, ii. 112, 150, 189.

Pink, ii. 8.

Pievish, ii. 88.

Pimple, iii. 83.

Pliny, ii. 118.

Plato, ii. 148, 248 : iii. 58.

Pope, iii. 66, 156.

Porter, Endymion, i. 70, 124, ii. 136, 212 : iii. 70.*

Pot, i. 165.

Potter, Bp. of Carlisle, ii. 33.*

Potter, Mrs. Grace, iii. 43.

Porter, Amie, ii. 288.

Portman, Mrs., iii. 73.

Prat, ii. 227.

Prew, ii. 80, 268.

Prigg, i. 123 : ii. 66.

Prickles, iii. 9.

* Notices of Porter will be found in Mr. Huth's "Inedited Poetical Miscellanies" 1870. Notes, sig. Ff. Randolph's "Pareneticon" to him is finely touched.

* The " three brave brothers " celebrated, were—
    (1) George Stuart, Lord D'Aubigny, slain at Edgehill 23 Oct., 1642.
    (2) Lord John Stuart, killed at the battle of Alresford in 1644.
    (3) Lord Bernard Stuart, who fell at Rowton Heath in 1655. They were sons of Esme, 3d duke of Lennox.

† Further research has not elicited more on this name. Could it be a character-name?

* The poem here promised is as follows :—
　　"Those oaks that most obdurate are,
　　　　Shall willingly their arms unwind ;
　　And by themselves engraven, wear
　　　　My verse upon their Leaves, and Rind :
　　And every Tree, whose Top prefers
　　To Heaven these sacred Characters,
　　　　No storms shall offer to invade.
　　For whilst thus charm'd, the rough Winds may
　　Hope with more ease, to snatch away
　　　　Their fastned Roots, or fleeting shade."
† He was the only surviving son of John Stone, Sergeant at Law, brother of Mrs. Herrick, the poet's mother. He was Se-

Sudds, i. 170.
Swetnaham, iii. 76.

T.

Tanner, farting, ii. 86.
Tap, ii. 285.
Tennyson, i. 44, 62, 64, 93,
  173 : ii. 20, 94, 95, 204,
  302.
Thamasis, iii. 56.
Tibullus, i. 140.
Titian, ii. 79.
Tintoretto, ii. 79.
Topsell, ii. 234.
Tooly, ii. 171.
Tracie, Lady, ii. 191.
Trap, iii. 72.
Trapp, iii. 192.
Trasy, ii. 241 : iii. 33.
Tradescant, ii. 217.
Trencherman, ii. 274.
Trigg, ii. 230.
Truggin, ii. 304.
Trundell, Tim, ii. 87.

Tubbs, iii. 34.
Tuck, ii. 228.

U.

Umber, ii. 172.
Urbin, 79.
Ursley, ii. 159, 217.
Urles, ii. 177.

V.

Valentine, St., i. 52, 53, 96:
  ii. 77.
Vandike, ii. 79.
Vaughan, Henry, ii. 136.
Venus, i. 95: ii. 55, 58: iii.
  52, *et passim.*
Villars, Lady Mary, ii. 56.*
Vineger, iii. 32.
Virgil, i. 77, 97, 135, 181 :
  ii. 237, 274 : iii. 49, 79.
Vulcan, ii. 188.

W.

Warr, i. 81 : ii. 166.†

condary of Wood Street Compter in London. He died 20th September, 1660.

* This was a Villiers; and her Letters abound—showing all the family capacity and eke their strange spelling even for the period.

† Randolph has an " Epitaph upon his honoured Friend, Master Warre." It begins :—

" Here lies the knowing head, the honest heart,

> Fair blood and courteous hands, and every part
> Of gentle Warre," &c.

Probably the same with Herrick's friend.   Warre and Weare were also (I think) identical.

* I had hoped to give further details on the Wheelers ; but nothing of any value has resulted from somewhat extensive inquiries. The Herricks and Wheelers were related by marriage.

‡ Barnabas Potter, Herrick's predecessor and appointed Bp. of Carlisle, married Elizabeth Yard, d. of Lady Giles by her first husband, and widow of Edward Yard (mother of the 'witty' Mrs Lettice Yard), and it is probable therefore that he and his family continued to maintain rare intercourse with the parish. Hence our Poet's celebration of members of the Potter family. (For Potter see ii. 33.)

The Yardes at present hold the Giles Estates at Dean Prior. In our own day the name has been splendidly in honour.

FINIS.

ROBERT ROBERTS, PRINTER, BOSTON

A List of Books

PUBLISHED BY

CHATTO & WINDUS,

214, Piccadilly, London, W.

Sold by all Booksellers, or sent post-free for the published price by the Publishers.

ABOUT.—THE FELLAH: An Egyptian Novel. By EDMOND ABOUT. Translated by Sir RANDAL ROBERTS. Post 8vo, illustrated boards, **2s.**

ADAMS (W. DAVENPORT), WORKS BY.
A DICTIONARY OF THE DRAMA. Being a comprehensive Guide to the Plays, Playwrights, Players, and Playhouses of the United Kingdom and America. Crown 8vo, half-bound, **12s. 6d.** [*Preparing.*
QUIPS AND QUIDDITIES. Selected by W. D. ADAMS. Post 8vo, cloth limp, **2s. 6d.**

ADAMS (W. H. D.).—WITCH, WARLOCK, AND MAGICIAN: Historical Sketches of Magic and Witchcraft in England and Scotland. By W. H. DAVENPORT ADAMS. Demy 8vo, cloth extra, **12s.**

AGONY COLUMN (THE) OF "THE TIMES," from 1800 to 1870. Edited, with an Introduction, by ALICE CLAY. Post 8vo, cloth limp, **2s. 6d.**

AIDE (HAMILTON), WORKS BY. Post 8vo, illustrated boards, **2s.** each.
CARR OF CARRLYON. | **CONFIDENCES.**

ALEXANDER (MRS.), NOVELS BY. Post 8vo, illustrated boards, **2s.** each.
MAID, WIFE, OR WIDOW? | **VALERIE'S FATE.**

ALLEN (GRANT), WORKS BY. Crown 8vo, cloth extra, **6s.** each.
THE EVOLUTIONIST AT LARGE. | **COLIN CLOUT'S CALENDAR.**
VIGNETTES FROM NATURE.

Crown 8vo, cloth extra, **6s.** each; post 8vo, illustrated boards., **2s.** each.
STRANGE STORIES. With a Frontispiece by GEORGE DU MAURIER.
THE BECKONING HAND. With a Frontispiece by TOWNLEY GREEN.

Crown 8vo, cloth extra, **3s. 6d.** each; post 8vo, illustrated boards, **2s.** each
PHILISTIA. | **FOR MAIMIE'S SAKE.** | **THIS MORTAL COIL.**
BABYLON. | **IN ALL SHADES.** | **THE TENTS OF SHEM.**
| **THE DEVIL'S DIE.** |

THE GREAT TABOO. Crown 8vo, cloth extra, **3s. 6d.**

AMERICAN LITERATURE, A LIBRARY OF, from the Earliest Settlement to the Present Time. Compiled and Edited by EDMUND CLARENCE STEDMAN and ELLEN MACKAY HUTCHINSON. Eleven Vols., royal 8vo, cloth extra. A few copies are for sale by Messrs. CHATTO & WINDUS (published in New York by C. L. WEBSTER & Co.), price **£6 12s.** the set.

ARCHITECTURAL STYLES, A HANDBOOK OF. By A. ROSENGARTEN. Translated by W COLLETT-SANDARS. With 639 Illusts. Cr. 8vo, cl ex, **7s. 6d.**

ART (THE) OF AMUSING: A Collection of Graceful Arts, GAMES, Tricks, Puzzles, and Charades. By FRANK BELLEW. 300 Illusts. Cr. 8vo, cl. ex., **4s. 6d.**

ARNOLD (EDWIN LESTER), WORKS BY.
THE WONDERFUL ADVENTURES OF PHRA THE PHŒNICIAN. With Introduction by Sir EDWIN ARNOLD, K.C.I.E., and 12 Illusts. by H. M. PAGET. Three Vols.
BIRD LIFE IN ENGLAND. Crown 8vo. cloth extra. 6s.

ARTEMUS WARD'S WORKS: The Works of CHARLES FARRER BROWNE,
better known as ARTEMUS WARD. With Portrait and Facsimile. Crown 8vo, cloth extra, 7s. 6d.—Also a POPULAR EDITION, post 8vo, picture boards, 2s.
THE GENIAL SHOWMAN: Life and Adventures of ARTEMUS WARD. By EDWARD P. HINGSTON. With a Frontispiece. Crown 8vo, cloth extra, 3s. 6d.

ASHTON (JOHN), WORKS BY. Crown 8vo, cloth extra, 7s. 6d. each.
HISTORY OF THE CHAP-BOOKS OF THE 18th CENTURY. With 334 Illusts.
SOCIAL LIFE IN THE REIGN OF QUEEN ANNE. With 85 Illustrations.
HUMOUR, WIT, AND SATIRE OF SEVENTEENTH CENTURY. With 82 Illusts.
ENGLISH CARICATURE AND SATIRE ON NAPOLEON THE FIRST. 115 Illusts.
MODERN STREET BALLADS. With 57 Illustrations

BACTERIA.—A SYNOPSIS OF THE BACTERIA AND YEAST
FUNGI AND ALLIED SPECIES. By W. B. GROVE, B.A. With 87 Illustrations.
Crown 8vo, cloth extra, 3s. 6d.

BARDSLEY (REV. C. W.), WORKS BY.
ENGLISH SURNAMES: Their Sources and Significations. Cr. 8vo, cloth, 7s. 6d.
CURIOSITIES OF PURITAN NOMENCLATURE. Crown 8vo. cloth extra, 6s.

BARING GOULD (S., Author of "John Herring," &c.), NOVELS BY.
Crown 8vo, cloth extra, 3s. 6d. each, post 8vo, illustrated boards, 2s. each.
RED SPIDER. | EVE.

BARRETT (FRANK, Author of "Lady Biddy Fane,") NOVELS BY.
FETTERED FOR LIFE. Post 8vo, illustrated boards, 2s.; cloth, 2s. 6d.
BETWEEN LIFE AND DEATH. Three Vols., crown 8vo.

BEACONSFIELD, LORD: A Biography. By T. P. O'CONNOR, M.P.
Sixth Edition, with an Introduction. Crown 8vo, cloth extra, 5s.

BEAUCHAMP.—GRANTLEY GRANGE: A Novel. By SHELSLEY
BEAUCHAMP. Post 8vo, illustrated boards, 2s.

BEAUTIFUL PICTURES BY BRITISH ARTISTS: A Gathering of
Favourites from our Picture Galleries, beautifully engraved on Steel. With Notices of the Artists by SYDNEY ARMYTAGE, M.A. Imperial 4to, cloth extra, gilt edges, 21s.

BECHSTEIN.—AS PRETTY AS SEVEN, and other German Stories.
Collected by LUDWIG BECHSTEIN. With Additional Tales by the Brothers GRIMM, and 98 Illustrations by RICHTER. Square 8vo, cloth extra, 6s. 6d.; gilt edges, 7s. 6d.

BEERBOHM.—WANDERINGS IN PATAGONIA; or, Life among the
Ostrich Hunters. By JULIUS BEERBOHM. With Illusts. Cr. 8vo, cl. extra, 3s. 6d.

BESANT (WALTER), NOVELS BY.
Cr. 8vo, cl. ex., 3s. 6d. each; post 8vo, illust. bds., 2s. each; cl. limp, 2s. 6d. each.
ALL SORTS AND CONDITIONS OF MEN. With Illustrations by FRED. BARNARD.
THE CAPTAINS' ROOM, &c. With Frontispiece by E. J. WHEELER.
ALL IN A GARDEN FAIR. With 6 Illustrations by HARRY FURNISS.
DOROTHY FORSTER. With Frontispiece by CHARLES GREEN.
UNCLE JACK, and other Stories | CHILDREN OF GIBEON.
THE WORLD WENT VERY WELL THEN. With 12 Illustrations by A. FORESTIER.
HERR PAULUS: His Rise, his Greatness, and his Fall.
FOR FAITH AND FREEDOM. With Illustrations by A. FORESTIER and F. WADDY.

Crown 8vo, cloth extra, 3s. 6d. each.
TO CALL HER MINE, &c. With 9 Illustrations by A. FORESTIER.
THE BELL OF ST. PAUL'S.

THE HOLY ROSE, &c. With Frontispiece by F. BARNARD. Cr. 8vo, cloth extra, 6s.
ARMOREL OF LYONESSE: A Romance of To-day. Three Vols., crown 8vo
ST. KATHERINE'S BY THE TOWER. With 12 full-page Illustrations by C. GREEN. Three Vols., crown 8vo. [May.
FIFTY YEARS AGO. With 137 Plates and Woodcuts. Demy 8vo, cloth extra, 16s.
THE EULOGY OF RICHARD JEFFERIES. With Portrait. Cr. 8vo, cl. extra, 6s.
THE ART OF FICTION. Demy 8vo, 1s.

BESANT (WALTER) AND JAMES RICE, NOVELS BY.

Cr. 8vo, cl. ex., **3s. 6d.** each ; post 8vo, illust bds., **2s.** each; cl. limp, **2s. 6d.** each.

READY-MONEY MORTIBOY.
MY LITTLE GIRL.
WITH HARP AND CROWN.
THIS SON OF VULCAN.
THE GOLDEN BUTTERFLY.
THE MONKS OF THELEMA.

BY CELIA'S ARBOUR.
THE CHAPLAIN OF THE FLEET.
THE SEAMY SIDE.
THE CASE OF MR. LUCRAFT, &c.
'TWAS IN TRAFALGAR'S BAY, &c.
THE TEN YEARS' TENANT, &c.

⁎⁎⁎ There is also a LIBRARY EDITION of the above Twelve Volumes, handsomely set in new type, on a large crown 8vo page, and bound in cloth extra, **6s.** each.

BENNETT (W. C., LL.D.), WORKS BY. Post 8vo, cloth limp, **2s.** each.

A BALLAD HISTORY OF ENGLAND. | SONGS FOR SAILORS.

BEWICK (THOMAS) AND HIS PUPILS. By AUSTIN DOBSON. With
95 Illustrations. Square 8vo, cloth extra, **6s.**

BLACKBURN'S (HENRY) ART HANDBOOKS.

ACADEMY NOTES, separate years, from 1875-1887, 1889, and 1890, each **1s.**
ACADEMY NOTES, 1891. With Illustrations. **1s.**   [May.
ACADEMY NOTES, 1875-79. Complete in One Vol., with 600 Illusts. Cloth limp, **6s.**
ACADEMY NOTES, 1880-84. Complete in One Vol., with 700 Illusts. Cloth limp, **6s.**
GROSVENOR NOTES, 1877. **6d.**
GROSVENOR NOTES, separate years, from 1878 to 1890, each **1s.**
GROSVENOR NOTES, Vol. I, 1877-82. With 300 Illusts Demy 8vo, cloth limp, **6s.**
GROSVENOR NOTES, Vol II., 1883-87. With 300 Illusts Demy 8vo, cloth limp, **6s.**
THE NEW GALLERY, 1888-1890. With numerous Illustrations, each **1s.**
THE NEW GALLERY, 1891. With Illustrations **1s.**   [May
ENGLISH PICTURES AT THE NATIONAL GALLERY. 114 Illustrations, **1s.**
OLD MASTERS AT THE NATIONAL GALLERY. 128 Illustrations. **1s. 6d.**
ILLUSTRATED CATALOGUE TO THE NATIONAL GALLERY. 242 Illusts. cl., **3s.**

THE PARIS SALON, 1891. With Facsimile Sketches. **3s.**   [May.
THE PARIS SOCIETY OF FINE ARTS, 1891. With Sketches. **3s. 6d.**   [May.

BLAKE (WILLIAM): India-proof Etchings from his Works by WILLIAM
BELL SCOTT. With descriptive Text. Folio, half-bound boards, **21s.**

BLIND.—THE ASCENT OF MAN: A Poem. By MATHILDE BLIND.
Crown 8vo, printed on hand-made paper cloth extra, **5s.**

BOURNE (H. R. FOX), WORKS BY.

ENGLISH MERCHANTS: Memoirs in Illustration of the Progress of British Commerce. With numerous Illustrations. Crown 8vo, cloth extra, **7s. 6d.**
ENGLISH NEWSPAPERS: The History of Journalism. Two Vols , demy 8vo, cl., **25s.**
THE OTHER SIDE OF THE EMIN PASHA RELIEF EXPEDITION. Crown 8vo, cloth extra, **6s.**

BOWERS' (G.) HUNTING SKETCHES. Oblong 4to, hf.-bd. bds., **21s.** each.

CANTERS IN CRAMPSHIRE. | LEAVES FROM A HUNTING JOURNAL.

BOYLE (FREDERICK), WORKS BY. Post 8vo, illustrated boards, **2s.** each.

CHRONICLES OF NO-MAN'S LAND. | CAMP NOTES.
SAVAGE LIFE. Crown 8vo, cloth extra, **3s. 6d.**; post 8vo, picture boards, **2s.**

BRAND'S OBSERVATIONS ON POPULAR ANTIQUITIES; chiefly
illustrating the Origin of our Vulgar Customs, Ceremonies, and Superstitions. With the Additions of Sir HENRY ELLIS, and Illustrations. Cr. 8vo, cloth extra, **7s. 6d.**

BREWER (REV. DR.), WORKS BY.

THE READER'S HANDBOOK OF ALLUSIONS, REFERENCES, PLOTS, AND STORIES. Fifteenth Thousand. Crown 8vo, cloth extra, **7s. 6d.**
AUTHORS AND THEIR WORKS, WITH THE DATES: Being the Appendices to "The Reader's Handbook," separately printed. Crown 8vo, cloth limp, **2s.**
A DICTIONARY OF MIRACLES. Crown 8vo, cloth extra, **7s. 6d.**

BREWSTER (SIR DAVID), WORKS BY. Post 8vo, cl ex., **4s. 6d.** each.

MORE WORLDS THAN ONE: Creed of Philosopher and Hope of Christian Plates.
THE MARTYRS OF SCIENCE: Galileo, Tycho Brahe, and Kepler. With Portraits.
LETTERS ON NATURAL MAGIC. With numerous Illustrations.

BRET HARTE, WORKS BY.
LIBRARY EDITION, Complete in Six Volumes, crown 8vo, cloth extra, **6s.** each.
BRET HARTE'S COLLECTED WORKS. Arranged and Revised by the Author.
  Vol. I. COMPLETE POETICAL AND DRAMATIC WORKS. With Steel Portrait.
  Vol. II. LUCK OF ROARING CAMP—BOHEMIAN PAPERS—AMERICAN LEGENDS.
  Vol. III. TALES OF THE ARGONAUTS—EASTERN SKETCHES.
  Vol. IV. GABRIEL CONROY.
  Vol. V. STORIES—CONDENSED NOVELS, &c.
  Vol. VI. TALES OF THE PACIFIC SLOPE.

THE SELECT WORKS OF BRET HARTE, in Prose and Poetry. With Introductory Essay by J. M. BELLEW, Portrait of Author, and 50 Illusts. Cr. 8vo, cl. ex.. **7s. 6d.**
BRET HARTE'S POETICAL WORKS. Hand-made paper & buckram. Cr.8vo, **4s.6d.**
THE QUEEN OF THE PIRATE ISLE. With 28 original Drawings by KATE GREENAWAY, reproduced in Colours by EDMUND EVANS. Small 4to, cloth, **5s.**

Crown 8vo, cloth extra, **3s. 6d.** each.
A WAIF OF THE PLAINS. With 60 Illustrations by STANLEY L. WOOD.
A WARD OF THE GOLDEN GATE. With 59 Illustrations by STANLEY L. WOOD.
A SAPPHO OF GREEN SPRINGS, &c. With Two Illustrations by HUME NISBET.

Post 8vo, illustrated boards, **2s.** each.
GABRIEL CONROY. | **THE LUCK OF ROARING CAMP,** &c.
AN HEIRESS OF RED DOG, &c. | **CALIFORNIAN STORIES.**

Post 8vo, illustrated boards, **2s.** each; cloth limp, **2s. 6d.** each.
FLIP. | **MARUJA.** | **A PHYLLIS OF THE SIERRAS.**

Fcap. 8vo, picture cover, **1s.** each.
THE TWINS OF TABLE MOUNTAIN. | **JEFF BRIGGS'S LOVE STORY.**

BRILLAT-SAVARIN.—GASTRONOMY AS A FINE ART. By BRILLAT-SAVARIN. Translated by R. E. ANDERSON, M.A. Post 8vo, half-bound, **2s.**

BRYDGES.—UNCLE SAM AT HOME. By HAROLD BRYDGES. Post 8vo, illustrated boards, **2s.**; cloth limp, **2s. 6d.**

BUCHANAN'S (ROBERT) WORKS. Crown 8vo, cloth extra, **6s.** each.
SELECTED POEMS OF ROBERT BUCHANAN. With Frontispiece by T. DALZIEL.
THE EARTHQUAKE; or, Six Days and a Sabbath.
THE CITY OF DREAM: An Epic Poem. With Two Illustrations by P. MACNAB.
THE OUTCAST: A Rhyme for the Time. With 12 Full-page Illustrations and numerous Vignettes. Crown 8vo, cloth extra, **8s.**

ROBERT BUCHANAN'S COMPLETE POETICAL WORKS. With Steel-plate Portrait. Crown 8vo, cloth extra, **7s. 6d.**

Crown 8vo, cloth extra, **3s. 6d.** each; post 8vo, illustrated boards, **2s.** each.
THE SHADOW OF THE SWORD. | **LOVE ME FOR EVER.** Frontispiece.
A CHILD OF NATURE. Frontispiece. | **ANNAN WATER.** | **FOXGLOVE MANOR.**
GOD AND THE MAN. With 11 Illustrations by FRED. BARNARD. | **THE NEW ABELARD.**
THE MARTYRDOM OF MADELINE. | **MATT:** A Story of a Caravan Front.
With Frontispiece by A. W. COOPER | **THE MASTER OF THE MINE.** Front.
| **THE HEIR OF LINNE.**

BURTON (CAPTAIN). — THE BOOK OF THE SWORD: Being a History of the Sword and its Use in all Countries, from the Earliest Times. By RICHARD F. BURTON. With over 400 Illustrations. Square 8vo, cloth extra, **32s.**

BURTON (ROBERT).
THE ANATOMY OF MELANCHOLY: A New Edition, with translations of the Classical Extracts. Demy 8vo, cloth extra, **7s. 6d.**
MELANCHOLY ANATOMISED: Being an Abridgment, for popular use, of BURTON's ANATOMY OF MELANCHOLY. Post 8vo, cloth limp, **2s. 6d.**

CAINE (T. HALL), NOVELS BY. Crown 8vo, cloth extra, **3s. 6d.** each; post 8vo, illustrated boards, **2s.** each; cloth limp, **2s. 6d.** each.
SHADOW OF A CRIME. | **A SON OF HAGAR.** | **THE DEEMSTER.**

CAMERON (COMMANDER). — THE CRUISE OF THE "BLACK PRINCE" PRIVATEER. By V. LOVETT CAMERON, R.N., C.B. With Two Illustrations by P. MACNAB. Crown 8vo, cloth extra, **5s.**; post 8vo, illustrated boards, **2s.**

CAMERON (MRS. H. LOVETT), NOVELS BY.
Crown 8vo, cloth extra, **3s. 6d.** each; post 8vo, illustrated boards, **2s.** each.
JULIET'S GUARDIAN. | **DECEIVERS EVER.**

CARLYLE (THOMAS) ON THE CHOICE OF BOOKS. With Life by R. H. SHEPHERD, and Three Illustrations. Post 8vo, cloth extra, **1s. 6d.**
THE CORRESPONDENCE OF THOMAS CARLYLE AND RALPH WALDO EMERSON, 1834 to 1872. Edited by CHARLES ELIOT NORTON. With Portraits. Two Vols., crown 8vo. cloth extra, **24s.**

CARLYLE (JANE WELSH), LIFE OF. By Mrs. ALEXANDER IRELAND. With Portrait and Facsimile Letter. Small demy 8vo, cloth extra, **7s. 6d.**

CHAPMAN'S (GEORGE) WORKS. Vol. I. contains the Plays complete, including the doubtful ones. Vol II, the Poems and Minor Translations, with an Introductory Essay by ALGERNON CHARLES SWINBURNE. Vol. III., the Translations of the Iliad and Odyssey. Three Vols., crown 8vo, cloth extra, **6s.** each.

CHATTO AND JACKSON.—A TREATISE ON WOOD ENGRAVING, Historical and Practical. By WILLIAM ANDREW CHATTO and JOHN JACKSON. With an Additional Chapter by HENRY G. BOHN, and 450 fine Illusts Large 4to, hf.-bd., **28s.**

CHAUCER FOR CHILDREN: A Golden Key. By Mrs. H. R. HAWEIS. With 8 Coloured Plates and 30 Woodcuts. Small 4to, cloth extra, **6s.**
CHAUCER FOR SCHOOLS. By Mrs. H. R. HAWEIS. Demy 8vo, cloth limp. **2s. 6d.**

CLARE.—FOR THE LOVE OF A LASS: A Tale of Tynedale. By AUSTIN CLARE. Post 8vo, picture boards, **2s.**; cloth limp, **2s. 6d.**

CLIVE (MRS. ARCHER), NOVELS BY. Post 8vo, illust. boards, **2s.** each.
PAUL FERROLL. | **WHY PAUL FERROLL KILLED HIS WIFE.**

CLODD (EDW., F.R.A.S.).—MYTHS AND DREAMS. Cr. 8vo, cl. ex., **5s.**

COBBAN.—THE CURE OF SOULS: A Story. By J. MACLAREN COBBAN. Post 8vo, illustrated boards, **2s.**

COLEMAN (JOHN), WORKS BY.
PLAYERS AND PLAYWRIGHTS I HAVE KNOWN. Two Vols., 8vo, cloth, **24s.**
CURLY: An Actor's Story. With 21 Illusts. by J. C DOLLMAN. Cr. 8vo, cl, **1s. 6d.**

COLLINS (C. ALLSTON).—THE BAR SINISTER. Post 8vo, **2s.**

COLLINS (MORTIMER AND FRANCES), NOVELS BY.
Crown 8vo, cloth extra, **3s. 6d.** each, post 8vo, illustrated boards, **2s.** each.
SWEET ANNE PAGE. | **FROM MIDNIGHT TO MIDNIGHT.** | **TRANSMIGRATION.**
BLACKSMITH AND SCHOLAR. | **YOU PLAY ME FALSE.** | **VILLAGE COMEDY.**

Post 8vo, illustrated boards, **2s.** each.
A FIGHT WITH FORTUNE. | **SWEET AND TWENTY.** | **FRANCES.**

COLLINS (WILKIE), NOVELS BY.
Cr 8vo, cl. ex., **3s. 6d.** each, post 8vo, illust bds., **2s.** each; cl. limp, **2s. 6d.** each.
ANTONINA. With a Frontispiece by Sir JOHN GILBERT, R.A.
BASIL. Illustrated by Sir JOHN GILBERT, R.A., and J. MAHONEY.
HIDE AND SEEK. Illustrated by Sir JOHN GILBERT, R.A., and J. MAHONEY.
AFTER DARK. With Illustrations by A. B. HOUGHTON.
THE DEAD SECRET. With a Frontispiece by Sir JOHN GILBERT, R A.
QUEEN OF HEARTS. With a Frontispiece by Sir JOHN GILBERT, R.A.
THE WOMAN IN WHITE. With Illusts. by Sir J. GILBERT, R.A., and F. A. FRASER.
NO NAME. With Illustrations by Sir J. E. MILLAIS, R.A., and A. W. COOPER.
MY MISCELLANIES. With a Steel-plate Portrait of WILKIE COLLINS.
ARMADALE. With Illustrations by G. H. THOMAS.
THE MOONSTONE. With Illustrations by G Du MAURIER and F. A. FRASER.
MAN AND WIFE. With Illustrations by WILLIAM SMALL.
POOR MISS FINCH. Illustrated by G. Du MAURIER and EDWARD HUGHES.
MISS OR MRS.? With Illusts by S. L. FILDES, R.A., and HENRY WOODS, A.R.A.
THE NEW MAGDALEN. Illustrated by G. Du MAURIER and C S. REINHARDT.
THE FROZEN DEEP. Illustrated by G. Du MAURIER and J. MAHONEY.
THE LAW AND THE LADY. Illusts. by S. L. FILDES, R.A., and SYDNEY HALL.
THE TWO DESTINIES.
THE HAUNTED HOTEL. Illustrated by ARTHUR HOPKINS
THE FALLEN LEAVES. | **HEART AND SCIENCE.** | **THE EVIL GENIUS.**
JEZEBEL'S DAUGHTER. | **"I SAY NO."** | **LITTLE NOVELS.**
THE BLACK ROBE. | **A ROGUE'S LIFE.** | **THE LEGACY OF CAIN.**

BLIND LOVE. With a Preface by WALTER BESANT, and 36 Illustrations by A. FORESTIER. Crown 8vo, cloth extra, **3s. 6d.**

COLLINS (CHURTON).—A MONOGRAPH ON DEAN SWIFT. By J. CHURTON COLLINS. Crown 8vo, cloth extra, 8s. [*Shortly.*

COLMAN'S HUMOROUS WORKS: "Broad Grins," "My Nightgown and Slippers," and other Humorous Works of GEORGE COLMAN. With Life by G. B. BUCKSTONE, and Frontispiece by HOGARTH. Crown 8vo, cloth extra, 7s. 6d.

COLQUHOUN.—EVERY INCH A SOLDIER: A Novel. By M. J. COLQUHOUN. Post 8vo, illustrated boards, 2s.

CONVALESCENT COOKERY: A Family Handbook. By CATHERINE RYAN. Crown 8vo, 1s.; cloth limp, 1s. 6d.

CONWAY (MONCURE D.), WORKS BY.
DEMONOLOGY AND DEVIL-LORE. With 65 Illustrations. Third Edition. Two Vols., demy 8vo. cloth extra, 28s.
A NECKLACE OF STORIES. 25 Illusts. by W. J. HENNESSY. Sq. 8vo, cloth, 6s.
PINE AND PALM: A Novel. Two Vols., crown 8vo, cloth extra, 21s.
GEORGE WASHINGTON'S RULES OF CIVILITY Traced to their Sources and Restored. Fcap. 8vo, Japanese vellum, 2s. 6d.

COOK (DUTTON), NOVELS BY.
PAUL FOSTER'S DAUGHTER. Cr. 8vo, cl. ex., 3s. 6d.; post 8vo, illust. boards, 2s.
LEO. Post 8vo, illustrated boards, 2s.

CORNWALL.—POPULAR ROMANCES OF THE WEST OF ENG-LAND; or, The Drolls, Traditions, and Superstitions of Old Cornwall. Collected by ROBERT HUNT, F.R.S. Two Steel-plates by GEO. CRUIKSHANK. Cr. 8vo, cl., 7s. 6d.

CRADDOCK.—THE PROPHET OF THE GREAT SMOKY MOUN-TAINS. By CHARLES EGBERT CRADDOCK. Post 8vo, illust. bds., 2s.; cl. limp, 2s. 6d.

CRUIKSHANK'S COMIC ALMANACK. Complete in TWO SERIES: The FIRST from 1835 to 1843; the SECOND from 1844 to 1853. A Gathering of the BEST HUMOUR of THACKERAY, HOOD, MAYHEW, ALBERT SMITH, A'BECKETT, ROBERT BROUGH, &c. With numerous Steel Engravings and Woodcuts by CRUIK-SHANK, HINE, LANDELLS, &c. Two Vols., crown 8vo, cloth gilt, 7s. 6d. each.
THE LIFE OF GEORGE CRUIKSHANK. By BLANCHARD JERROLD. With 84 Illustrations and a Bibliography Crown 8vo, cloth extra, 7s. 6d.

CUMMING (C. F. GORDON), WORKS BY. Demy 8vo, cl. ex., 8s. 6d. each.
IN THE HEBRIDES. With Autotype Facsimile and 23 Illustrations.
IN THE HIMALAYAS AND ON THE INDIAN PLAINS. With 42 Illustrations.

VIA CORNWALL TO EGYPT. With Photogravure Frontis. Demy 8vo, cl., 7s. 6d.

CUSSANS.—A HANDBOOK OF HERALDRY; with Instructions for Tracing Pedigrees and Deciphering Ancient MSS., &c. By JOHN E. CUSSANS. With 408 Woodcuts, Two Coloured and Two Plain Plates. Crown 8vo, cloth extra, 7s. 6d.

CYPLES (W.)—HEARTS of GOLD. Cr. 8vo, cl., 3s. 6d.; post 8vo, bds., 2s.

DANIEL.—MERRIE ENGLAND IN THE OLDEN TIME. By GEORGE DANIEL. With Illustrations by ROBERT CRUIKSHANK. Crown 8vo, cloth extra, 3s. 6d.

DAUDET.—THE EVANGELIST; or, Port Salvation. By ALPHONSE DAUDET. Crown 8vo, cloth extra, 3s. 6d.; post 8vo, illustrated boards, 2s.

DAVENANT.—HINTS FOR PARENTS ON THE CHOICE OF A PRO-FESSION FOR THEIR SONS. By F. DAVENANT, M.A. Post 8vo, 1s.; cl., 1s. 6d.

DAVIES (DR. N. E. YORKE-), WORKS BY.
Crown 8vo, 1s. each; cloth limp, 1s. 6d. each.
ONE THOUSAND MEDICAL MAXIMS AND SURGICAL HINTS.
NURSERY HINTS: A Mother's Guide in Health and Disease.
FOODS FOR THE FAT: A Treatise on Corpulency, and a Dietary for its Cure.

AIDS TO LONG LIFE. Crown 8vo, 2s.; cloth limp, 2s. 6d.

DAVIES' (SIR JOHN) COMPLETE POETICAL WORKS, including Psalms I. to L. in Verse, and other hitherto Unpublished MSS., for the first time Collected and Edited, with Memorial-Introduction and Notes, by the Rev. A. B. GROSART, D.D. Two Vols., crown 8vo, cloth boards, 12s.

DE MAISTRE.—A JOURNEY ROUND MY ROOM. By XAVIER DE MAISTRE. Translated by HENRY ATTWELL. Post 8vo. cloth limp, **2s. 6d.**

DE MILLE.—A CASTLE IN SPAIN. By JAMES DE MILLE. With a Frontispiece. Crown 8vo, cloth extra, **3s. 6d.**; post 8vo, illustrated boards, **2s.**

DERBY (THE).—THE BLUE RIBBON OF THE TURF: A Chronicle of the RACE FOR THE DERBY, from Diomed to Donovan. With Notes on the Winning Horses, the Men who trained them, Jockeys who rode them, and Gentlemen to whom they belonged; also Notices of the Betting and Betting Men of the period, and Brief Accounts of THE OAKS. By LOUIS HENRY CURZON. Cr. 8vo, cloth extra, **6s.**

DERWENT (LEITH), NOVELS BY. Cr. 8vo, cl., **3s. 6d.** ea.; post 8vo, bds., **2s. ea.**
OUR LADY OF TEARS. | CIRCE'S LOVERS.

DICKENS (CHARLES), NOVELS BY. Post 8vo, illustrated boards, **2s.** each.
SKETCHES BY BOZ. | NICHOLAS NICKLEBY.
THE PICKWICK PAPERS. | OLIVER TWIST.

THE SPEECHES OF CHARLES DICKENS, 1841-1870. With a New Bibliography. Edited by RICHARD HERNE SHEPHERD. Crown 8vo, cloth extra, **6s.**—Also a SMALLER EDITION, in the *Mayfair Library*, post 8vo, cloth limp, **2s. 6d.**
ABOUT ENGLAND WITH DICKENS. By ALFRED RIMMER. With 57 Illustrations by C. A. VANDERHOOF, ALFRED RIMMER, and others. Sq. 8vo, cloth extra, **7s. 6d.**

DICTIONARIES.
A DICTIONARY OF MIRACLES: Imitative, Realistic, and Dogmatic. By the Rev. E. C. BREWER, LL.D. Crown 8vo, cloth extra, **7s. 6d.**
THE READER'S HANDBOOK OF ALLUSIONS, REFERENCES, PLOTS, AND STORIES. By the Rev. E. C. BREWER, LL.D. With an ENGLISH BIBLIOGRAPHY. Fifteenth Thousand. Crown 8vo, cloth extra, **7s. 6d.**
AUTHORS AND THEIR WORKS, WITH THE DATES. Cr. 8vo, cloth limp, **2s.**
FAMILIAR SHORT SAYINGS OF GREAT MEN. With Historical and Explanatory Notes. By SAMUEL A. BENT, A.M. Crown 8vo, cloth extra, **7s. 6d.**
SLANG DICTIONARY: Etymological, Historical, and Anecdotal. Cr. 8vo, cl., **6s. 6d.**
WOMEN OF THE DAY: A Biographical Dictionary. By F. HAYS. Cr. 8vo, cl., **5s.**
WORDS, FACTS, AND PHRASES: A Dictionary of Curious, Quaint, and Out-of-the-Way Matters. By ELIEZER EDWARDS. Crown 8vo, cloth extra, **7s. 6d.**

DIDEROT.—THE PARADOX OF ACTING. Translated, with Annotations, from Diderot's "Le Paradoxe sur le Comédien," by WALTER HERRIES POLLOCK. With a Preface by HENRY IRVING. Crown 8vo, parchment, **4s. 6d.**

DOBSON (AUSTIN), WORKS BY.
THOMAS BEWICK & HIS PUPILS. With 95 Illustrations. Square 8vo, cloth, **6s.**
FOUR FRENCHWOMEN: MADEMOISELLE DE CORDAY, MADAME ROLAND, THE PRINCESS DE LAMBALLE; MADAME DE GENLIS. Fcap. 8vo, hf. roxburghe, **2s. 6d.**

DOBSON (W. T.), WORKS BY. Post 8vo, cloth limp, **2s. 6d.** each.
LITERARY FRIVOLITIES, FANCIES, FOLLIES, AND FROLICS.
POETICAL INGENUITIES AND ECCENTRICITIES.

DONOVAN (DICK), DETECTIVE STORIES BY.
Post 8vo, illustrated boards, **2s.** each, cloth limp, **2s. 6d.** each.
THE MAN-HUNTER. | TRACKED AND TAKEN.
CAUGHT AT LAST! | WHO POISONED HETTY DUNCAN?
A DETECTIVE'S TRIUMPHS. [*Preparing.*
THE MAN FROM MANCHESTER. With 23 Illustrations. Crown 8vo, cloth, **6s.**; post 8vo, illustrated boards, **2s.**

DOYLE (A. CONAN, Author of "Micah Clarke"), NOVELS BY.
THE FIRM OF GIRDLESTONE. Crown 8vo, cloth extra, **6s.**
STRANGE SECRETS. Told by CONAN DOYLE, PERCY FITZGERALD, FLORENCE MARRYAT, &c. Cr. 8vo, cl. ex., Eight Illusts., **6s.**; post 8vo, illust. bds., **2s.**

DRAMATISTS, THE OLD. With Vignette Portraits. Cr. 8vo, cl. ex., **6s.** per Vol.
BEN JONSON'S WORKS. With Notes Critical and Explanatory, and a Biographical Memoir by WM. GIFFORD. Edited by Col. CUNNINGHAM. Three Vols.
CHAPMAN'S WORKS. Complete in Three Vols. Vol. I. contains the Plays complete; Vol. II., Poems and Minor Translations, with an Introductory Essay by A. C. SWINBURNE; Vol. III., Translations of the Iliad and Odyssey.
MARLOWE'S WORKS. Edited, with Notes, by Col. CUNNINGHAM. One Vol.
MASSINGER'S PLAYS. From Gifford's Text. Edit. by Col. CUNNINGHAM. One Vol.

DUNCAN (SARA JEANNETTE), WORKS BY.
A SOCIAL DEPARTURE: How Orthodocia and I Went round the World by Ourselves. With 111 Illustrations by F. H. TOWNSEND. Crown 8vo, cloth, 7s. 6d.
AN AMERICAN GIRL IN LONDON. With 80 Illustrations by F. H. TOWNSEND. Crown 8vo, cloth extra, 7s. 6d. [*Preparing.*

DYER.—THE FOLK-LORE OF PLANTS. By Rev. T. F. THISELTON DYER, M.A. Crown 8vo, cloth extra, 6s.

EARLY ENGLISH POETS. Edited, with Introductions and Annotations, by Rev. A. B. GROSART, D.D. Crown 8vo, cloth boards, 6s. per Volume.
FLETCHER'S (GILES) COMPLETE POEMS. One Vol.
DAVIES' (SIR JOHN) COMPLETE POETICAL WORKS. Two Vols.
HERRICK'S (ROBERT) COMPLETE COLLECTED POEMS. Three Vols.
SIDNEY'S (SIR PHILIP) COMPLETE POETICAL WORKS. Three Vols.

EDGCUMBE.—ZEPHYRUS : A Holiday in Brazil and on the River Plate.
By E. R. PEARCE EDGCUMBE. With 41 Illustrations. Crown 8vo, cloth extra, 5s.

EDWARDES (MRS. ANNIE), NOVELS BY:
A POINT OF HONOUR. Post 8vo, illustrated boards, 2s.
ARCHIE LOVELL. Crown 8vo, cloth extra, 3s. 6d. ; post 8vo, illust. boards, 2s.

EDWARDS (ELIEZER).—WORDS, FACTS, AND PHRASES: A
Dictionary of Curious, Quaint, and Out-of-the-Way Matters. By ELIEZER EDWARDS. Crown 8vo, cloth extra, 7s. 6d.

EDWARDS (M. BETHAM-), NOVELS BY.
KITTY. Post 8vo, illustrated boards, 2s. ; cloth limp, 2s. 6d.
FELICIA. Post 8vo, illustrated boards, 2s.

EGGLESTON (EDWARD).—ROXY : A Novel. Post 8vo, illust. bds., 2s.

EMANUEL.—ON DIAMONDS AND PRECIOUS STONES: Their History, Value, and Properties ; with Simple Tests for ascertaining their Reality. By HARRY EMANUEL, F.R.G.S. With Illustrations, tinted and plain. Cr. 8vo, cl. ex., 6s.

ENGLISHMAN'S HOUSE, THE: A Practical Guide to all interested in Selecting or Building a House ; with Estimates of Cost, Quantities, &c. By C. J. RICHARDSON. With Coloured Frontispiece and 600 Illusts. Crown 8vo, cloth, 7s. 6d.

EWALD (ALEX. CHARLES, F.S.A.), WORKS BY.
THE LIFE AND TIMES OF PRINCE CHARLES STUART, Count of Albany (THE YOUNG PRETENDER). With a Portrait. Crown 8vo, cloth extra, 7s. 6d.
STORIES FROM THE STATE PAPERS. With an Autotype. Crown 8vo, cloth, 6s.

EYES, OUR : How to Preserve Them from Infancy to Old Age. By JOHN BROWNING, F.R.A.S. With 70 Illusts. Eleventh Edition. Crown 8vo, cl., 1s.

FAMILIAR SHORT SAYINGS OF GREAT MEN. By SAMUEL ARTHUR BENT, A.M. Fifth Edition, Revised and Enlarged. Crown 8vo, cloth extra, 7s. 6d.

FARADAY (MICHAEL), WORKS BY. Post 8vo, cloth extra, 4s. 6d. each.
THE CHEMICAL HISTORY OF A CANDLE: Lectures delivered before a Juvenile Audience. Edited by WILLIAM CROOKES, F.C.S. With numerous Illustrations.
ON THE VARIOUS FORCES OF NATURE, AND THEIR RELATIONS TO EACH OTHER. Edited by WILLIAM CROOKES, F.C.S. With Illustrations.

FARRER (J. ANSON), WORKS BY.
MILITARY MANNERS AND CUSTOMS. Crown 8vo, cloth extra, 6s.
WAR: Three Essays, reprinted from "Military Manners." Cr. 8vo, 1s.; cl., 1s. 6d.

FELLOW (A) OF TRINITY : A Novel. By ALAN ST. AUBYN. With a "Note" by OLIVER WENDELL HOLMES, and a Frontispiece. Crown 8vo, cloth extra, 3s. 6d. ; post 8vo, illustrated boards, 2s.

FICTION.—A CATALOGUE OF NEARLY SIX HUNDRED WORKS OF FICTION published by CHATTO & WINDUS, with a Short Critical Notice of each (40 pages, demy 8vo), will be sent free upon application.

FIN-BEC.—THE CUPBOARD PAPERS: Observations on the Art of Living and Dining. By FIN-BEC. Post 8vo, cloth limp, 2s. 6d.

FIREWORKS, THE COMPLETE ART OF MAKING ; or, The Pyro-
technist's Treasury. By THOMAS KENTISH. With 267 Illustrations. Cr. 8vo, cl., 5s.

FITZGERALD (PERCY, M.A., F.S.A.), WORKS BY.
THE WORLD BEHIND THE SCENES. Crown 8vo, cloth extra, 3s. 6d.
LITTLE ESSAYS: Passages from Letters of CHARLES LAMB. Post 8vo, cl., 2s. 6d.
A DAY'S TOUR: Journey through France and Belgium. With Sketches. Cr. 4to, 1s.
FATAL ZERO. Crown 8vo, cloth extra, 3s. 6d.; post 8vo, illustrated boards, 2s.

Post 8vo, illustrated boards, 2s. each.
BELLA DONNA. | LADY OF BRANTOME. | THE SECOND MRS. TILLOTSON.
POLLY. | NEVER FORGOTTEN. | SEVENTY-FIVE BROOKE STREET.

LIFE OF JAMES BOSWELL (of Auchinleck). With an Account of his Sayings,
Doings, and Writings. Two Vols., demy 8vo, cloth extra, with Illustrations,
24s. [*Preparing.*

FLETCHER'S (GILES, B.D.) COMPLETE POEMS: Christ's Victorie
in Heaven, Christ's Victorie on Earth, Christ's Triumph over Death, and Minor
Poems. With Notes by Rev. A. B GROSART, D D. Crown 8vo, cloth boards, 6s.

FLUDYER (HARRY) AT CAMBRIDGE: A Series of Family Letters.
Post 8vo, picture cover, 1s.; cloth limp, 1s. 6d.

FONBLANQUE (ALBANY).—FILTHY LUCRE. Post 8vo, illust bds., 2s.

FRANCILLON (R. E.), NOVELS BY.
Crown 8vo, cloth extra, 3s. 6d. each, post 8vo, illustrated boards, 2s. each.
ONE BY ONE. | QUEEN COPHETUA. | A REAL QUEEN. | KING OR KNAVE?
OLYMPIA. Post 8vo, illust bds., 2s. | ESTHER'S GLOVE. Fcap. 8vo, pict. cover, 1s.
ROMANCES OF THE LAW. Crown 8vo, cloth, 6s.; post 8vo, illust boards, 2s.

FREDERIC (HAROLD), NOVELS BY.
SETH'S BROTHER'S WIFE. Post 8vo, illustrated boards, 2s.
THE LAWTON GIRL. With Frontispiece by F. BARNARD. Cr. 8vo, cloth ex., 6s.;
post 8vo, illustrated boards, 2s.

FRENCH LITERATURE, A HISTORY OF. By HENRY VAN LAUN.
Three Vols., demy 8vo, cloth boards, 7s. 6d. each.

FRENZENY.—FIFTY YEARS ON THE TRAIL: Adventures of JOHN
Y. NELSON, Scout, Guide, and Interpreter. By HARRINGTON O'REILLY. With 100
Illustrations by PAUL FRENZENY. Crown 8vo, 3s. 6d.; cloth extra, 4s. 6d.

FRERE.—PANDURANG HARI; or, Memoirs of a Hindoo. With a
Preface by Sir H. BARTLE FRERE, G.C.S.I., &c. Crown 8vo, cloth extra, 3s. 6d.

FRISWELL (HAIN).—ONE OF TWO: A Novel. Post 8vo, illust bds., 2s.

FROST (THOMAS), WORKS BY. Crown 8vo, cloth extra, 3s. 6d. each.
CIRCUS LIFE AND CIRCUS CELEBRITIES. | LIVES OF THE CONJURERS.
THE OLD SHOWMEN AND THE OLD LONDON FAIRS.

FRY'S (HERBERT) ROYAL GUIDE TO THE LONDON CHARITIES.
Showing their Name, Date of Foundation, Objects, Income, Officials, &c. Edited
by JOHN LANE. Published Annually. Crown 8vo, cloth, 1s. 6d.

GARDENING BOOKS. Post 8vo, 1s. each; cloth limp, 1s. 6d. each.
A YEAR'S WORK IN GARDEN AND GREENHOUSE: Practical Advice as to the
Management of the Flower, Fruit, and Frame Garden. By GEORGE GLENNY.
OUR KITCHEN GARDEN: Plants, and How we Cook Them. By TOM JERROLD.
HOUSEHOLD HORTICULTURE. By TOM and JANE JERROLD. Illustrated.
THE GARDEN THAT PAID THE RENT. By TOM JERROLD.

MY GARDEN WILD, AND WHAT I GREW THERE. By FRANCIS G. HEATH.
Crown 8vo, cloth extra, gilt edges, 6s.

GARRETT.—THE CAPEL GIRLS: A Novel. By EDWARD GARRETT.
Crown 8vo, cloth extra 3s. 6d.; post 8vo, illustrated boards, 2s.

GENTLEMAN'S MAGAZINE, THE. 1s. Monthly. In addition to the
Articles upon subjects in Literature, Science, and Art, for which this Magazine has
so high a reputation, "TABLE TALK" by SYLVANUS URBAN appears monthly.
** Bound Volumes for recent years kept in stock, 8s. 6d. each. Cases for binding, 2s.

GENTLEMAN'S ANNUAL, THE. Published Annually in November. 1s.

GERMAN POPULAR STORIES. Collected by the Brothers GRIMM and Translated by EDGAR TAYLOR. With Introduction by JOHN RUSKIN, and 22 Steel Plates by GEORGE CRUIKSHANK. Square 8vo. cloth, **6s. 6d.**; gilt edges, **7s. 6d.**

GIBBON (CHARLES), NOVELS BY. Crown 8vo, cloth extra, **3s. 6d.** each; post 8vo, illustrated boards, **2s.** each.

ROBIN GRAY. | LOVING A DREAM.
QUEEN OF THE MEADOW.
THE FLOWER OF THE FOREST.

THE GOLDEN SHAFT.
OF HIGH DEGREE.
IN HONOUR BOUND.

Post 8vo, illustrated boards, **2s.** each.

THE DEAD HEART.
FOR LACK OF GOLD.
WHAT WILL THE WORLD SAY?
FOR THE KING. | BLOOD-MONEY.
IN PASTURES GREEN.
IN LOVE AND WAR.

A HEART'S PROBLEM.
BY MEAD AND STREAM.
THE BRAES OF YARROW.
FANCY FREE.
A HARD KNOT.
HEART'S DELIGHT.

GIBNEY (SOMERVILLE).—SENTENCED! Cr. 8vo, 1s.; cl, 1s. 6d.

GILBERT (WILLIAM), NOVELS BY. Post 8vo, illustrated boards, **2s.** each.

DR. AUSTIN'S GUESTS.
THE WIZARD OF THE MOUNTAIN.

JAMES DUKE, COSTERMONGER.

GILBERT (W. S.), ORIGINAL PLAYS BY. In Two Series, each complete in itself, price **2s. 6d.** each. The FIRST SERIES contains: The Wicked World—Pygmalion and Galatea—Charity—The Princess—The Palace of Truth—Trial by Jury. The SECOND SERIES. Broken Hearts—Engaged—Sweethearts—Gretchen—Dan'l Druce—Tom Cobb—H.M.S. "Pinafore"—The Sorcerer—Pirates of Penzance.

EIGHT ORIGINAL COMIC OPERAS written by W. S. GILBERT. Containing: The Sorcerer—H.M.S. "Pinafore"—Pirates of Penzance—Iolanthe—Patience—Princess Ida—The Mikado—Trial by Jury. Demy 8vo, cloth limp, **2s. 6d.**

THE **"GILBERT AND SULLIVAN" BIRTHDAY BOOK:** Quotations for Every Day in the Year, Selected from Plays by W. S. GILBERT set to Music by SIR A. SULLIVAN. Compiled by ALEX. WATSON. Royal 16mo. Jap. leather, **2s. 6d.**

GLANVILLE.—THE LOST HEIRESS: A Tale of Love and Battle. By ERNEST GLANVILLE. 2 Illusts. by HUME NISBET. Cr. 8vo, cloth extra, **3s. 6d.**

GLENNY.—A YEAR'S WORK IN GARDEN AND GREENHOUSE: Practical Advice to Amateur Gardeners as to the Management of the Flower, Fruit, and Frame Garden. By GEORGE GLENNY. Post 8vo, **1s.**; cloth limp, **1s. 6d.**

GODWIN.—LIVES OF THE NECROMANCERS. By WILLIAM GODWIN. Post 8vo, cloth limp, **2s.**

GOLDEN TREASURY OF THOUGHT, THE: An Encyclopædia of QUOTATIONS. Edited by THEODORE TAYLOR. Crown 8vo, cloth gilt, **7s. 6d.**

GOWING.—FIVE THOUSAND MILES IN A SLEDGE: A Midwinter Journey Across Siberia. By LIONEL F. GOWING. With 30 Illustrations by C. J. UREN, and a Map by E. WELLER. Large crown 8vo, cloth extra. **8s.**

GRAHAM. — THE PROFESSOR'S WIFE: A Story. By LEONARD GRAHAM. Fcap. 8vo, picture cover, **1s.**

GREEKS AND ROMANS, THE LIFE OF THE, described from Antique Monuments By ERNST GUHL and W. KONER. Edited by Dr. F. HUEFFER. With 545 Illustrations. Large crown 8vo, cloth extra, **7s. 6d.**

GREENWOOD (JAMES), WORKS BY. Cr. 8vo, cloth extra, **3s. 6d.** each.
THE WILDS OF LONDON. | LOW-LIFE DEEPS.

GREVILLE (HENRY), NOVELS BY:
NIKANOR. Translated by ELIZA E. CHASE With 8 Illusts Cr. 8vo, cl. extra, **6s.**
A NOBLE WOMAN. Translated by ALBERT D VANDAM. Crown 8vo, cloth extra **5s.**; post 8vo, illustrated boards, **2s.**

HABBERTON (JOHN, Author of "Helen's Babies"). **NOVELS BY,** Post 8vo, illustrated boards **2s.** each, cloth limp, **2s. 6d.** each.
BRUETON'S BAYOU. | COUNTRY LUCK.

HAIR, THE : Its Treatment in Health, Weakness, and Disease. Translated from the German of Dr. J. PINCUS. Crown 8vo, **1s.**; cloth limp, **1s. 6d.**

HAKE (DR. THOMAS GORDON), POEMS BY. Cr. 8vo, cl. ex., **6s.** each.
NEW SYMBOLS. | LEGENDS OF THE MORROW. | THE SERPENT PLAY.

MAIDEN ECSTASY. Small 4to, cloth extra, **8s.**

HALL.—SKETCHES OF IRISH CHARACTER. By Mrs. S. C. HALL. With numerous Illustrations on Steel and Wood by MACLISE, GILBERT, HARVEY, and GEORGE CRUIKSHANK. Medium 8vo, cloth extra, **7s. 6d.**

HALLIDAY (ANDR.).—EVERY-DAY PAPERS. Post 8vo, bds., 2s.

HANDWRITING, THE PHILOSOPHY OF. With over 100 Facsimiles and Explanatory Text. By DON FELIX DE SALAMANCA. Post 8vo, cloth limp, **2s. 6d.**

HANKY-PANKY : A Collection of Very Easy Tricks, Very Difficult Tricks, White Magic, Sleight of Hand. &c. Edited by W. H. CREMER. With 200 Illustrations. Crown 8vo, cloth extra, **4s. 6d.**

HARDY (LADY DUFFUS). — PAUL WYNTER'S SACRIFICE. By Lady DUFFUS HARDY. Post 8vo, illustrated boards, **2s.**

HARDY (THOMAS). — UNDER THE GREENWOOD TREE. By THOMAS HARDY, Author of "Far from the Madding Crowd." Post 8vo, illust bds , **2s.**

HARWOOD.—THE TENTH EARL. By J. BERWICK HARWOOD. Post 8vo, illustrated boards, **2s.**

HAWEIS (MRS. H. R.), WORKS BY. Square 8vo, cloth extra, **6s.** each.
THE ART OF BEAUTY. With Coloured Frontispiece and 91 Illustrations.
THE ART OF DECORATION. With Coloured Frontispiece and 74 Illustrations.
CHAUCER FOR CHILDREN. With 8 Coloured Plates and 30 Woodcuts.

THE ART OF DRESS. With 32 Illustrations. Post 8vo, **1s.** ; cloth, **1s. 6d.**
CHAUCER FOR SCHOOLS. Demy 8vo, cloth limp, **2s. 6d.**

HAWEIS (Rev. H. R., M.A.). —AMERICAN HUMORISTS : WASHINGTON IRVING, OLIVER WENDELL HOLMES, JAMES RUSSELL LOWELL, ARTEMUS WARD, MARK TWAIN, and BRET HARTE. Third Edition. Crown 8vo, cloth extra. **6s.**

HAWLEY SMART.—WITHOUT LOVE OR LICENCE : A Novel. By HAWLEY SMART Crown 8vo, cloth extra, **3s. 6d.**

HAWTHORNE. — OUR OLD HOME. By NATHANIEL HAWTHORNE. Annotated with Passages from the Author's Note-book, and Illustrated with 31 Photogravures. Two Vols., crown 8vo, buckram, gilt top, **15s.**

HAWTHORNE (JULIAN), NOVELS BY. Crown 8vo, cloth extra, **3s. 6d.** each ; post 8vo, illustrated boards, **2s.** each.
GARTH. | ELLICE QUENTIN. | BEATRIX RANDOLPH. | DUST.
SEBASTIAN STROME. | DAVID POINDEXTER.
FORTUNE'S FOOL. | THE SPECTRE OF THE CAMERA.
Post 8vo, illustrated boards, **2s.** each.
MISS CADOGNA. | LOVE—OR A NAME.

MRS. GAINSBOROUGH'S DIAMONDS. Fcap. 8vo, illustrated cover, **1s.**
A DREAM AND A FORGETTING. Post 8vo, cloth limp, **1s. 6d.**

HAYS.—WOMEN OF THE DAY : A Biographical Dictionary of Notable Contemporaries. By FRANCES HAYS. Crown 8vo, cloth extra, **5s.**

HEATH.—MY GARDEN WILD, AND WHAT I GREW THERE. By FRANCIS GEORGE HEATH. Crown 8vo, cloth extra, gilt edges, **6s.**

HELPS (SIR ARTHUR), WORKS BY. Post 8vo, cloth limp, **2s. 6d.** each.
ANIMALS AND THEIR MASTERS. | SOCIAL PRESSURE.

IVAN DE BIRON : A Novel. Cr. 8vo, cl. extra, **3s. 6d.** ; post 8vo, illust. bds , **2s.**

HENDERSON.—AGATHA PAGE : A Novel. By ISAAC HENDERSON. Crown 8vo, cloth extra, **3s. 6d.**

HERRICK'S (ROBERT) HESPERIDES, NOBLE NUMBERS, AND COMPLETE COLLECTED POEMS. With Memorial-Introduction and Notes by the Rev. A. B. GROSART, D.D.; Steel Portrait, &c. Three Vols., crown 8vo, cl. bds., **18s.**

HERTZKA.—FREELAND : A Social Anticipation. By Dr. THEODOR HERTZKA. Translated by ARTHUR RANSOM. Crown 8vo, cloth extra, **6s.**

HESSE-WARTEGG.—TUNIS : The Land and the People. By Chevalier ERNST VON HESSE-WARTEGG. With 22 Illustrations. Cr. 8vo, cloth extra, **3s. 6d.**

HINDLEY (CHARLES), WORKS BY.
TAVERN ANECDOTES AND SAYINGS: Including the Origin of Signs, and Reminiscences connected with Taverns, Coffee Houses, Clubs, &c. With Illustrations. Crown 8vo, cloth extra, **3s. 6d.**
THE LIFE AND ADVENTURES OF A CHEAP JACK. By ONE OF THE FRATERNITY. Edited by CHARLES HINDLEY. Crown 8vo, cloth extra, **3s. 6d.**

HOEY.—THE LOVER'S CREED. By Mrs. CASHEL HOEY. Post 8vo, illustrated boards, **2s.**

HOLLINGSHEAD (JOHN).—NIAGARA SPRAY. Crown 8vo, **1s.**

HOLMES.—THE SCIENCE OF VOICE PRODUCTION AND VOICE PRESERVATION: A Popular Manual for the Use of Speakers and Singers. By GORDON HOLMES, M.D. With Illustrations. Crown 8vo, **1s.;** cloth, **1s. 6d.**

HOLMES (OLIVER WENDELL), WORKS BY.
THE AUTOCRAT OF THE BREAKFAST-TABLE. Illustrated by J. GORDON THOMSON. Post 8vo, cloth limp, **2s. 6d.**—Another Edition, in smaller type, with an Introduction by G. A. SALA. Post 8vo, cloth limp, **2s.**
THE PROFESSOR AT THE BREAKFAST-TABLE. Post 8vo, cloth limp, **2s.**

HOOD'S (THOMAS) CHOICE WORKS, in Prose and Verse. With Life of the Author, Portrait, and 200 Illustrations. Crown 8vo, cloth extra, **7s. 6d.**
HOOD'S WHIMS AND ODDITIES. With 85 Illustrations. Post 8vo, printed on laid paper and half-bound, **2s.**

HOOD (TOM).—FROM NOWHERE TO THE NORTH POLE: A Noah's Arkæological Narrative. By TOM HOOD. With 25 Illustrations by W. BRUNTON and E. C. BARNES. Square 8vo, cloth extra, gilt edges, **6s.**

HOOK'S (THEODORE) CHOICE HUMOROUS WORKS; including his Ludicrous Adventures, Bons Mots, Puns, and Hoaxes. With Life of the Author, Portraits, Facsimiles, and Illustrations. Crown 8vo, cloth extra, **7s. 6d.**

HOOPER.—THE HOUSE OF RABY : A Novel. By Mrs. GEORGE HOOPER. Post 8vo, illustrated boards, **2s.**

HOPKINS.—"'TWIXT LOVE AND DUTY :" A Novel. By TIGHE HOPKINS. Post 8vo, illustrated boards, **2s.**

HORNE. — ORION : An Epic Poem. By RICHARD HENGIST HORNE. With Photographic Portrait by SUMMERS. Tenth Edition. Cr 8vo, cloth extra, **7s.**

HORSE (THE) AND HIS RIDER : An Anecdotic Medley. By "THORMANBY." Crown 8vo, cloth extra, **6s.**

HUNT.—ESSAYS BY LEIGH HUNT : A TALE FOR A CHIMNEY CORNER, and other Pieces. Edited, with an Introduction, by EDMUND OLLIER. Post 8vo, printed on laid paper and half-bd., **2s.** Also in sm. sq. 8vo, cl. extra, at same price.

HUNT (MRS. ALFRED), NOVELS BY.
Crown 8vo, cloth extra, **3s. 6d.** each; post 8vo, illustrated boards, **2s.** each.
THE LEADEN CASKET. | SELF-CONDEMNED. | THAT OTHER PERSON.
THORNICROFT'S MODEL. Post 8vo, illustrated boards, **2s.**

HYDROPHOBIA : An Account of M. PASTEUR's System. Containing a Translation of all his Communications on the Subject, the Technique of his Method, and Statistics. By RENAUD SUZOR, M.B. Crown 8vo, cloth extra, **6s.**

INGELOW (JEAN).—FATED TO BE FREE. With 24 Illustrations by G. J. PINWELL. Cr. 8vo, cloth extra, **3s. 6d.;** post 8vo, illustrated boards, **2s.**

INDOOR PAUPERS. By ONE OF THEM. Crown 8vo, **1s.;** cloth, **1s. 6d.**

IRISH WIT AND HUMOUR, SONGS OF. Collected and Edited by A. PERCEVAL GRAVES. Post 8vo, cloth limp, **2s. 6d.**

JAMES.—A ROMANCE OF THE QUEEN'S HOUNDS. By CHARLES JAMES. Post 8vo, picture cover, **1s.**; cloth limp, **1s. 6d.**

JANVIER.—PRACTICAL KERAMICS FOR STUDENTS. By CATHERINE A. JANVIER. Crown 8vo, cloth extra, **6s.**

JAY (HARRIETT), NOVELS BY. Post 8vo, illustrated boards, **2s.** each.
THE DARK COLLEEN. | THE QUEEN OF CONNAUGHT.

JEFFERIES (RICHARD), WORKS BY. Post 8vo, cloth limp, **2s. 6d.** each
NATURE NEAR LONDON. | THE LIFE OF THE FIELDS. | THE OPEN AIR.
THE EULOGY OF RICHARD JEFFERIES. By WALTER BESANT. Second Edition. With a Photograph Portrait. Crown 8vo, cloth extra, **6s.**

JENNINGS (H. J.), WORKS BY.
CURIOSITIES OF CRITICISM. Post 8vo, cloth limp, **2s. 6d.**
LORD TENNYSON: A Biographical Sketch. With a Photograph. Cr. 8vo, cl, **6s.**

JEROME. — STAGELAND: Curious Habits and Customs of its Inhabitants. By JEROME K. JEROME. With 64 Illustrations by J. BERNARD PARTRIDGE. Sixteenth Thousand. Fcap. 4to, cloth extra, **3s. 6d.**

JERROLD.—THE BARBER'S CHAIR; & THE HEDGEHOG LETTERS. By DOUGLAS JERROLD. Post 8vo, printed on laid paper and half-bound, **2s.**

JERROLD (TOM), WORKS BY. Post 8vo, **1s.** each; cloth limp, **1s. 6d.** each.
THE GARDEN THAT PAID THE RENT.
HOUSEHOLD HORTICULTURE: A Gossip about Flowers. Illustrated.
OUR KITCHEN GARDEN: The Plants we Grow, and How we Cook Them.

JESSE.—SCENES AND OCCUPATIONS OF A COUNTRY LIFE. By EDWARD JESSE. Post 8vo, cloth limp, **2s.**

JONES (WILLIAM, F.S.A.), WORKS BY. Cr. 8vo, cl. extra, **7s. 6d.** each.
FINGER-RING LORE: Historical, Legendary, and Anecdotal. With nearly 300 Illustrations. Second Edition, Revised and Enlarged.
CREDULITIES, PAST AND PRESENT. Including the Sea and Seamen, Miners, Talismans, Word and Letter Divination, Exorcising and Blessing of Animals, Birds, Eggs, Luck, &c. With an Etched Frontispiece.
CROWNS AND CORONATIONS: A History of Regalia. With 100 Illustrations.

JONSON'S (BEN) WORKS. With Notes Critical and Explanatory, and a Biographical Memoir by WILLIAM GIFFORD. Edited by Colonel CUNNINGHAM. Three Vols., crown 8vo cloth extra, **6s.** each.

JOSEPHUS, THE COMPLETE WORKS OF. Translated by WHISTON. Containing "The Antiquities of the Jews" and "The Wars of the Jews." With 52 Illustrations and Maps. Two Vols., demy 8vo, half-bound, **12s. 6d.**

KEMPT.—PENCIL AND PALETTE: Chapters on Art and Artists. By ROBERT KEMPT. Post 8vo, cloth limp, **2s. 6d.**

KERSHAW. — COLONIAL FACTS AND FICTIONS: Humorous Sketches. By MARK KERSHAW. Post 8vo, illustrated boards, **2s.**; cloth, **2s. 6d.**

KEYSER. — CUT BY THE MESS: A Novel. By ARTHUR KEYSER. Crown 8vo, picture cover, **1s.**; cloth limp, **1s. 6d.**

KING (R. ASHE), NOVELS BY. Cr. 8vo, cl., **3s. 6d.** ea., post 8vo, bds., **2s.** ea.
A DRAWN GAME. | "THE WEARING OF THE GREEN."
PASSION'S SLAVE. Post 8vo, illustrated boards, **2s.**
BELL BARRY. 2 vols., crown 8vo.

KINGSLEY (HENRY), NOVELS BY.
OAKSHOTT CASTLE. Post 8vo, illustrated boards, **2s.**
NUMBER SEVENTEEN. Crown 8vo, cloth extra, **3s. 6d.**

KNIGHTS (THE) OF THE LION: A Romance of the Thirteenth Century. Edited, with an Introduction, by the MARQUESS of LORNE, K.T. Cr. 8vo, cl. ex., **6s.**

KNIGHT.—THE PATIENT'S VADE MECUM: How to Get Most
Benefit from Medical Advice. By WILLIAM KNIGHT, M.R.C.S., and EDWARD
KNIGHT, L.R.C.P. Crown 8vo, 1s.; cloth limp, 1s. 6d.

LAMB'S (CHARLES) COMPLETE WORKS, in Prose and Verse.
Edited, with Notes and Introduction, by R. H. SHEPHERD. With Two Portraits
and Facsimile of a page of the "Essay on Roast Pig." Cr. 8vo, cl. ex., 7s. 6d.
THE ESSAYS OF ELIA. Post 8vo, printed on laid paper and half-bound, 2s.
LITTLE ESSAYS: Sketches and Characters by CHARLES LAMB, selected from his
Letters by PERCY FITZGERALD. Post 8vo, cloth limp, 2s. 6d.

LANDOR.—CITATION AND EXAMINATION OF WILLIAM SHAKS-
PEARE, &c., before Sir THOMAS LUCY, touching Deer-stealing, 19th September, 1582.
To which is added, A CONFERENCE OF MASTER EDMUND SPENSER with the
Earl of Essex, touching the State of Ireland, 1595. By WALTER SAVAGE LANDOR.
Fcap. 8vo, half-Roxburghe, 2s. 6d.

LANE.—THE THOUSAND AND ONE NIGHTS, commonly called in
England THE ARABIAN NIGHTS' ENTERTAINMENTS. Translated from the
Arabic, with Notes, by EDWARD WILLIAM LANE. Illustrated by many hundred
Engravings from Designs by HARVEY. Edited by EDWARD STANLEY POOLE. With a
Preface by STANLEY LANE-POOLE. Three Vols., demy 8vo, cloth extra, 7s. 6d. each.

LARWOOD (JACOB), WORKS BY.
THE STORY OF THE LONDON PARKS. With Illusts. Cr. 8vo, cl. extra, 3s. 6d.
ANECDOTES OF THE CLERGY: The Antiquities, Humours, and Eccentricities of
the Cloth. Post 8vo, printed on laid paper and half-bound, 2s.

Post 8vo, cloth limp, 2s. 6d. each.
FORENSIC ANECDOTES. | THEATRICAL ANECDOTES.

LEIGH (HENRY S.), WORKS BY.
CAROLS OF COCKAYNE. Printed on hand-made paper, bound in buckram, 5s.
JEUX D'ESPRIT. Edited by HENRY S. LEIGH. Post 8vo, cloth limp, 2s. 6d.

LEYS (JOHN).—THE LINDSAYS: A Romance. Post 8vo, illust. bds., 2s.

LIFE IN LONDON; or, The History of JERRY HAWTHORN and COR-
INTHIAN TOM. With CRUIKSHANK's Coloured Illustrations. Crown 8vo, cloth extra,
7s. 6d.   [New Edition preparing.

LINSKILL.—IN EXCHANGE FOR A SOUL. By MARY LINSKILL.
Post 8vo, illustrated boards, 2s.

LINTON (E. LYNN), WORKS BY.   Post 8vo, cloth limp, 2s. 6d. each.
WITCH STORIES. | OURSELVES: ESSAYS ON WOMEN.

Crown 8vo, cloth extra, 3s. 6d. each; post 8vo, illustrated boards, 2s. each.

SOWING THE WIND.	UNDER WHICH LORD?
PATRICIA KEMBALL.	"MY LOVE!"	IONE.
ATONEMENT OF LEAM DUNDAS.	PASTON CAREW, Millionaire & Miser.
THE WORLD WELL LOST.	

Post 8vo, illustrated boards, 2s. each.
THE REBEL OF THE FAMILY. | WITH A SILKEN THREAD.

LONGFELLOW'S POETICAL WORKS. With numerous Illustrations
on Steel and Wood. Crown 8vo, cloth extra, 7s. 6d.

LUCY.—GIDEON FLEYCE: A Novel. By HENRY W. LUCY. Crown
8vo, cloth extra, 3s. 6d.; post 8vo, illustrated boards, 2s.

LUSIAD (THE) OF CAMOENS. Translated into English Spenserian
Verse by ROBERT FFRENCH DUFF. With 14 Plates. Demy 8vo, cloth boards, 18s.

MACALPINE (AVERY), NOVELS BY.
TERESA ITASCA, and other Stories. Crown 8vo, bound in canvas, 2s. 6d.
BROKEN WINGS. With 6 Illusts. by W. J. HENNESSY. Crown 8vo, cloth extra, 6s.

MACCOLL (HUGH), NOVELS BY.
MR. STRANGER'S SEALED PACKET. Second Edition. Crown 8vo, cl. extra, 5s.
EDNOR WHITLOCK. Crown 8vo, cloth extra, 6s.

McCARTHY (JUSTIN, M.P.), WORKS BY.

A HISTORY OF OUR OWN TIMES, from the Accession of Queen Victoria to the General Election of 1880. Four Vols. demy 8vo, cloth extra, **12s.** each.—Also a POPULAR EDITION, in Four Vols., crown 8vo, cloth extra, **6s.** each.—And a JUBILEE EDITION, with an Appendix of Events to the end of 1886, in Two Vols., large crown 8vo, cloth extra, **7s. 6d.** each.

A SHORT HISTORY OF OUR OWN TIMES. One Vol., crown 8vo, cloth extra, **6s.** —Also a CHEAP POPULAR EDITION, post 8vo, cloth limp, **2s. 6d.**

A HISTORY OF THE FOUR GEORGES. Four Vols. demy 8vo, cloth extra, **12s.** each. [Vols. I. & II. *ready*.

Crown 8vo, cloth extra, **3s. 6d.** each; post 8vo, illustrated boards, **2s.** each.

THE WATERDALE NEIGHBOURS.	**MISS MISANTHROPE.**
MY ENEMY'S DAUGHTER.	**DONNA QUIXOTE.**
A FAIR SAXON.	**THE COMET OF A SEASON.**
LINLEY ROCHFORD.	**MAID OF ATHENS.**
DEAR LADY DISDAIN.	**CAMIOLA:** A Girl with a Fortune.

"THE RIGHT HONOURABLE." By JUSTIN McCARTHY, M.P., and Mrs. CAMPBELL-PRAED. Fourth Edition. Crown 8vo, cloth extra, **6s.**

McCARTHY (JUSTIN H., M.P.), WORKS BY.

THE FRENCH REVOLUTION. Four Vols., 8vo, **12s.** each. [Vols. I. & II. *ready*.
AN OUTLINE OF THE HISTORY OF IRELAND. Crown 8vo, **1s.** : cloth, **1s. 6d.**
IRELAND SINCE THE UNION : Irish History, 1798-1886. Crown 8vo, cloth, **6s.**
ENGLAND UNDER GLADSTONE, 1880-85. Crown 8vo, cloth extra, **6s.**

HAFIZ IN LONDON : Poems. Small 8vo, gold cloth, **3s. 6d.**
HARLEQUINADE : Poems. Small 4to, Japanese vellum, **8s.**

OUR SENSATION NOVEL. Crown 8vo, picture cover, **1s.** ; cloth limp, **1s. 6d.**
DOOM ! An Atlantic Episode. Crown 8vo, picture cover, **1s.**
DOLLY : A Sketch. Crown 8vo, picture cover, **1s.** ; cloth limp, **1s. 6d.**
LILY LASS : A Romance. Crown 8vo, picture cover, **1s.** ; cloth limp, **1s. 6d.**

MACDONALD.— WORKS OF FANCY AND IMAGINATION. By GEORGE MACDONALD, LL.D. Ten Vols., cloth extra, gilt edges, in cloth case, **21s.** Or the Vols. may be had separately, bound in grolier cloth, at **2s. 6d.** each.

Vol. I. WITHIN AND WITHOUT.—THE HIDDEN LIFE.
,, II. THE DISCIPLE.—THE GOSPEL WOMEN.—BOOK OF SONNETS.—ORGAN SONGS.
,, III. VIOLIN SONGS.—SONGS OF THE DAYS AND NIGHTS.—A BOOK OF DREAMS.—ROADSIDE POEMS.—POEMS FOR CHILDREN.
,, IV. PARABLES—BALLADS.—SCOTCH SONGS.
,, V. & VI. PHANTASTES: A Faerie Romance. | Vol. VII. THE PORTENT.
,, VIII. THE LIGHT PRINCESS.—THE GIANT'S HEART.—SHADOWS.
,, IX. CROSS PURPOSES.—THE GOLDEN KEY.—THE CARASOYN.—LITTLE DAYLIGHT.
,, X. THE CRUEL PAINTER.—THE WOW O' RIVVEN.—THE CASTLE.—THE BROKEN SWORDS.—THE GRAY WOLF—UNCLE CORNELIUS.

MACDONELL.—QUAKER COUSINS : A Novel. By AGNES MACDONELL. Crown 8vo, cloth extra, **3s. 6d.** ; post 8vo, illustrated boards, **2s.**

MACGREGOR. — PASTIMES AND PLAYERS : Notes on Popular Games. By ROBERT MACGREGOR. Post 8vo, cloth limp, **2s. 6d.**

MACKAY.—INTERLUDES AND UNDERTONES ; or, Music at Twilight. By CHARLES MACKAY, LL.D. Crown 8vo, cloth extra, **6s.**

MACLISE PORTRAIT GALLERY (THE) OF ILLUSTRIOUS LITER-ARY CHARACTERS : 85 PORTRAITS ; with Memoirs — Biographical, Critical, Bibliographical, and Anecdotal—illustrative of the Literature of the former half of the Present Century, by WILLIAM BATES, B.A. Crown 8vo, cloth extra, **7s. 6d.**

MACQUOID (MRS.), WORKS BY. Square 8vo, cloth extra, **7s. 6d.** each.

IN THE ARDENNES. With 50 Illustrations by THOMAS R. MACQUOID.
PICTURES AND LEGENDS FROM NORMANDY AND BRITTANY. With 34 Illustrations by THOMAS R. MACQUOID.
THROUGH NORMANDY. With 92 Illustrations by T. R. MACQUOID, and a Map.
THROUGH BRITTANY. With 35 Illustrations by T. R. MACQUOID, and a Map.
ABOUT YORKSHIRE. With 67 Illustrations by T. R. MACQUOID.

Post 8vo, illustrated boards, **2s.** each.
THE EVIL EYE, and other Stories. | **LOST ROSE,**

MAGIC LANTERN, THE, and its Management: including full Practical Directions for producing the Limelight, making Oxygen Gas, and preparing Lantern Slides. By T. C. HEPWORTH. With 10 Illustrations. Cr. 8vo. **1s.**; cloth. **1s. 6d.**

MAGICIAN'S OWN BOOK, THE: Performances with Cups and Balls, Eggs, Hats, Handkerchiefs, &c. All from actual Experience. Edited by W. H. CREMER. With 200 Illustrations. Crown 8vo, cloth extra, **4s. 6d.**

MAGNA CHARTA: An Exact Facsimile of the Original in the British Museum, 3 feet by 2 feet, with Arms and Seals emblazoned in Gold and Colours, **5s.**

MALLOCK (W. H.), WORKS BY.
THE NEW REPUBLIC. Post 8vo, picture cover, **2s.**; cloth limp, **2s. 6d.**
THE NEW PAUL & VIRGINIA: Positivism on an Island. Post 8vo, cloth, **2s. 6d.**
POEMS. Small 4to, parchment, **8s.**
IS LIFE WORTH LIVING? Crown 8vo, cloth extra, **6s.**

MALLORY'S (SIR THOMAS) MORT D'ARTHUR: The Stories of King Arthur and of the Knights of the Round Table. (A Selection.) Edited by B. MONTGOMERIE RANKING. Post 8vo, cloth limp, **2s.**

MARK TWAIN, WORKS BY. Crown 8vo, cloth extra, **7s. 6d.** each.
THE CHOICE WORKS OF MARK TWAIN. Revised and Corrected throughout by the Author. With Life, Portrait, and numerous Illustrations.
ROUGHING IT, and INNOCENTS AT HOME. With 200 Illusts. by F. A. FRASER.
THE GILDED AGE. By MARK TWAIN and C. D. WARNER. With 212 Illustrations.
MARK TWAIN'S LIBRARY OF HUMOUR. With 197 Illustrations.
A YANKEE AT THE COURT OF KING ARTHUR. With 220 Illusts. by BEARD.

Crown 8vo, cloth extra (illustrated), **7s. 6d.** each; post 8vo, illust. boards, **2s.** each.
THE INNOCENTS ABROAD; or, New Pilgrim's Progress. With 234 Illustrations. (The Two-Shilling Edition is entitled MARK TWAIN'S PLEASURE TRIP.)
THE ADVENTURES OF TOM SAWYER. With 111 Illustrations.
A TRAMP ABROAD. With 314 Illustrations.
THE PRINCE AND THE PAUPER. With 190 Illustrations.
LIFE ON THE MISSISSIPPI. With 300 Illustrations.
ADVENTURES OF HUCKLEBERRY FINN. With 174 Illusts. by E. W. KEMBLE.

THE STOLEN WHITE ELEPHANT, &c. Cr. 8vo, cl., **6s.**; post 8vo, illust. bds., **2s.**

MARLOWE'S WORKS. Including his Translations. Edited, with Notes and Introductions, by Col. CUNNINGHAM. Crown 8vo, cloth extra, **6s.**

MARRYAT (FLORENCE), NOVELS BY. Post 8vo, illust. boards, **2s.** each.
A HARVEST OF WILD OATS. | WRITTEN IN FIRE. | FIGHTING THE AIR.
OPEN! SESAME! Crown 8vo, cloth extra, **3s. 6d.**; post 8vo, picture boards, **2s.**

MASSINGER'S PLAYS. From the Text of WILLIAM GIFFORD. Edited by Col. CUNNINGHAM. Crown 8vo, cloth extra, **6s.**

MASTERMAN.—HALF-A-DOZEN DAUGHTERS: A Novel. By J. MASTERMAN. Post 8vo, illustrated boards, **2s.**

MATTHEWS.—A SECRET OF THE SEA, &c. By BRANDER MATTHEWS. Post 8vo, illustrated boards, **2s.**; cloth limp, **2s. 6d.**

MAYHEW.—LONDON CHARACTERS AND THE HUMOROUS SIDE OF LONDON LIFE. By HENRY MAYHEW. With Illusts. Crown 8vo, cloth, **3s. 6d.**

MENKEN.—INFELICIA: Poems by ADAH ISAACS MENKEN. With Biographical Preface, Illustrations by F. E. LUMMIS and F. O. C. DARLEY, and Facsimile of a Letter from CHARLES DICKENS. Small 4to, cloth extra, **7s. 6d.**

MEXICAN MUSTANG (ON A), through Texas to the Rio Grande. By A. E. SWEET and J. ARMOY KNOX. With 265 Illusts. Cr. 8vo, cloth extra, **7s. 6d.**

MIDDLEMASS (JEAN), NOVELS BY. Post 8vo, illust. boards, **2s.** each.
TOUCH AND GO. | MR. DORILLION.

MILLER.—PHYSIOLOGY FOR THE YOUNG; or, The House of Life: Human Physiology, with its application to the Preservation of Health. By Mrs. F. FENWICK MILLER. With numerous Illustrations. Post 8vo, cloth limp, **2s. 6d.**

MILTON (J. L.), WORKS BY. Post 8vo, 1s. each; cloth, 1s. 6d. each.
THE HYGIENE OF THE SKIN. With Directions for Diet, Soaps, Baths, &c.
THE BATH IN DISEASES OF THE SKIN.
THE LAWS OF LIFE, AND THEIR RELATION TO DISEASES OF THE SKIN.
THE SUCCESSFUL TREATMENT OF LEPROSY. Demy 8vo, 1s.

MINTO (WM.)—WAS SHE GOOD OR BAD? Cr. 8vo, 1s. ; cloth, 1s. 6d.

MOLESWORTH (MRS.), NOVELS BY.
HATHERCOURT RECTORY. Post 8vo, illustrated boards, 2s.
THAT GIRL IN BLACK. Crown 8vo, picture cover, 1s. ; cloth, 1s. 6d.

MOORE (THOMAS), WORKS BY.
THE EPICUREAN; and ALCIPHRON. Post 8vo, half-bound, 2s.
PROSE AND VERSE, Humorous, Satirical, and Sentimental, by THOMAS MOORE,
with Suppressed Passages from the MEMOIRS OF LORD BYRON. Edited by R.
HERNE SHEPHERD. With Portrait. Crown 8vo, cloth extra, 7s. 6d.

MUDDOCK (J. E.), STORIES BY.
STORIES WEIRD AND WONDERFUL. Post 8vo, illust boards, 2s. ; cloth, 2s. 6d.
THE DEAD MAN'S SECRET; or, The Valley of Gold: A Narrative of Strange
Adventure. With a Frontispiece by F. BARNARD. Crown 8vo, cloth extra, 5s. ;
post 8vo, illustrated boards, 2s.

MURRAY (D. CHRISTIE), NOVELS BY.
Crown 8vo, cloth extra, 3s. 6d. each; post 8vo, illustrated boards, 2s. each.

A LIFE'S ATONEMENT.	A MODEL FATHER.	A BIT OF HUMAN NATURE.
JOSEPH'S COAT.	HEARTS.	FIRST PERSON SINGULAR.
COALS OF FIRE.	THE WAY OF THE	CYNIC FORTUNE.
VAL STRANGE.	WORLD.	

BY THE GATE OF THE SEA. Post 8vo, picture boards, 2s.
OLD BLAZER'S HERO. With Three Illustrations by A. McCORMICK. Crown 8vo,
cloth extra, 6s. ; post 8vo, illustrated boards. 2s.

MURRAY (D. CHRISTIE) & HENRY HERMAN, WORKS BY.
Crown 8vo, cloth extra, 6s. each; post 8vo, illustrated boards, 2s. each.
ONE TRAVELLER RETURNS.
PAUL JONES'S ALIAS. With 13 Illustrations by A. FORESTIER and G. NICOLET.
THE BISHOPS' BIBLE. Crown 8vo, cloth extra, 3s. 6d.

MURRAY.—A GAME OF BLUFF: A Novel. By HENRY MURRAY.
Post 8vo, picture boards, 2s. ; cloth limp, 2s. 6d.

NISBET.—"BAIL UP!" A Romance of BUSHRANGERS AND BLACKS.
By HUME NISBET. With Frontispiece and Vignette. Crown 8vo, cloth extra, 3s. 6d.

NOVELISTS.—HALF-HOURS WITH THE BEST NOVELISTS OF
THE CENTURY. Edit. by H. T. MACKENZIE BELL. Cr. 8vo, cl, 3s. 6d. [Preparing.

O'CONNOR. — LORD BEACONSFIELD: A Biography. By T. P.
O'CONNOR, M.P. Sixth Edition, with an Introduction. Crown 8vo, cloth extra, 5s.

O'HANLON (ALICE), NOVELS BY. Post 8vo, illustrated boards, 2s. each.
THE UNFORESEEN. | CHANCE? OR FATE?

OHNET (GEORGES), NOVELS BY.
DOCTOR RAMEAU. Translated by Mrs. CASHEL HOEY With 9 Illustrations by
E. BAYARD. Crown 8vo, cloth extra, 6s. ; post 8vo, illustrated boards, 2s.
A LAST LOVE. Translated by ALBERT D. VANDAM. Crown 8vo, cloth extra, 5s. ;
post 8vo, illustrated boards, 2s.
A WEIRD GIFT. Translated by ALBERT D. VANDAM. Crown 8vo, cloth, 3s. 6d.

OLIPHANT (MRS.), NOVELS BY. Post 8vo, illustrated boards, 2s. each.
THE PRIMROSE PATH. | THE GREATEST HEIRESS IN ENGLAND.
WHITELADIES. With Illustrations by ARTHUR HOPKINS and HENRY WOODS,
A.R.A. Crown 8vo, cloth extra, 3s. 6d. ; post 8vo, illustrated boards, 2s.

O'REILLY (MRS.).—PHŒBE'S FORTUNES. Post 8vo, illust. bds. • 2s.

O'SHAUGHNESSY (ARTHUR), POEMS BY.
LAYS OF FRANCE. Crown 8vo, cloth extra, 10s. 6d.
MUSIC AND MOONLIGHT. Fcap. 8vo, cloth extra, 7s. 6d.
SONGS OF A WORKER. Fcap. 8vo, cloth extra, 7s. 6d.

OUIDA, NOVELS BY. Cr. 8vo, cl., **3s. 6d.** each; post 8vo, illust. bds., **2s.** each.

HELD IN BONDAGE.	FOLLE-FARINE.	MOTHS.
TRICOTRIN.	A DOG OF FLANDERS.	PIPISTRELLO.
STRATHMORE.	PASCAREL.	A VILLAGE COMMUNE.
CHANDOS.	TWO LITTLE WOODEN	IN MAREMMA.
CECIL CASTLEMAINE'S	SHOES.	BIMBI.
GAGE.	SIGNA.	WANDA.
IDALIA.	IN A WINTER CITY.	FRESCOES.
UNDER TWO FLAGS.	ARIADNE.	PRINCESS NAPRAXINE.
PUCK.	FRIENDSHIP.	OTHMAR. | GUILDEROY.

Crown 8vo, cloth extra, **3s. 6d.** each.

SYRLIN. | RUFFINO.

WISDOM, WIT, AND PATHOS, selected from the Works of OUIDA by F. SYDNEY MORRIS. Post 8vo, cloth extra, **5s.**— CHEAP EDITION, Illustrated boards, **2s.**

PAGE (H. A.), WORKS BY.
THOREAU: His Life and Aims. With Portrait. Post 8vo, cloth limp, **2s. 6d.**
ANIMAL ANECDOTES. Arranged on a New Principle. Crown 8vo, cloth extra, **5s.**

PASCAL'S PROVINCIAL LETTERS. A New Translation, with His-
torical Introduction and Notes by T. M'CRIE, D.D. Post 8vo, cloth limp, **2s.**

PAUL.—GENTLE AND SIMPLE. By MARGARET A. PAUL. With Frontis-
piece by HELEN PATERSON. Crown 8vo, cloth, **3s. 6d.**; post 8vo, illust. boards, **2s.**

PAYN (JAMES), NOVELS BY.
Crown 8vo, cloth extra, **3s. 6d.** each; post 8vo, illustrated boards, **2s.** each.

LOST SIR MASSINGBERD.	A GRAPE FROM A THORN.
WALTER'S WORD.	FROM EXILE.
LESS BLACK THAN WE'RE	SOME PRIVATE VIEWS.
PAINTED.	THE CANON'S WARD.
BY PROXY.	THE TALK OF THE TOWN.
HIGH SPIRITS.	HOLIDAY TASKS.
UNDER ONE ROOF.	GLOW-WORM TALES.
A CONFIDENTIAL AGENT.	THE MYSTERY OF MIRBRIDGE.

Post 8vo, illustrated boards, **2s.** each.

HUMOROUS STORIES.	THE CLYFFARDS OF CLYFFE.
THE FOSTER BROTHERS.	FOUND DEAD.
THE FAMILY SCAPEGRACE.	GWENDOLINE'S HARVEST.
MARRIED BENEATH HIM.	A MARINE RESIDENCE.
BENTINCK'S TUTOR.	MIRK ABBEY.
A PERFECT TREASURE.	NOT WOOED, BUT WON.
A COUNTY FAMILY.	TWO HUNDRED POUNDS REWARD.
LIKE FATHER, LIKE SON.	THE BEST OF HUSBANDS.
A WOMAN'S VENGEANCE.	HALVES.
CARLYON'S YEAR. | CECIL'S TRYST.	FALLEN FORTUNES.
MURPHY'S MASTER.	WHAT HE COST HER.
AT HER MERCY.	KIT: A MEMORY. | FOR CASH ONLY.

IN PERIL AND PRIVATION: Stories of MARINE ADVENTURE Re-told. With 17 Illustrations. Crown 8vo, cloth extra, **3s. 6d.**
NOTES FROM THE "NEWS." Crown 8vo, portrait cover, **1s.**; cloth, **1s. 6d.**
THE BURNT MILLION. Crown 8vo, cloth extra, **3s. 6d.**
THE WORD AND THE WILL. Three Vols., crown 8vo.
SUNNY STORIES, and some SHADY ONES. With a Frontispiece by FRED. BARNARD. Crown 8vo, cloth extra, **3s. 6d.** [Shortly.

PENNELL (H. CHOLMONDELEY), WORKS BY. Post 8vo, cl., **2s. 6d.** each.
PUCK ON PEGASUS. With Illustrations.
PEGASUS RE-SADDLED. With Ten full-page Illustrations by G. DU MAURIER.
THE MUSES OF MAYFAIR. Vers de Société, Selected by H. C. PENNELL.

PHELPS (E. STUART), WORKS BY. Post 8vo, **1s.** each; cloth, **1s. 6d.** each.
BEYOND THE GATES. By the Author | AN OLD MAID'S PARADISE.
of "The Gates Ajar." | BURGLARS IN PARADISE.

JACK THE FISHERMAN. Illustrated by C. W. REED. Cr 8vo, **1s.**; cloth, **1s. 6d.**

PIRKIS (C. L.), NOVELS BY.
TROOPING WITH CROWS. Fcap. 8vo, picture cover, **1s.**
LADY LOVELACE. Post 8vo, illustrated boards, **2s.**

PLANCHE (J. R.), WORKS BY.
THE PURSUIVANT OF ARMS; or, Heraldry Founded upon Facts. With Coloured Frontispiece, Five Plates, and 209 Illusts. Crown 8vo, cloth, 7s. 6d.
SONGS AND POEMS, 1819-1879. Introduction by Mrs MACKARNESS. Cr. 8vo, cl, 6s.

PLUTARCH'S LIVES OF ILLUSTRIOUS MEN. Translated from the Greek, with Notes Critical and Historical, and a Life of Plutarch, by JOHN and WILLIAM LANGHORNE. With Portraits. Two Vols., demy 8vo, half-bound, 10s. 6d.

POE'S (EDGAR ALLAN) CHOICE WORKS, in Prose and Poetry. Introduction by CHAS. BAUDELAIRE, Portrait, and Facsimiles. Cr. 8vo, cloth, 7s. 6d.
THE MYSTERY OF MARIE ROGET, &c. Post 8vo, illustrated boards, 2s.

POPE'S POETICAL WORKS. Post 8vo, cloth limp, 2s.

PRICE (E. C.), NOVELS BY.
Crown 8vo, cloth extra, 3s. 6d. each; post 8vo, illustrated boards, 2s. each.
VALENTINA. | THE FOREIGNERS. | MRS. LANCASTER'S RIVAL.
GERALD. Post 8vo, illustrated boards, 2s.

PRINCESS OLGA.—RADNA; or, The Great Conspiracy of 1881. By the Princess OLGA. Crown 8vo, cloth extra, 6s.

PROCTOR (RICHARD A., B.A.), WORKS BY.
FLOWERS OF THE SKY. With 55 Illusts. Small crown 8vo, cloth extra, 3s. 6d.
EASY STAR LESSONS. With Star Maps for Every Night in the Year, Drawings of the Constellations, &c. Crown 8vo, cloth extra, 6s.
FAMILIAR SCIENCE STUDIES. Crown 8vo, cloth extra, 6s.
SATURN AND ITS SYSTEM. With 13 Steel Plates. Demy 8vo, cloth ex, 10s. 6d.
MYSTERIES OF TIME AND SPACE. With Illustrations Cr. 8vo, cloth extra, 6s.
THE UNIVERSE OF SUNS. With numerous Illustrations. Cr. 8vo, cloth ex., 6s.
WAGES AND WANTS OF SCIENCE WORKERS. Crown 8vo, 1s. 6d.

RAMBOSSON.—POPULAR ASTRONOMY. By J RAMBOSSON, Laureate of the Institute of France. With numerous Illusts. Crown 8vo, cloth extra, 7s. 6d.

RANDOLPH.—AUNT ABIGAIL DYKES: A Novel. By Lt.-Colonel GEORGE RANDOLPH, U.S.A. Crown 8vo, cloth extra, 7s. 6d.

READE (CHARLES), NOVELS BY.
Crown 8vo, cloth extra, illustrated, 3s. 6d. each; post 8vo, illust. bds., 2s. each.
PEG WOFFINGTON. Illustrated by S. L. FILDES, R.A.—Also a POCKET EDITION, set in New Type, in Elzevir style, fcap. 8vo, half-leather, 2s. 6d.
CHRISTIE JOHNSTONE. Illustrated by WILLIAM SMALL.—Also a POCKET EDITION, set in New Type, in Elzevir style, fcap. 8vo, half-leather, 2s. 6d.
IT IS NEVER TOO LATE TO MEND. Illustrated by G. J. PINWELL.
THE COURSE OF TRUE LOVE NEVER DID RUN SMOOTH. Illustrated by HELEN PATERSON.
THE AUTOBIOGRAPHY OF A THIEF, &c. Illustrated by MATT STRETCH.
LOVE ME LITTLE, LOVE ME LONG. Illustrated by M. ELLEN EDWARDS.
THE DOUBLE MARRIAGE. Illusts. by Sir JOHN GILBERT, R.A., and C. KEENE
THE CLOISTER AND THE HEARTH. Illustrated by CHARLES KEENE.
HARD CASH. Illustrated by F. W. LAWSON.
GRIFFITH GAUNT. Illustrated by S. L. FILDES, R A., and WILLIAM SMALL.
FOUL PLAY. Illustrated by GEORGE DU MAURIER.
PUT YOURSELF IN HIS PLACE. Illustrated by ROBERT BARNES.
A TERRIBLE TEMPTATION. Illustrated by EDWARD HUGHES and A. W. COOPER.
A SIMPLETON. Illustrated by KATE CRAUFURD.
THE WANDERING HEIR. Illustrated by HELEN PATERSON, S. L. FILDES, R.A., C. GREEN, and HENRY WOODS, A.R.A.
A WOMAN-HATER. Illustrated by THOMAS COULDERY.
SINGLEHEART AND DOUBLEFACE. Illustrated by P. MACNAB.
GOOD STORIES OF MEN AND OTHER ANIMALS. Illustrated by E. A. ABBEY, PERCY MACQUOID, R.W.S., and JOSEPH NASH.
THE JILT, and other Stories. Illustrated by JOSEPH NASH.
READIANA. With a Steel-plate Portrait of CHARLES READE.
BIBLE CHARACTERS: Studies of David, Paul, &c. Fcap. 8vo, leatherette, 1s.
SELECTIONS FROM THE WORKS OF CHARLES READE. With an Introduction by Mrs. ALEX. IRELAND, and a Steel-Plate Portrait. Crown 8vo, buckram, gilt top, 6s. [Preparing.

RIDDELL (MRS. J. H.), NOVELS BY.
Crown 8vo, cloth extra, 3s. 6d. each; post 8vo, Illustrated boards, 2s. each.
HER MOTHER'S DARLING. | WEIRD STORIES.
THE PRINCE OF WALES'S GARDEN PARTY.

Post 8vo, illustrated boards, 2s. each.
UNINHABITED HOUSE. | FAIRY WATER. | MYSTERY IN PALACE GARDENS.

RIMMER (ALFRED), WORKS BY. Square 8vo, cloth gilt, 7s. 6d. each.
OUR OLD COUNTRY TOWNS. With 55 Illustrations.
RAMBLES ROUND ETON AND HARROW. With 50 Illustrations.
ABOUT ENGLAND WITH DICKENS. With 58 Illusts. by C. A. VANDERHOOF, &c.

ROBINSON CRUSOE. By DANIEL DEFOE. (MAJOR'S EDITION.) With 37 Illustrations by GEORGE CRUIKSHANK. Post 8vo, half-bound, 2s.

ROBINSON (F. W.), NOVELS BY.
Crown 8vo, cloth extra, 3s. 6d. each; post 8vo, illustrated boards, 2s. each.
WOMEN ARE STRANGE. | THE HANDS OF JUSTICE.

ROBINSON (PHIL), WORKS BY. Crown 8vo, cloth extra, 7s. 6d. each.
THE POETS' BIRDS. | THE POETS' BEASTS.
THE POETS AND NATURE: REPTILES, FISHES, INSECTS. [Preparing.

ROCHEFOUCAULD'S MAXIMS AND MORAL REFLECTIONS. With Notes, and an Introductory Essay by SAINTE-BEUVE. Post 8vo, cloth limp, 2s.

ROLL OF BATTLE ABBEY, THE : A List of the Principal Warriors who came from Normandy with William the Conqueror, and Settled in this Country, A.D 1066-7. With Arms emblazoned in Gold and Colours. Handsomely printed, 5s.

ROWLEY (HON. HUGH), WORKS BY. Post 8vo, cloth, 2s. 6d. each.
PUNIANA: RIDDLES AND JOKES. With numerous Illustrations.
MORE PUNIANA. Profusely Illustrated.

RUNCIMAN (JAMES), STORIES BY.
Post 8vo, illustrated boards, 2s. each; cloth limp, 2s. 6d. each.
SKIPPERS AND SHELLBACKS. | GRACE BALMAIGN'S SWEETHEART.
SCHOOLS AND SCHOLARS.

RUSSELL (W. CLARK), BOOKS AND NOVELS BY :
Crown 8vo, cloth extra, 6s. each; post 8vo, illustrated boards, 2s. each.
ROUND THE GALLEY-FIRE. | A BOOK FOR THE HAMMOCK.
IN THE MIDDLE WATCH. | MYSTERY OF THE "OCEAN STAR."
A VOYAGE TO THE CAPE. | THE ROMANCE OF JENNY HARLOWE.

ON THE FO'K'SLE HEAD. Post 8vo, illustrated boards, 2s.
AN OCEAN TRAGEDY. Cr. 8vo, cloth extra, 3s. 6d.; post 8vo, Illust. bds., 2s.
MY SHIPMATE LOUISE. Three Vols., crown 8vo.

SALA.—GASLIGHT AND DAYLIGHT. By GEORGE AUGUSTUS SALA. Post 8vo, illustrated boards. 2s.

SANSON.—SEVEN GENERATIONS OF EXECUTIONERS : Memoirs of the Sanson Family (1688 to 1847). Crown 8vo, cloth extra, 3s. 6d.

SAUNDERS (JOHN), NOVELS BY.
Crown 8vo, cloth extra, 3s. 6d. each; post 8vo, illustrated boards, 2s. each.
GUY WATERMAN. | THE LION IN THE PATH. | THE TWO DREAMERS.
BOUND TO THE WHEEL. Crown 8vo, cloth extra, 3s. 6d.

SAUNDERS (KATHARINE), NOVELS BY.
Crown 8vo, cloth extra, 3s. 6d. each; post 8vo, illustrated boards, 2s. each.
MARGARET AND ELIZABETH. | HEART SALVAGE.
THE HIGH MILLS. | SEBASTIAN.

JOAN MERRYWEATHER. Post 8vo, illustrated boards, 2s.
GIDEON'S ROCK. Crown 8vo, cloth extra, 3s. 6d.

SCIENCE-GOSSIP : An Illustrated Medium of Interchange for Students and Lovers of Nature. Edited by Dr. J. E. TAYLOR, F.L.S., &c. Devoted to Geology, Botany, Physiology, Chemistry, Zoology, Microscopy, Telescopy, Physiography, Photography, &c. Price 4d. Monthly: or 5s. per year, post-free. Vols. I. to XIX. may be had, 7s. 6d. each; Vols. XX. to date, 5s. each. Cases for Binding, 1s. 6d.

SECRET OUT, THE: One Thousand Tricks with Cards; with Entertaining Experiments in Drawing-room or "White Magic." By W. H. Cremer. With 300 Illustrations. Crown 8vo, cloth extra, 4s. 6d.

SEGUIN (L. G.), WORKS BY.
THE COUNTRY OF THE PASSION PLAY (OBERAMMERGAU) and the Highlands of Bavaria. With Map and 37 Illustrations. Crown 8vo, cloth extra, 3s. 6d.
WALKS IN ALGIERS. With 2 Maps and 16 Illusts. Crown 8vo, cloth extra, 6s.

SENIOR (WM.).—BY STREAM AND SEA. Post 8vo, cloth, 2s. 6d.

SHAKESPEARE, THE FIRST FOLIO.—Mr William Shakespeare's Comedies, Histories, and Tragedies. Published according to the true Originall Copies. London, Printed by Isaac Iaggard and Ed Blount. 1623— A reduced Photographic Reproduction. Small 8vo, half-Roxburghe. 7s. 6d.
SHAKESPEARE FOR CHILDREN: LAMB'S TALES FROM SHAKESPEARE. With Illustrations, coloured and plain, by J. Moyr Smith. Crown 4to, cloth, 6s.

SHARP.—CHILDREN OF TO-MORROW: A Novel. By William Sharp. Crown 8vo, cloth extra, 6s.

SHELLEY.—THE COMPLETE WORKS IN VERSE AND PROSE OF PERCY BYSSHE SHELLEY. Edited, Prefaced, and Annotated by R. Herne Shepherd. Five Vols., crown 8vo, cloth boards, 3s. 6d. each.
POETICAL WORKS, in Three Vols. :
Vol. I. Introduction by the Editor; Posthumous Fragments of Margaret Nicholson; Shelley's Correspondence with Stockdale; The Wandering Jew, Queen Mab, with the Notes, Alastor, and other Poems, Rosalind and Helen, Prometheus Unbound, Adonais, &c.
Vol II Laon and Cythna, The Cenci, Julian and Maddalo, Swellfoot the Tyrant, The Witch of Atlas; Epipsychidion Hellas
Vol III. Posthumous Poems, The Masque of Anarchy, and other Pieces.
PROSE WORKS, in Two Vols :
Vol. I. The Two Romances of Zastrozzi and St Irvyne; the Dublin and Marlow Pamphlets, A Refutation of Deism, Letters to Leigh Hunt, and some Minor Writings and Fragments
Vol. II The Essays; Letters from Abroad, Translations and Fragments, Edited by Mrs Shelley, With a Bibliography of Shelley, and an Index of the Prose Works.

SHERARD.—ROGUES: A Novel. By R. H. Sherard. Crown 8vo, picture cover, 1s.: cloth, 1s. 6d.

SHERIDAN (GENERAL). — PERSONAL MEMOIRS OF GENERAL P. H. SHERIDAN. With Portraits and Facsimiles. Two Vols., demy 8vo, cloth, 24s.

SHERIDAN'S (RICHARD BRINSLEY) COMPLETE WORKS. With Life and Anecdotes. Including his Dramatic Writings, his Works in Prose and Poetry, Translations, Speeches, Jokes, &c With 10 Illusts. Cr. 8vo, cl, 7s. 6d.
THE RIVALS, THE SCHOOL FOR SCANDAL, and other Plays. Post 8vo, printed on laid paper and half bound, 2s.
SHERIDAN'S COMEDIES: THE RIVALS and THE SCHOOL FOR SCANDAL. Edited, with an Introduction and Notes to each Play, and a Biographical Sketch, by Brander Matthews. With Illustrations. Demy 8vo, half-parchment, 12s. 6d.

SIDNEY'S (SIR PHILIP) COMPLETE POETICAL WORKS, including all those in "Arcadia." With Portrait, Memorial-Introduction, Notes, &c. by the Rev. A. B. Grosart, D D. Three Vols., crown 8vo, cloth boards, 18s.

SIGNBOARDS: Their History. With Anecdotes of Famous Taverns and Remarkable Characters. By Jacob Larwood and John Camden Hotten. With Coloured Frontispiece and 94 Illustrations. Crown 8vo, cloth extra, 7s. 6d.

SIMS (GEORGE R.), WORKS BY.
Post 8vo, illustrated boards, 2s. each, cloth limp, 2s. 6d. each.
ROGUES AND VAGABONDS. | MARY JANE MARRIED.
THE RING O' BELLS. | TALES OF TO-DAY.
MARY JANE'S MEMOIRS. | DRAMAS OF LIFE. With 60 Illustrations.
TINKLETOP'S CRIME. With a Frontispiece by Maurice Greiffenhagen.
Crown 8vo, picture cover, 1s. each, cloth, 1s. 6d. each.
HOW THE POOR LIVE; and HORRIBLE LONDON.
THE DAGONET RECITER AND READER: being Readings and Recitations in Prose and Verse, selected from his own Works by George R. Sims.
THE CASE OF GEORGE CANDLEMAS.

SISTER DORA: A Biography. By Margaret Lonsdale. With Four Illustrations. Demy 8vo, picture cover, 4d.; cloth, 6d.

SKETCHLEY.—A MATCH IN THE DARK. By ARTHUR SKETCHLEY.
Post 8vo, illustrated boards, 2s.

SLANG DICTIONARY (THE): Etymological, Historical, and Anecdotal. Crown 8vo, cloth extra, 6s. 6d.

SMITH (J. MOYR), WORKS BY.
THE PRINCE OF ARGOLIS. With 130 Illusts. Post 8vo, cloth extra, 3s. 6d.
TALES OF OLD THULE. With numerous Illustrations. Crown 8vo, cloth gilt, 6s.
THE WOOING OF THE WATER WITCH. Illustrated. Post 8vo, cloth, 6s.

SOCIETY IN LONDON. By A FOREIGN RESIDENT. Crown 8vo,
1s.; cloth, 1s. 6d.

SOCIETY IN PARIS: The Upper Ten Thousand. A Series of Letters
from Count PAUL VASILI to a Young French Diplomat. Crown 8vo. cloth, 6s.

SOMERSET. — SONGS OF ADIEU. By Lord HENRY SOMERSET.
Small 4to, Japanese vellum, 6s.

SPALDING.—ELIZABETHAN DEMONOLOGY: An Essay on the Belief
in the Existence of Devils. By T. A. SPALDING, LL.B. Crown 8vo, cloth extra, 5s.

SPEIGHT (T. W.), NOVELS BY.
Post 8vo, illustrated boards, 2s. each.

| THE MYSTERIES OF HERON DYKE. | THE GOLDEN HOOP. |
| BY DEVIOUS WAYS, and A BARREN TITLE. | HOODWINKED; and THE SANDY-CROFT MYSTERY. |

Post 8vo, cloth limp, 1s. 6d. each.

| A BARREN TITLE. | WIFE OR NO WIFE? |

THE SANDYCROFT MYSTERY. Crown 8vo, picture cover, 1s.

SPENSER FOR CHILDREN. By M. H. TOWRY. With Illustrations
by WALTER J. MORGAN. Crown 4to, cloth gilt, 6s.

STARRY HEAVENS (THE): A POETICAL BIRTHDAY BOOK. Royal
16mo, cloth extra, 2s. 6d.

STAUNTON.—THE LAWS AND PRACTICE OF CHESS. With an
Analysis of the Openings. By HOWARD STAUNTON. Edited by ROBERT B. WORMALD.
Crown 8vo, cloth extra, 5s.

STEDMAN (E. C.), WORKS BY.
VICTORIAN POETS. Thirteenth Edition. Crown 8vo, cloth extra, 9s.
THE POETS OF AMERICA. Crown 8vo, cloth extra, 9s.

STERNDALE. — THE AFGHAN KNIFE: A Novel. By ROBERT
ARMITAGE STERNDALE. Cr. 8vo, cloth extra, 3s. 6d.; post 8vo, illust. boards, 2s.

STEVENSON (R. LOUIS), WORKS BY. Post 8vo, cl. limp, 2s. 6d. each.
TRAVELS WITH A DONKEY. Eighth Edit. With a Frontis. by WALTER CRANE.
AN INLAND VOYAGE. Fourth Edition. With a Frontispiece by WALTER CRANE.

Crown 8vo, buckram, gilt top, 6s. each.
FAMILIAR STUDIES OF MEN AND BOOKS. Fifth Edition.
THE SILVERADO SQUATTERS. With a Frontispiece. Third Edition.
THE MERRY MEN. Second Edition. | UNDERWOODS: Poems. Fifth Edition.
MEMORIES AND PORTRAITS. Third Edition.
VIRGINIBUS PUERISQUE, and other Papers. Fifth Edition. | BALLADS.

Crown 8vo, buckram, gilt top, 6s. each; post 8vo, illustrated boards, 2s. each.
NEW ARABIAN NIGHTS. Eleventh Edition. | PRINCE OTTO. Sixth Edition.

FATHER DAMIEN: An Open Letter to the Rev. Dr. Hyde. Second Edition.
Crown 8vo, hand-made and brown paper, 1s.

STODDARD. — SUMMER CRUISING IN THE SOUTH SEAS. By
C. WARREN STODDARD. Illustrated by WALLIS MACKAY. Cr. 8vo, cl. extra, 3s. 6d.

STORIES FROM FOREIGN NOVELISTS. With Notices by HELEN and
ALICE ZIMMERN. Crown 8vo, cloth extra, 3s. 6d.; post 8vo, illustrated boards, 2s.

STRANGE MANUSCRIPT (A) FOUND IN A COPPER CYLINDER. With 19 Illustrations by GILBERT GAUL. Third Edition. Crown 8vo, cloth extra, **5s.**

STRUTT'S SPORTS AND PASTIMES OF THE PEOPLE OF ENGLAND; including the Rural and Domestic Recreations, May Games, Mummeries, Shows, &c., from the Earliest Period to the Present Time. Edited by WILLIAM HONE. With 140 Illustrations. Crown 8vo, cloth extra, **7s. 6d.**

SUBURBAN HOMES (THE) OF LONDON : A Residential Guide. With a Map, and Notes on Rental, Rates, and Accommodation Crown 8vo, cloth, **7s. 6d.**

SWIFT'S (DEAN) CHOICE WORKS, in Prose and Verse. With Memoir, Portrait, and Facsimiles of the Maps in "Gulliver's Travels." Cr. 8vo, cl., **7s. 6d.**
 GULLIVER'S TRAVELS, and **A TALE OF A TUB.** Post 8vo, printed on laid paper and half-bound, **2s.**
 A MONOGRAPH ON SWIFT. By J. CHURTON COLLINS. Cr. 8vo, cloth, **8s.** [*Shortly*.

SWINBURNE (ALGERNON C.), WORKS BY.

SELECTIONS FROM POETICAL WORKS OF A. C. SWINBURNE. Fcap. 8vo, **6s.**
ATALANTA IN CALYDON. Cr. 8vo, **6s.**
CHASTELARD: A Tragedy. Cr. 8vo, **7s.**
NOTES ON POEMS AND REVIEWS. Demy 8vo, **1s.**
POEMS AND BALLADS. FIRST SERIES. Crown 8vo or fcap 8vo, **9s.**
POEMS AND BALLADS. SECOND SERIES. Crown 8vo or fcap. 8vo, **9s.**
POEMS AND BALLADS. THIRD SERIES. Crown 8vo, **7s.**
SONGS BEFORE SUNRISE. Crown 8vo, **10s. 6d.**
BOTHWELL: A Tragedy. Crown 8vo, **12s. 6d.**
SONGS OF TWO NATIONS. Cr 8vo, **6s.**

GEORGE CHAPMAN. (*See* Vol. II. of G. CHAPMAN's Works) Crown 8vo, **6s.**
ESSAYS AND STUDIES. Cr. 8vo, **12s.**
ERECHTHEUS: A Tragedy Cr. 8vo, **6s.**
SONGS OF THE SPRINGTIDES. Crown 8vo. **6s.**
STUDIES IN SONG. Crown 8vo, **7s.**
MARY STUART: A Tragedy. Cr. 8vo **8s.**
TRISTRAM OF LYONESSE. Cr 8vo, **9s.**
A CENTURY OF ROUNDELS. Sm. 4to, **8s.**
A MIDSUMMER HOLIDAY. Cr. 8vo, **7s.**
MARINO FALIERO: A Tragedy. Crown 8vo, **6s.**
A STUDY OF VICTOR HUGO. Cr. 8vo, **6s.**
MISCELLANIES. Crown 8vo, **12s.**
LOCRINE: A Tragedy. Cr 8vo, **6s.**
A STUDY OF BEN JONSON. Cr. 8vo, **7s.**

SYMONDS.—WINE, WOMEN, AND SONG : Mediæval Latin Students' Songs. With Essay and Trans by J. ADDINGTON SYMONDS. Fcap. 8vo, parchment, **6s.**

SYNTAX'S (DR.) THREE TOURS : In Search of the Picturesque, in Search of Consolation, and in Search of a Wife. With ROWLANDSON's Coloured Illustrations, and Life of the Author by J. C. HOTTEN. Crown 8vo, cloth extra, **7s. 6d.**

TAINE'S HISTORY OF ENGLISH LITERATURE. Translated by HENRY VAN LAUN. Four Vols., medium 8vo, cloth boards, **30s.**—POPULAR EDITION, Two Vols , large crown 8vo, cloth extra, **15s.**

TAYLOR'S (BAYARD) DIVERSIONS OF THE ECHO CLUB : Burlesques of Modern Writers. Post 8vo, cloth limp, **2s.**

TAYLOR (DR. J. E., F.L.S.), WORKS BY. Cr. 8vo, cl. ex , **7s. 6d.** each.
 THE SAGACITY AND MORALITY OF PLANTS: A Sketch of the Life and Conduct of the Vegetable Kingdom. With a Coloured Frontispiece and 100 Illustrations.
 OUR COMMON BRITISH FOSSILS, and Where to Find Them. 331 Illustrations.

 THE PLAYTIME NATURALIST. With 366 Illustrations. Crown 8vo, cloth, **5s.**

TAYLOR'S (TOM) HISTORICAL DRAMAS. Containing "Clancarty," "Jeanne Darc," "'Twixt Axe and Crown," "The Fool's Revenge," "Arkwright's Wife," "Anne Boleyn," " Plot and Passion." Crown 8vo, cloth extra, **7s. 6d.**
 . The Plays may also be had separately, at **1s.** each.

TENNYSON (LORD): A Biographical Sketch. By H. J. JENNINGS. With a Photograph-Portrait. Crown 8vo, cloth extra, **6s.**

THACKERAYANA : Notes and Anecdotes. Illustrated by Hundreds of Sketches by WILLIAM MAKEPEACE THACKERAY, depicting Humorous Incidents in his School-life, and Favourite Characters in the Books of his Every-day Reading. With a Coloured Frontispiece. Crown 8vo, cloth extra, **7s. 6d.**

THAMES.—A NEW PICTORIAL HISTORY OF THE THAMES. By A. S. KRAUSSE. With 340 Illustrations Post 8vo, **1s.**; cloth, **1s. 6d.**

THOMAS (BERTHA), NOVELS BY. Cr. 8vo, cl., **3s. 6d.** ea. ; post 8vo, **2s.** ea.
CRESSIDA. | THE VIOLIN-PLAYER. | PROUD MAISIE.

THOMSON'S SEASONS, and CASTLE OF INDOLENCE. Introduction
by ALLAN CUNNINGHAM, and Illustrations on Steel and Wood. Cr. 8vo, cl., **7s. 6d.**

THORNBURY (WALTER), WORKS BY. Cr. 8vo, cl. extra, **7s. 6d.** each.
THE LIFE AND CORRESPONDENCE OF J. M. W. TURNER. Founded upon
Letters and Papers furnished by his Friends. With Illustrations in Colours.
HAUNTED LONDON. Edit. by E. WALFORD, M.A. Illusts. by F. W. FAIRHOLT, F.S.A.

Post 8vo, illustrated boards, **2s.** each.
OLD STORIES RE-TOLD. | TALES FOR THE MARINES.

TIMBS (JOHN), WORKS BY. Crown 8vo, cloth extra, **7s. 6d.** each.
THE HISTORY OF CLUBS AND CLUB LIFE IN LONDON: Anecdotes of its
Famous Coffee-houses, Hostelries, and Taverns. With 42 Illustrations.
ENGLISH ECCENTRICS AND ECCENTRICITIES: Stories of Wealth and Fashion,
Delusions, Impostures, and Fanatic Missions, Sporting Scenes, Eccentric Artists,
Theatrical Folk, Men of Letters. &c. With 48 Illustrations.

TROLLOPE (ANTHONY), NOVELS BY.
Crown 8vo, cloth extra, **3s. 6d.** each ; post 8vo, illustrated boards, **2s.** each.
THE WAY WE LIVE NOW.   MARION FAY.
KEPT IN THE DARK.   MR. SCARBOROUGH'S FAMILY.
FRAU FROHMANN.   THE LAND-LEAGUERS.

Post 8vo, illustrated boards, **2s.** each.
GOLDEN LION OF GRANPERE. | JOHN CALDIGATE. | AMERICAN SENATOR.

TROLLOPE (FRANCES E.), NOVELS BY.
Crown 8vo, cloth extra, **3s. 6d.** each, post 8vo, illustrated boards, **2s.** each.
LIKE SHIPS UPON THE SEA. | MABEL'S PROGRESS. | ANNE FURNESS.

TROLLOPE (T. A.).—DIAMOND CUT DIAMOND. Post 8vo, illust. bds., **2s.**

TROWBRIDGE.—FARNELL'S FOLLY: A Novel. By J. T. TROW-
BRIDGE. Post 8vo, illustrated boards, **2s.**

TYTLER (C. C. FRASER-).—MISTRESS JUDITH: A Novel. By
C. C. FRASER-TYTLER. Crown 8vo, cloth extra, **3s. 6d.** ; post 8vo, illust. boards, **2s.**

TYTLER (SARAH), NOVELS BY.
Crown 8vo, cloth extra, **3s. 6d.** each ; post 8vo, illustrated boards, **2s.** each.
WHAT SHE CAME THROUGH.   LADY BELL.
THE BRIDE'S PASS.   BURIED DIAMONDS.
NOBLESSE OBLIGE.   THE BLACKHALL GHOSTS.

Post 8vo, illustrated boards, **2s.** each.
SAINT MUNGO'S CITY.   DISAPPEARED.
BEAUTY AND THE BEAST.   THE HUGUENOT FAMILY.
CITOYENNE JACQUELINE.

VILLARI.—A DOUBLE BOND. By LINDA VILLARI. Fcap. 8vo, picture
cover **1s.**

WALT WHITMAN, POEMS BY. Edited, with Introduction, by
WILLIAM M. ROSSETTI. With Portrait. Cr. 8vo, hand-made paper and buckram, **6s.**

WALTON AND COTTON'S COMPLETE ANGLER; or, The Con-
templative Man's Recreation, by IZAAK WALTON ; and Instructions how to Angle for a
Trout or Grayling in a clear Stream, by CHARLES COTTON. With Memoirs and Notes
by Sir HARRIS NICOLAS, and 61 Illustrations. Crown 8vo, cloth antique, **7s. 6d.**

WARD (HERBERT), WORKS BY.
FIVE YEARS WITH THE CONGO CANNIBALS. With 92 Illustrations by the
Author, VICTOR PERARD, and W. B. DAVIS. Third ed. Roy. 8vo, cloth ex., **14s.**
MY LIFE WITH STANLEY'S REAR GUARD. With a Map by F. S. WELLER,
F.R.G.S. Post 8vo, **1s.** ; cloth, **1s. 6d.**

WARNER.—A ROUNDABOUT JOURNEY. By CHARLES DUDLEY
WARNER. Crown 8vo, cloth extra, **6s.**

WALFORD (EDWARD, M.A.), WORKS BY.

WALFORD'S COUNTY FAMILIES OF THE UNITED KINGDOM (1891). Containing the Descent, Birth, Marriage, Education, &c., of 12,000 Heads of Families, their Heirs, Offices, Addresses, Clubs, &c. Royal 8vo, cloth gilt, **50s.**

WALFORD'S SHILLING PEERAGE (1891). Containing a List of the House of Lords, Scotch and Irish Peers, &c. 32mo, cloth, **1s.**

WALFORD'S SHILLING BARONETAGE (1891). Containing a List of the Baronets of the United Kingdom, Biographical Notices, Addresses, &c. 32mo, cloth, **1s.**

WALFORD'S SHILLING KNIGHTAGE (1891). Containing a List of the Knights of the United Kingdom, Biographical Notices, Addresses, &c. 32mo, cloth, **1s.**

WALFORD'S SHILLING HOUSE OF COMMONS (1891). Containing a List of all Members of Parliament, their Addresses, Clubs, &c. 32mo, cloth, **1s.**

WALFORD'S COMPLETE PEERAGE, BARONETAGE, KNIGHTAGE, AND HOUSE OF COMMONS (1891). Royal 32mo, cloth extra, gilt edges, **5s.**

WALFORD'S WINDSOR PEERAGE, BARONETAGE, AND KNIGHTAGE (1891). Crown 8vo, cloth extra, **12s. 6d.**

TALES OF OUR GREAT FAMILIES. Crown 8vo, cloth extra, **3s. 6d.**

WILLIAM PITT: A Biography. Post 8vo, cloth extra, **5s.**

WARRANT TO EXECUTE CHARLES I. A Facsimile, with the 59 Signatures and Seals. Printed on paper 22 in. by 14 in. **2s.**

WARRANT TO EXECUTE MARY QUEEN OF SCOTS. A Facsimile, including Queen Elizabeth's Signature and the Great Seal. **2s.**

WEATHER, HOW TO FORETELL THE, WITH POCKET SPECTROSCOPE. By F. W. CORY. With 10 Illustrations. Cr 8vo, **1s.**; cloth, **1s. 6d.**

WESTROPP.—HANDBOOK OF POTTERY AND PORCELAIN. By HODDER M. WESTROPP. With Illusts. and List of Marks Cr. 8vo, cloth, **4s. 6d.**

WHIST.—HOW TO PLAY SOLO WHIST. By ABRAHAM S WILKS and CHARLES F. PARDON. Crown 8vo, cloth extra, **3s. 6d.**

WHISTLER'S (MR.) TEN O'CLOCK. Cr. 8vo, hand-made paper, 1s.

WHITE.—THE NATURAL HISTORY OF SELBORNE. By GILBERT WHITE, M.A. Post 8vo, printed on laid paper and half-bound, **2s.**

WILLIAMS (W. MATTIEU, F.R.A.S.), WORKS BY.

SCIENCE IN SHORT CHAPTERS. Crown 8vo, cloth extra, **7s. 6d.**

A SIMPLE TREATISE ON HEAT. With Illusts. Cr. 8vo, cloth limp, **2s. 6d.**

THE CHEMISTRY OF COOKERY. Crown 8vo, cloth extra, **6s.**

THE CHEMISTRY OF IRON AND STEEL MAKING. Crown 8vo, cloth extra, **9s.**

WILSON (DR. ANDREW, F.R.S.E.), WORKS BY.

CHAPTERS ON EVOLUTION. With 259 Illustrations Cr. 8vo, cloth extra, **7s. 6d.**

LEAVES FROM A NATURALIST'S NOTE-BOOK. Post 8vo, cloth limp, **2s. 6d.**

LEISURE-TIME STUDIES. With Illustrations. Crown 8vo, cloth extra, **6s.**

STUDIES IN LIFE AND SENSE. With numerous Illusts. Cr. 8vo, cl. ex., **6s.**

COMMON ACCIDENTS: HOW TO TREAT THEM. Illusts. Cr 8vo, **1s.**; cl., **1s. 6d.**

GLIMPSES OF LIFE AND NATURE. Crown 8vo, cloth extra, **3s. 6d.** [Shortly.

WINTER (J. S.), STORIES BY. Post 8vo, illustrated boards, 2s. each.
CAVALRY LIFE. | **REGIMENTAL LEGENDS.**

WOOD.—SABINA: A Novel. By Lady WOOD. Post 8vo, boards, 2s.

WOOD (H. F.), DETECTIVE STORIES BY.
Crown 8vo, cloth extra, 6s. each; post 8vo, illustrated boards, 2s. each.
PASSENGER FROM SCOTLAND YARD. | **ENGLISHMAN OF THE RUE CAIN.**

WOOLLEY.—RACHEL ARMSTRONG; or, Love and Theology. By CELIA PARKER WOOLLEY. Post 8vo, illustrated boards, 2s.; cloth, 2s. 6d.

WRIGHT (THOMAS), WORKS BY. Crown 8vo, cloth extra, 7s. 6d. each.
CARICATURE HISTORY OF THE GEORGES. With 400 Pictures, Caricatures, Squibs, Broadsides, Window Pictures, &c.

HISTORY OF CARICATURE AND OF THE GROTESQUE IN ART, LITERATURE, SCULPTURE, AND PAINTING. Illustrated by F. W. FAIRHOLT, F.S.A.

YATES (EDMUND), NOVELS BY. Post 8vo, illustrated boards, 2s. each.
LAND AT LAST. | **THE FORLORN HOPE.** | **CASTAWAY.**

LISTS OF BOOKS CLASSIFIED IN SERIES.

. *For full cataloguing, see alphabetical arrangement, pp.* 1-25.

THE MAYFAIR LIBRARY.   Post 8vo, cloth limp, **2s. 6d.** per Volume.

A Journey Round My Room. By XAVIER DE MAISTRE

Quips and Quiddities. By W. D. ADAMS.

The Agony Column of "The Times."

Melancholy Anatomised: Abridgment of "Burton's Anatomy of Melancholy."

The Speeches of Charles Dickens.

Literary Frivolities, Fancies, Follies, and Frolics. By W. T. DOBSON.

Poetical Ingenuities. By W. T. DOBSON.

The Cupboard Papers. By FIN-BEC.

W. S. Gilbert's Plays. FIRST SERIES

W. S. Gilbert's Plays. SECOND SERIES.

Songs of Irish Wit and Humour.

Animals and Masters. By SIR A. HELPS.

Social Pressure. By SIR A. HELPS.

Curiosities of Criticism. H. J. JENNINGS.

Holmes's Autocrat of Breakfast-Table.

Pencil and Palette. By R. KEMPT.

Little Essays: from LAMB's Letters.

Forensic Anecdotes. By JACOB LARWOOD

Theatrical Anecdotes. JACOB LARWOOD.

Jeux d'Esprit. Edited by HENRY S. LEIGH.

Witch Stories. By E. LYNN LINTON.

Ourselves. By E. LYNN LINTON.

Pastimes & Players. By R. MACGREGOR.

New Paul and Virginia. W. H. MALLOCK.

New Republic. By W. H. MALLOCK.

Puck on Pegasus. By H. C. PENNELL.

Pegasus Re-Saddled. By H. C. PENNELL.

Muses of Mayfair. Ed. H. C. PENNELL.

Thoreau: His Life & Aims. By H. A. PAGE.

Puniana. By Hon. HUGH ROWLEY.

More Puniana. By Hon. HUGH ROWLEY.

The Philosophy of Handwriting.

By Stream and Sea. By WM. SENIOR.

Leaves from a Naturalist's Note-Book. By Dr. ANDREW WILSON.

THE GOLDEN LIBRARY.   Post 8vo, cloth limp, **2s.** per Volume.

Bayard Taylor's Diversions of the Echo Club.

Bennett's Ballad History of England.

Bennett's Songs for Sailors.

Godwin's Lives of the Necromancers.

Pope's Poetical Works.

Holmes's Autocrat of Breakfast Table.

Holmes's Professor at Breakfast Table.

Jesse's Scenes of Country Life.

Leigh Hunt's Tale for a Chimney Corner.

Mallory's Mort d'Arthur: Selections.

Pascal's Provincial Letters.

Rochefoucauld's Maxims & Reflections.

THE WANDERER'S LIBRARY.   Crown 8vo, cloth extra, **3s. 6d.** each.

Wanderings in Patagonia. By JULIUS BEERBOHM. Illustrated.

Camp Notes. By FREDERICK BOYLE.

Savage Life. By FREDERICK BOYLE.

Merrie England in the Olden Time. By G. DANIEL. Illustrated by CRUIKSHANK.

Circus Life. By THOMAS FROST.

Lives of the Conjurers. THOMAS FROST.

The Old Showmen and the Old London Fairs. By THOMAS FROST.

Low-Life Deeps. By JAMES GREENWOOD.

Wilds of London. JAMES GREENWOOD.

Tunis. Chev. HESSE-WARTEGG. 22 Illusts.

Life and Adventures of a Cheap Jack.

World Behind the Scenes. P. FITZGERALD.

Tavern Anecdotes and Sayings.

The Genial Showman. By E. P. HINGSTON

Story of London Parks. JACOB LARWOOD.

London Characters. By HENRY MAYHEW.

Seven Generations of Executioners.

Summer Cruising in the South Seas. By C. WARREN STODDARD. Illustrated.

POPULAR SHILLING BOOKS.

Harry Fludyer at Cambridge.

Jeff Briggs's Love Story. BRET HARTE.

Twins of Table Mountain. BRET HARTE.

A Day's Tour. By PERCY FITZGERALD.

Esther's Glove. By R. E. FRANCILLON.

Sentenced! By SOMERVILLE GIBNEY.

The Professor's Wife. By L. GRAHAM.

Mrs. Gainsborough's Diamonds. By JULIAN HAWTHORNE.

Niagara Spray. By J. HOLLINGSHEAD.

A Romance of the Queen's Hounds. By CHARLES JAMES.

The Garden that Paid the Rent. By TOM JERROLD.

Cut by the Mess. By ARTHUR KEYSER.

Our Sensation Novel. J. H. McCARTHY.

Doom! By JUSTIN H. McCARTHY, M.P.

Dolly. By JUSTIN H. McCARTHY, M.P.

Lily Lass. JUSTIN H. McCARTHY, M.P.

Was She Good or Bad? By W. MINTO.

That Girl in Black. Mrs. MOLESWORTH.

Notes from the "News." By JAS. PAYN.

Beyond the Gates. By E. S. PHELPS.

Old Maid's Paradise. By E. S. PHELPS.

Burglars in Paradise. By E. S. PHELPS.

Jack the Fisherman. By E. S. PHELPS.

Trooping with Crows. By C. L. PIRKIS.

Bible Characters. By CHARLES READE.

Rogues. By R. H. SHERARD.

The Dagonet Reciter. By G. R. SIMS.

How the Poor Live. By G. R. SIMS.

Case of George Candlemas. G. R. SIMS.

Sandycroft Mystery. T. W. SPEIGHT.

Hoodwinked. By T. W. SPEIGHT.

Father Damien. By R. L. STEVENSON.

A Double Bond. By LINDA VILLARI.

My Life with Stanley's Rear Guard. By HERBERT WARD.

MY LIBRARY.

Choice Works, printed on laid paper, bound half-Roxburghe, 3s. 6d. each.

Four Frenchwomen. By AUSTIN DOBSON.
Citation and Examination of William Shakspeare. By W. S. LANDOR.
Christie Johnstone. By CHARLES READE. With a Photogravure Frontispiece.
Peg Woffington. By CHARLES READE.

THE POCKET LIBRARY.
Post 8vo, printed on laid paper and hf-bd, 2s. each.

The Essays of Elia. By CHARLES LAMB.
Robinson Crusoe. Edited by JOHN MAJOR. With 37 Illusts. by GEORGE CRUIKSHANK.
Whims and Oddities. By THOMAS HOOD. With 85 Illustrations.
The Barber's Chair, and The Hedgehog Letters. By DOUGLAS JERROLD.
Gastronomy as a Fine Art. By BRILLAT-SAVARIN. Trans. R. E. ANDERSON, M.A.
The Epicurean, &c. By THOMAS MOORE.
Leigh Hunt's Essays. Ed E. OLLIER.
The Natural History of Selborne. By GILBERT WHITE.
Gulliver's Travels, and The Tale of a Tub. By Dean SWIFT.
The Rivals, School for Scandal, and other Plays by RICHARD BRINSLEY SHERIDAN.
Anecdotes of the Clergy. J. LARWOOD.

THE PICCADILLY NOVELS.

LIBRARY EDITIONS OF NOVELS BY THE BEST AUTHORS, many Illustrated, crown 8vo, cloth extra, 3s. 6d. each.

By GRANT ALLEN.
Philistia. | For Maimie's Sake.
Babylon | The Devil's Die.
In all Shades. | This Mortal Coil.
The Tents of Shem. | The Great Taboo.

By ALAN ST. AUBYN.
A Fellow of Trinity.

By Rev. S. BARING GOULD.
Red Spider. | Eve.

By W. BESANT & J. RICE.
My Little Girl. | By Celia's Arbour.
Case of Mr.Lucraft. | Monks of Thelema.
This Son of Vulcan. | The Seamy Side.
Golden Butterfly. | Ten Years' Tenant.
Ready-Money Mortiboy.
With Harp and Crown.
'Twas in Trafalgar's Bay.
The Chaplain of the Fleet.

By WALTER BESANT.
All Sorts and Conditions of Men.
The Captains' Room.
All in a Garden Fair
The World Went Very Well Then.
For Faith and Freedom.
Dorothy Forster. | Herr Paulus.
Uncle Jack. | Bell of St. Paul's.
Children of Gibeon. | To Call Her Mine.

By ROBERT BUCHANAN.
The Shadow of the Sword.
A Child of Nature.
The Martyrdom of Madeline.
God and the Man. | The New Abelard.
Love Me for Ever. | Foxglove Manor.
Annan Water. | Master of the Mine.
Matt. | Heir of Linne.

By HALL CAINE.
The Shadow of a Crime.
A Son of Hagar. | The Deemster.

MORT. & FRANCES COLLINS.
Sweet Anne Page. | Transmigration.
From Midnight to Midnight.
Blacksmith and Scholar.
Village Comedy. | You Play Me False

By Mrs. H. LOVETT CAMERON.
Juliet's Guardian. | Deceivers Ever.

By WILKIE COLLINS.
Armadale. | The Frozen Deep.
After Dark. | The Two Destinies.
No Name. | Law and the Lady.
Antonina. | Basil. | Haunted Hotel.
Hide and Seek. | The Fallen Leaves.
The Dead Secret. | Jezebel's Daughter.
Queen of Hearts. | The Black Robe.
My Miscellanies. | Heart and Science.
Woman in White. | "I Say No."
The Moonstone. | Little Novels.
Man and Wife. | The Evil Genius.
Poor Miss Finch. | The Legacy of Cain
Miss or Mrs? | A Rogue's Life.
New Magdalen. | Blind Love.

By DUTTON COOK.
Paul Foster's Daughter.

By WILLIAM CYPLES.
Hearts of Gold.

By ALPHONSE DAUDET.
The Evangelist; or, Port Salvation

By JAMES DE MILLE.
A Castle in Spain.

By J. LEITH DERWENT.
Our Lady of Tears. | Circe's Lovers.

By Mrs. ANNIE EDWARDES.
Archie Lovell.

By PERCY FITZGERALD.
Fatal Zero.

By R. E. FRANCILLON.
Queen Cophetua. | A Real Queen.
One by One. | King or Knave?

Pref. by Sir BARTLE FRERE.
Pandurang Hari.

By EDWARD GARRETT.
The Capel Girls.

THE PICCADILLY (3/6) NOVELS—*continued.*

By CHARLES GIBBON.

Robin Gray.	The Golden Shaft.
In Honour Bound.	Of High Degree.

Loving a Dream.
Queen of the Meadow.
The Flower of the Forest.

By JULIAN HAWTHORNE.

Garth.	Dust.
Ellice Quentin.	Fortune's Fool.
Sebastian Strome.	Beatrix Randolph.

David Poindexter's Disappearance.
The Spectre of the Camera.

By Sir A. HELPS.

Ivan de Biron.

By ISAAC HENDERSON.

Agatha Page.

By Mrs. ALFRED HUNT.

The Leaden Casket. | Self-Condemned.
That other Person.

By JEAN INGELOW.

Fated to be Free.

By R. ASHE KING.

A Drawn Game.
"The Wearing of the Green."

By HENRY KINGSLEY.

Number Seventeen.

By E. LYNN LINTON.

Patricia Kemball.	Ione.
Under which Lord?	Paston Carew.
"My Love!"	Sowing the Wind.

The Atonement of Leam Dundas.
The World Well Lost.

By HENRY W. LUCY.

Gideon Fleyce.

By JUSTIN McCARTHY.

A Fair Saxon.	Donna Quixote.
Linley Rochford.	Maid of Athens.
Miss Misanthrope.	Camiola.

The Waterdale Neighbours.
My Enemy's Daughter.
Dear Lady Disdain.
The Comet of a Season.

By AGNES MACDONELL.

Quaker Cousins.

By FLORENCE MARRYAT.

Open! Sesame!

By D. CHRISTIE MURRAY.

Life's Atonement.	Coals of Fire.
Joseph's Coat.	Val Strange.
A Model Father.	Hearts.

A Bit of Human Nature.
First Person Singular.
Cynic Fortune.
The Way of the World.

By MURRAY & HERMAN.

The Bishops' Bible.

By GEORGES OHNET.

A Weird Gift.

THE PICCADILLY (3/6) NOVELS—*continued.*

By Mrs. OLIPHANT.

Whiteladies.

By OUIDA.

Held in Bondage.	Two Little Wooden
Strathmore.	Shoes.
Chandos.	In a Winter City.
Under Two Flags.	Ariadne.
Idalia.	Friendship.
CecilCastlemaine's	Moths. Ruffino.
Gage.	Pipistrello.
Tricotrin. Puck.	A Village Commune
Folle Farine.	Bimbi. Wanda.
A Dog of Flanders.	Frescoes.
Pascarel. Signa.	In Maremma.
Princess Naprax-	Othmar. Syrlin.
ine.	Guilderoy.

By MARGARET A. PAUL.

Gentle and Simple.

By JAMES PAYN.

Lost Sir Massingberd.
Less Black than We're Painted.
A Confidential Agent.
A Grape from a Thorn.
Some Private Views.
In Peril and Privation.
The Mystery of Mirbridge.
The Canon's Ward.

Walter's Word.	Glow-worm Tales.
By Proxy.	Talk of the Town.
High Spirits.	Holiday Tasks.
Under One Roof.	The Burnt Million.
From Exile.	Sunny Stories.

By E. C. PRICE.

Valentina.	The Foreigners.

Mrs. Lancaster's Rival.

By CHARLES READE.

It is Never Too Late to Mend.
The Double Marriage.
Love Me Little, Love Me Long.
The Cloister and the Hearth.
The Course of True Love.
The Autobiography of a Thief.
Put Yourself in his Place.
A Terrible Temptation.
Singleheart and Doubleface.
Good Stories of Men and other Animals.

Hard Cash.	Wandering Heir.
Peg Woffington.	A Woman-Hater.
Christie Johnstone.	A Simpleton.
Griffith Gaunt.	Readiana.
Foul Play.	The Jilt.

By Mrs. J. H. RIDDELL.

Her Mother's Darling.
Prince of Wales's Garden Party.
Weird Stories.

By F. W. ROBINSON.

Women are Strange.
The Hands of Justice.

By W. CLARK RUSSELL.

An Ocean Tragedy.

By JOHN SAUNDERS.

Guy Waterman.	Two Dreamers.

Bound to the Wheel.
The Lion in the Path.

THE PICCADILLY (3/6) NOVELS —*continued.*

By KATHARINE SAUNDERS.
Margaret and Elizabeth.
Gideon's Rock. | Heart Salvage.
The High Mills. | Sebastian.

By HAWLEY SMART.
Without Love or Licence.

By R. A. STERNDALE.
The Afghan Knife.

By BERTHA THOMAS.
Proud Maisie. | Cressida.
The Violin-player.

By FRANCES E. TROLLOPE.
Like Ships upon the Sea.
Anne Furness. | Mabel's Progress.

THE PICCADILLY (3/6) NOVELS —*continued.*

By ANTHONY TROLLOPE.
Frau Frohmann. | Kept in the Dark.
Marion Fay. | Land-Leaguers.
The Way We Live Now.
Mr. Scarborough's Family.

By IVAN TURGENIEFF, &c.
Stories from Foreign Novelists.

By C. C. FRASER-TYTLER.
Mistress Judith.

By SARAH TYTLER.
The Bride's Pass. | Lady Bell.
Noblesse Oblige. | Buried Diamonds.
What She Came Through.
The Blackhall Ghosts.

CHEAP EDITIONS OF POPULAR NOVELS.

Post 8vo, Illustrated boards, 2s. each.

By ARTEMUS WARD.
Artemus Ward Complete.

By EDMOND ABOUT.
The Fellah.

By HAMILTON AIDE.
Carr of Carrlyon. | Confidences.

By Mrs. ALEXANDER.
Maid, Wife, or Widow? | Valerie's Fate.

By GRANT ALLEN.
Strange Stories. | The Devil's Die.
Philistia. | This Mortal Coil.
Babylon. | In all Shades.
The Beckoning Hand.
For Maimie's Sake. | Tents of Shem.

By ALAN ST. AUBYN.
A Fellow of Trinity.

By Rev. S. BARING GOULD.
Red Spider. | Eve.

By FRANK BARRETT.
Fettered for Life.

By SHELSLEY BEAUCHAMP.
Grantley Grange.

By W. BESANT & J. RICE.
This Son of Vulcan. | By Celia's Arbour.
My Little Girl. | Monks of Thelema.
Case of Mr. Lucraft. | The Seamy Side.
Golden Butterfly. | Ten Years' Tenant.
Ready-Money Mortiboy.
With Harp and Crown.
'Twas in Trafalgar's Bay.
The Chaplain of the Fleet.

By WALTER BESANT.
Dorothy Forster. | Uncle Jack.
Children of Gibeon. | Herr Paulus.
All Sorts and Conditions of Men.
The Captains' Room.
All in a Garden Fair.
The World Went Very Well Then.
For Faith and Freedom.

By FREDERICK BOYLE.
Camp Notes. | Savage Life.
Chronicles of No man's Land.

By BRET HARTE.
Flip. | Californian Stories
Maruja. | Gabriel Conroy.
An Heiress of Red Dog.
The Luck of Roaring Camp.
A Phyllis of the Sierras.

By HAROLD BRYDGES.
Uncle Sam at Home.

By ROBERT BUCHANAN.
The Shadow of the | The Martyrdom of
Sword. | Madeline.
A Child of Nature. | Annan Water.
God and the Man. | The New Abelard.
Love Me for Ever. | Matt.
Foxglove Manor. | The Hair of Linne.
The Master of the Mine.

By HALL CAINE.
The Shadow of a Crime.
A Son of Hagar. | The Deemster.

By Commander CAMERON.
The Cruise of the "Black Prince."

By Mrs. LOVETT CAMERON.
Deceivers Ever. | Juliet's Guardian

By AUSTIN CLARE.
For the Love of a Lass.

By Mrs. ARCHER CLIVE.
Paul Ferroll.
Why Paul Ferroll Killed his Wife.

By MACLAREN COBBAN.
The Cure of Souls.

By C. ALLSTON COLLINS.
The Bar Sinister.

By MORT. & FRANCES COLLINS
Sweet Anne Page. | Transmigration.
From Midnight to Midnight.
A Fight with Fortune.
Sweet and Twenty. | Village Comedy.
Frances. | You Play me False.
Blacksmith and Scholar.

Two-Shilling Novels—*continued.*

By WILKIE COLLINS.

Armadale.	A Rogue's Life.
After Dark.	My Miscellanies.
No Name.	Woman in White.
Antonina. | Basil.	The Moonstone.
Hide and Seek.	Man and Wife.
The Dead Secret.	Poor Miss Finch.
Queen of Hearts.	The Fallen Leaves.
Miss or Mrs?	Jezebel's Daughter
New Magdalen.	The Black Robe.
The Frozen Deep.	Heart and Science.
Law and the Lady.	"I Say No."
The Two Destinies.	The Evil Genius.
Haunted Hotel.	Little Novels.
Legacy of Cain.	

By M. J. COLQUHOUN.
Every Inch a Soldier.

By DUTTON COOK.
Leo. | Paul Foster's Daughter.

By C. EGBERT CRADDOCK.
Prophet of the Great Smoky Mountains.

By WILLIAM CYPLES.
Hearts of Gold.

By ALPHONSE DAUDET.
The Evangelist; or, Port Salvation.

By JAMES DE MILLE.
A Castle in Spain.

By J. LEITH DERWENT.
Our Lady of Tears. | Circe's Lovers.

By CHARLES DICKENS.

Sketches by Boz.	Oliver Twist.
Pickwick Papers.	Nicholas Nickleby.

By DICK DONOVAN.
The Man-Hunter. | Caught at Last!
Tracked and Taken.
Who Poisoned Hetty Duncan?
The Man from Manchester.
A Detective's Triumphs.

By CONAN DOYLE, &c.
Strange Secrets.

By Mrs. ANNIE EDWARDES.
A Point of Honour. | Archie Lovell.

By M. BETHAM-EDWARDS.
Felicia. | Kitty.

By EDWARD EGGLESTON.
Roxy.

By PERCY FITZGERALD.

Bella Donna.	Polly.
Never Forgotten.	Fatal Zero.
The Second Mrs. Tillotson.	
Seventy-five Brooke Street.	
The Lady of Brantome.	

ALBANY DE FONBLANQUE.
Filthy Lucre.

By R. E. FRANCILLON.

Olympia.	Queen Cophetua.
One by One.	King or Knave?
A Real Queen.	Romances of Law.

By HAROLD FREDERIC.
Seth's Brother's Wife.
The Lawton Girl.

Two-Shilling Novels—*continued.*

By HAIN FRISWELL.
One of Two.

By EDWARD GARRETT.
The Capel Girls.

By CHARLES GIBBON.

Robin Gray.	In Honour Bound.
Fancy Free.	Flower of Forest.
For Lack of Gold.	Braes of Yarrow.
What will the World Say?	The Golden Shaft.
	Of High Degree.
In Love and War.	Mead and Stream.
For the King.	Loving a Dream.
In Pastures Green.	A Hard Knot.
Queen of Meadow.	Heart's Delight.
A Heart's Problem.	Blood-Money.
The Dead Heart.	

By WILLIAM GILBERT.
Dr. Austin's Guests. | James Duke.
The Wizard of the Mountain.

By HENRY GREVILLE.
A Noble Woman.

By JOHN HABBERTON.
Brueton's Bayou. | Country Luck.

By ANDREW HALLIDAY.
Every-Day Papers.

By Lady DUFFUS HARDY.
Paul Wynter's Sacrifice.

By THOMAS HARDY.
Under the Greenwood Tree.

By J. BERWICK HARWOOD.
The Tenth Earl.

By JULIAN HAWTHORNE.

Garth.	Sebastian Strome.
Ellice Quentin.	Dust.
Fortune's Fool.	Beatrix Randolph.
Miss Cadogna.	Love—or a Name.
David Poindexter's Disappearance.	
The Spectre of the Camera.	

By Sir ARTHUR HELPS.
Ivan de Biron.

By Mrs. CASHEL HOEY.
The Lover's Creed.

By Mrs. GEORGE HOOPER.
The House of Raby.

By TIGHE HOPKINS.
'Twixt Love and Duty.

By Mrs. ALFRED HUNT.
Thornicroft's Model. | Self Condemned.
That Other Person. | Leaden Casket.

By JEAN INGELOW.
Fated to be Free.

By HARRIETT JAY.
The Dark Colleen.
The Queen of Connaught.

By MARK KERSHAW.
Colonial Facts and Fictions.

By R. ASHE KING.
A Drawn Game. | Passion's Slave.
"The Wearing of the Green."

TWO-SHILLING NOVELS—*continued.*

By HENRY KINGSLEY.
Oakshott Castle.

By JOHN LEYS.
The Lindsays.

By MARY LINSKILL.
In Exchange for a Soul.

By E. LYNN LINTON.
Patricia Kemball. | Paston Carew.
World Well Lost. | "My Love!"
Under which Lord? | Ione.
The Atonement of Leam Dundas.
With a Silken Thread.
The Rebel of the Family.
Sowing the Wind.

By HENRY W. LUCY.
Gideon Fleyce.

By JUSTIN McCARTHY.
A Fair Saxon. | Donna Quixote.
Linley Rochford. | Maid of Athens.
Miss Misanthrope. | Camiola.
Dear Lady Disdain.
The Waterdale Neighbours.
My Enemy's Daughter.
The Comet of a Season.

By AGNES MACDONELL.
Quaker Cousins.

KATHARINE S. MACQUOID.
The Evil Eye. | Lost Rose.

By W. H. MALLOCK.
The New Republic.

By FLORENCE MARRYAT.
Open! Sesame! | Fighting the Air.
A Harvest of Wild Oats.
Written in Fire.

By J. MASTERMAN
Half a-dozen Daughters.

By BRANDER MATTHEWS.
A Secret of the Sea.

By JEAN MIDDLEMASS.
Touch and Go. | Mr. Dorillion.

By Mrs. MOLESWORTH.
Hathercourt Rectory.

By J. E. MUDDOCK.
Stories Weird and Wonderful.
The Dead Man's Secret.

By D. CHRISTIE MURRAY.
A Model Father. | Old Blazer's Hero.
Joseph's Coat. | Hearts.
Coals of Fire. | Way of the World.
Val Strange. | Cynic Fortune.
A Life's Atonement.
By the Gate of the Sea.
A Bit of Human Nature.
First Person Singular.

By MURRAY and HERMAN.
One Traveller Returns.
Paul Jones's Alias.

By HENRY MURRAY.
A Game of Bluff.

By ALICE O'HANLON.
The Unforeseen. | Chance? or Fate?

By GEORGES OHNET.
Doctor Rameau. | A Last Love.

By Mrs. OLIPHANT.
Whiteladies. | The Primrose Path.
The Greatest Heiress in England.

By Mrs. ROBERT O'REILLY.
Phœbe's Fortunes.

By OUIDA.
Held in Bondage. | Two Little Wooden
Strathmore. | Shoes.
Chandos. | Ariadne.
Under Two Flags. | Friendship.
Idalia. | Moths.
CecilCastlemaine's | Pipistrello.
Gage. | A Village Com-
Tricotrin. | mune.
Puck. | Bimbi.
Folle Farine. | Wanda.
A Dog of Flanders. | Frescoes.
Pascarel. | In Maremma.
Signa. | Othmar.
Princess Naprax- | Guilderoy.
ine. | Ouida's Wisdom,
In a Winter City. | Wit, and Pathos.

MARGARET AGNES PAUL.
Gentle and Simple.

By JAMES PAYN.
Bentinck's Tutor. | £200 Reward.
Murphy's Master. | Marine Residence.
A County Family. | Mirk Abbey.
At Her Mercy. | By Proxy.
Cecil's Tryst. | Under One Roof.
Clyffards of Clyffe. | High Spirits.
Foster Brothers. | Carlyon's Year.
Found Dead. | From Exile.
Best of Husbands. | For Cash Only.
Walter's Word. | Kit.
Halves. | The Canon's Ward.
Fallen Fortunes. | Talk of the Town.
Humorous Stories. | Holiday Tasks.
Lost Sir Massingberd.
A Perfect Treasure.
A Woman's Vengeance.
The Family Scapegrace.
What He Cost Her.
Gwendoline's Harvest.
Like Father, Like Son.
Married Beneath Him.
Not Wooed, but Won.
Less Black than We're Painted.
A Confidential Agent.
Some Private Views.
A Grape from a Thorn.
Glow-worm Tales.
The Mystery of Mirbridge.

By C. L. PIRKIS.
Lady Lovelace.

By EDGAR A. POE.
The Mystery of Marie Roget.

By E. C. PRICE.
Valentina. | The Foreigners.
Mrs. Lancaster's Rival.
Gerald.

Two-Shilling Novels—*continued.*

By CHARLES READE.
It is Never Too Late to Mend.
Christie Johnstone.
Put Yourself in His Place.
The Double Marriage.
Love Me Little, Love Me Long.
The Cloister and the Hearth.
The Course of True Love.
Autobiography of a Thief.
A Terrible Temptation.
The Wandering Heir.
Singleheart and Doubleface.
Good Stories of Men and other Animals.

Hard Cash.	A Simpleton.
Peg Woffington.	Readiana.
Griffith Gaunt.	A Woman-Hater.
Foul Play.	The Jilt.

By Mrs. J. H. RIDDELL.
| Weird Stories. | Fairy Water. |
Her Mother's Darling.
Prince of Wales's Garden Party.
The Uninhabited House.
The Mystery in Palace Gardens.

By F. W. ROBINSON.
Women are Strange.
The Hands of Justice.

By JAMES RUNCIMAN.
Skippers and Shellbacks.
Grace Balmaign's Sweetheart.
Schools and Scholars.

By W. CLARK RUSSELL.
Round the Galley Fire.
On the Fo'k'sle Head.
In the Middle Watch.
A Voyage to the Cape.
A Book for the Hammock.
The Mystery of the "Ocean Star."
The Romance of Jenny Harlowe.
An Ocean Tragedy.

GEORGE AUGUSTUS SALA.
Gaslight and Daylight.

By JOHN SAUNDERS.
| Guy Waterman. | Two Dreamers. |
The Lion in the Path.

By KATHARINE SAUNDERS.
| Joan Merryweather. | Heart Salvage. |
| The High Mills. | Sebastian. |
Margaret and Elizabeth.

By GEORGE R. SIMS.
Rogues and Vagabonds.
The Ring o' Bells.
Mary Jane's Memoirs.
Mary Jane Married.
| Tales of To-day. | Dramas of Life. |
Tinkletop's Crime.

By ARTHUR SKETCHLEY.
A Match in the Dark.

By T. W. SPEIGHT.
The Mysteries of Heron Dyke.
| The Golden Hoop. | By Devious Ways. |
Hoodwinked, &c.

Two-Shilling Novels—*continued.*

By R. A. STERNDALE.
The Afghan Knife.

By R. LOUIS STEVENSON.
| New Arabian Nights. | Prince Otto. |

BY BERTHA THOMAS.
| Cressida. | Proud Maisie. |
The Violin-player.

By WALTER THORNBURY.
Tales for the Marines.
Old Stories Re-told.

T. ADOLPHUS TROLLOPE.
Diamond Cut Diamond.

By F. ELEANOR TROLLOPE.
Like Ships upon the Sea.
| Anne Furness. | Mabel's Progress. |

By ANTHONY TROLLOPE.
| Frau Frohmann. | Kept in the Dark. |
| Marion Fay. | John Caldigate. |
The Way We Live Now.
The American Senator.
Mr. Scarborough's Family.
The Land-Leaguers.
The Golden Lion of Granpere.

By J. T. TROWBRIDGE.
Farnell's Folly.

By IVAN TURGENIEFF, &c.
Stories from Foreign Novelists.

By MARK TWAIN.
| Tom Sawyer. | A Tramp Abroad. |
The Stolen White Elephant.
A Pleasure Trip on the Continent.
Huckleberry Finn.
Life on the Mississippi.
The Prince and the Pauper.

By C. C. FRASER-TYTLER.
Mistress Judith.

By SARAH TYTLER.
The Bride's Pass.	Noblesse Oblige.
Buried Diamonds.	Disappeared.
Saint Mungo's City.	Huguenot Family.
Lady Bell.	Blackhall Ghosts.
What She Came Through.
Beauty and the Beast.
Citoyenne Jaqueline.

By J. S. WINTER.
| Cavalry Life. | Regimental Legends. |

By H. F. WOOD.
The Passenger from Scotland Yard.
The Englishman of the Rue Cain.

By Lady WOOD.
Sabina.

CELIA PARKER WOOLLEY.
Rachel Armstrong; or, Love & Theology

By EDMUND YATES.
| The Forlorn Hope. | Land at Last. |
Castaway.

OGDEN, SMALE AND CO. LIMITED, PRINTERS, GREAT SAFFRON HILL, E.C.